# 5. SEA VENTURERS OF BRITAIN

*The Nautilus Library*

# THE NAUTILUS LIBRARY

# SEA VENTURERS
# OF BRITAIN

*by*

## "TAFFRAIL"
### (COMMANDER TAPRELL DORLING, D.S.O., R.N.)

*London*

PHILIP ALLAN & CO. LTD.

*Quality House, Great Russell Street, W.C.1*

*First published in The Nautilus Library, 1929*

910.3

*Made and Printed in Great Britain by*
UNWIN BROTHERS LIMITED, LONDON AND WOKING

# PREFACE

THERE is nothing new under the sun. The stories of John Hawkins, Drake, Anson, Cook, Franklin, the late Captain Scott, and other voyagers dealt with in this book have been told many times before. Biographies and volumes on voyages of exploration, however, are generally beyond the reach of the average reader, while short popular narratives are sometimes too sketchy in their detail to give a true picture.

In most cases I have obtained my material from contemporary accounts of the voyages written by those who took part in them, and I am indebted to W. G. Perrin, Esq., O.B.E., and the other officials of the Admiralty Library for their ever-ready willingness in helping me to make the fullest use of the many invaluable volumes in their care.

My thanks are due to L. G. Carr Laughton, Esq., the naval historian, and to Lieutenant Commander R. T. Gould, R.N. (retd.), for their welcome advice on many abstruse points. I am particularly grateful to Miss Monsie Scott, sister of the late Captain R. F. Scott; to Rear-Admiral E. R. G. R. Evans, C.B., D.S.O., R.N., and Captain Victor L. A. Campbell, D.S.O., O.B.E., R.N.—both of whom played a conspicuous part in the expedition in which Captain Scott and his companions lost their lives—for their great kindness in reading and criticizing my narrative of our greatest Antarctic explorer. Admiral Evans, moreover, gave me ready permission to make use of matter contained in his book, *South with Scott*.

"TAFFRAIL"

# CONTENTS

# INTRODUCTION

SUBSEQUENT to Columbus' first expedition in 1492, Pope Alexander VI, exercising his claim to dispose of the kingdoms of the earth, allocated to Spain all the newly found lands lying to the west of a meridian 370 leagues west of the Cape Verde Islands, and to Portugal all those to the east of it. This gave to Spain the West Indies, the Spanish Main, most of the eastern coast of South America, and the entire western coast from Cape Horn to California. Portugal, on the other hand, became the virtual mistress of the eastern hemisphere, from Cape Bojador—on the African coast near the Canary Islands—round the Cape of Good Hope to the Red Sea, and thence across the Indian Ocean to Macao, in China.

For the Spaniards, Pinzon found the great rivers leading into the heart of the South American continent. Cortez subdued Mexico, and Pizarro the Inca Empire of Peru. Florida was conquered and the Mississippi valley explored, and in the West Indies and on the Spanish Main the ports of Santiago de Cuba, Porto Rico, Nombre de Dios and Cartagena became flourishing trade centres. Every year the mule teams brought their loads of gold and jewels to the shores of the Gulf of Mexico, and each summer great fleets of treasure-laden galleons sailed across the Atlantic to replenish the coffers of Spain with the wealth of the New World.

For Portugal, Albuquerque founded a new empire in India, while trading-stations were established in the Spice Islands, in China and Japan, and at Pernambuco and Bahia in Brazil. Portuguese carracks and caravels, laden with the silks, spices and rich merchandise of the East, sailed regularly to and fro between their home country and India by the long route round the Cape of Good Hope. The island of St. Helena, now a British possession, was one of their ports of call.

On the annexation of Portugal by Spain in 1580, Philip II, besides being the ruler of Spain, Naples and Sicily, the Milanese territory of northern Italy, the province of Franche-Comté, the Netherlands and the new American colonies, found himself also the master of Portugal. At a single blow, as it were, he thereby added to his empire Brazil, the Azores, the Canary and Cape Verde Islands, Guinea, Angola and Mozambique, Goa and other possessions in India, Macao, Malacca, the Philippines, and a vast network of trade organized by the industrious Portuguese in the Far East. Never before in the history of the world had a single sovereign ruled over such world-wide dominions.

But the Spaniards were bad colonists. They practised a ruthless severity over conquered peoples instead of benevolent government. Moreover, they regarded gold as wealth in itself rather than as a means of exchange. It was an error which finally brought their splendid empire crashing to ruin. Yielding to the mad desire to grow rich without toil, Spain was eventually to find herself supplanted as a world-power by Britain, a country whose seamen and merchants, excluded by the Papal Bull from the gold-producing regions of the world, were driven instead to oversea trade and colonization.

Compared with mighty Spain, little Britain was one of the minor powers of Europe. Her mariners had long been recognized as expert seamen. She had an important and marketable commodity in her wool; but her trade had mainly been confined to the Mediterranean and northern Europe. Beyond a vague claim to Newfoundland and Labrador by right of Cabot's discovery in 1497, she had no oversea colonies or interests in America or the East. The great British Empire was still undreamt of.

The British navy was of early creation; but the foundations of our sea supremacy were laid by Henry VII (1485–1509) and Henry VIII (1509–1547) in their re-creation of the fighting Navy. It was during the reign of Queen Elizabeth (1558–1603), however, that the British really entered upon that wonderful career of nautical enterprise which, by the time of her death, placed their country at the head of the maritime nations.

An island race, the tang of the sea was in British nostrils as the salt was, and still is, in British blood. Stirred at the thought of fortunes to be made at the expense of Spain and Portugal, hardy mariners set forth from every port, from many a little fishing village, to reap the golden harvest of the sea.

They were not perfect, for pirates, smugglers and slave-traders many of them were. Some of the deeds carried out against their hapless enemies in those remote waters "beyond the line" were quite unjustifiable and barbarous. Nevertheless, the names of many of these men have passed down to history as national heroes.

Thirty years after Queen Elizabeth's accession Spain was punished by the shattering defeat of the Armada, a triumph which opened the ocean highways to British maritime endeavour, and, by the hardihood of generation after generation of seamen, no less than the bravery of British soldiers and the enterprise of British merchants and colonists, led in course of time to the establishment of a British Empire stretching over the entire globe.

Within the limited compass of a single book it is impossible to give more than the briefest outline of certain of the voyages, discoveries and exploits of a representative few of the greatest British navigators and explorers. The names of some, more famous than others, are known to us all.

But we are a maritime nation, and every successful navigator that ever sailed had his emulators. Where one man voyaged a hundred were sure to follow, and ever since the days when British ocean enterprise and commerce may be said to have fairly started, hosts of seamen have ventured to the uttermost parts of the earth, to return in due season to add their little contribution to our knowledge of the outer world and its resources and people.

Many, however, never returned. They perished instead: some fighting for their country's honour, some by shipwreck, others by thirst and famine and pestilence in the sweltering heat of the tropics, or the icy, windswept wastes of the Arctic and Antarctic. These lesser men have no monuments to commemorate their deeds—no books wherein their doings are recorded. Their tombstones are the foaming surges of the broad oceans, the coral reefs or golden sands of tropical islands, or, maybe, the icy pinnacles of the frozen north and south. Sea-birds wheel round the unknown resting-places of many, whose epitaphs are emblazoned across the sky in the trail of smoke from some passing steamer. Wherever the great ships go to-day on their lawful occasions British seamen have fought and ventured and given their lives.

This book deals with men with whose names we all are familiar; but it is to the persistent efforts of the obscure seamen, from captains to the men before the mast, as much as to the successes of those whose names are bywords in our language, that we are indebted for our present knowledge of the globe, our commercial prosperity and our greatness as an Oceanic Empire.

# SEA VENTURERS OF BRITAIN

## THE VOYAGES
## OF SIR JOHN HAWKINS

JOHN HAWKINS, or Hawkyns, born at Plymouth in 1532, was one of that little band of Elizabethan captains who helped to break the Spanish trade monopoly in the West Indies, and, by his share in the subsequent war against Spain, played no small part in the establishment of British maritime supremacy. In 1562, when he set out on his first really notable voyage, the Spanish flag was still predominant at sea, and Spain and Portugal between them owned the richest portions of the world. In 1595, when he died, the Spanish Armada had been defeated, supremacy at sea had passed from Spain to Britain, and the Spanish dream of subjugating Protestant England had passed for ever.

Hawkins lacked the fiery impulsive character and naval genius of Drake. He was undoubtedly an able administrator, a brave man, a valiant fighter and a seaman to his finger-tips; but while Drake was winning renown and riches by feats of unparalleled daring, Hawkins was enriching himself as a merchant and ship-owner. He was a blunt, stolid seaman of few words and gruff manners; but though preserving the strictest discipline was never tyrannical, and displayed a real solicitude for the men under his orders. History has rightly considered him as one of the pioneers of British seamanhood.

The Hawkins family had lived in Plymouth for generations. John was the second son of William Hawkins, a well-to-do ship-owner and merchant, who had made various voyages to the coast of Guinea and Brazil, and is described as one of the principal advisers on maritime affairs to King Henry VIII and one of the best known of the West Country sea captains.

On William Hawkins' death in 1555 his sons carried on the business, and in 1559 John, the younger of the two, married Katharine, the daughter of Benjamin Gonson, the Treasurer of the Navy. But he was not content to lead an easy life ashore. Inheriting his father's roving instincts he made several voyages to Spain, Portugal and the Canaries before reaching the age of thirty, and in those days voyages of this kind were regarded as something of an extraordinary adventure. It was during these expeditions that he formed friendships with merchants in the Canaries from whom he obtained much information of value about the Spanish trade, learning among other things that negro slaves were in great demand in the West Indies and that they might be obtained without great difficulty upon the coast of Guinea.

The slave trade was no novelty. The native races of Cuba and San Domingo had withered and died away during the ruthless Spanish occupation, and for years the Spaniards had made slaves of their Moorish and other native prisoners captured in war, and had sent them abroad under licence to work upon the plantations. John Hawkins was one of the first Englishmen to engage in the profitable business, a line of trade which according to modern ideas was not very honourable. In the sixteenth century, however, barter in human flesh was regarded as perfectly legitimate, while the English seamen of the day looked upon themselves as "the elect to whom God hath given the heathen for an inheritance." There was no idea that the traffic involved cruelty to the hapless natives upon whom it was practised, for they themselves were addicted to cannibalism and human sacrifice and were regarded as little better than brute beasts.

At the same time the Spanish laws against foreign "heretics" participating in the West Indian trade were very strict. Whether they came for honest trade or downright piracy they were all regarded as interlopers upon a preserve granted exclusively to Spain by virtue of the Papal Bull of 1494.

England strongly resented the Spanish claim to the absolute monopoly of the West Indies as an infringement of old treaty rights, and Hawkins, while transgressing the law of a foreign state, shocked no prejudices in his own country by slave-dealing. On the contrary he acquired considerable merit among his countrymen, not even excepting his Queen, for circumventing and harassing an arch-enemy who was trying her utmost to impose the rigours and barbarities of the Inquisition upon the whole world.

Religious hatred and commercial jealousy had superseded the former friendliness between England and Spain, and the severe, even cruel, enforcement of the trade monopoly on the one side was met, on the other, by smuggling and piracy. The profits to be made were enormous. The Spanish settlements were weakly held, and provided the intruders behaved warily and were prepared to back up their arguments with force if the necessity arose, the risks were not excessive.

In October 1562 three small private vessels manned by less than a hundred men sailed out of Plymouth Sound. They were the *Solomon* of one hundred and twenty tons, on board of which was John Hawkins himself; the *Swallow* of one hundred tons, commanded by Thomas Hampton; and the *Jonas* of forty tons.

Touching at Teneriffe, where, by reason of Hawkins' friendship with a merchant, they embarked a Spanish pilot for the West Indies, the little squadron passed on to Sierra Leone. Here they obtained, "partly by the sword and partly by other means," three hundred negroes together with what merchandise the country yielded. This done, the three ships stretched across the Atlantic to San Domingo, where, at the different ports in the island, Hawkins disposed of all his goods and most of the slaves, trusting the Spaniards no farther than "by his own strength he was able to master them."

The Spanish settlers themselves were by no means averse to trading, and slaves were particularly in demand. Indeed, the barter was so brisk and Hawkins received so much merchandise in the shape of hides, ginger, sugar and "some quantity of pearls," that he was forced to charter two vessels to carry it home. In bold assertion of the entire lawfulness of his actions the two chartered vessels were sent to Cadiz under Thomas Hampton, there to dispose of their cargoes. Hawkins himself arrived in London in September 1563, where his cargoes were sold at great profit. The merchandise on board the two ships sent to Spain, however, was promptly impounded as smuggled goods, while Hampton, flying from the country in danger of his life, found his way to London.

On hearing of his loss, which amounted to some 40,000 ducats, or roughly £20,000,[1] Hawkins was both astounded and furious. It is clear that he had no idea of offending Spain in undertaking the voyage, and he had even taken the precaution of obtaining a certificate of good conduct during his visit from the governor of San Domingo. Accordingly he

[1] Approximately £300,000 according to the present purchasing power of money.

he little *Tiger* of fifty tons. The vessels by 170 men and boys, and strict orders wn for the conduct of the fleet at sea. ips were instructed always to sail ahead dward of the *Jesus*, and to approach and er at least twice a day. If the *Jesus* hoisted n over the poop, or at night showed two l vessels were to come near and speak to ile if she showed three lights at night it she was about to tack. Two lights and a ot were to be used as a signal of distress, and y vessel lost touch she was, on rejoining, to v her identity by making three yaws and striking mizzen three times. The orders concluded with injunctions: "Serve God daily; love one another; eserve your victuals; beware of fire, and keep good ompany," the last, of course, meaning that the ships were not to straggle.

In the English Channel Hawkins fell in with the *Minion*, another Queen's ship, and the *St. John Baptist*, both bound to the coast of Guinea. Bad weather drove the squadron into the Spanish port of Ferrol, where they spent five days; but continuing the voyage on October 30th they reached Teneriffe five days later. Here Hawkins was well received by his old merchant friends, and on the night of November 15th, having victualled the squadron and repaired the damaged main-mast of the *Jesus*, he sailed again for the coast of Guinea.

After calling at Cape Blanco they arrived at Cape Verde on November 29th. No negroes were to be had, however, for the crew of the *Minion*, which had reached the coast some days before, had revealed the object of the voyage. After another futile attempt the first actual haul of slaves was made at an island called Sambula, where they stayed for some time, going "every day ashore, to take the inhabitants with burning, and spoiling their towns." The

made an indignant
the restitution of
of one hundr
lest any questi
payable upon th
writing to Philip
at Madrid to interce

But it was all usele
in Hawkins' voyage the
would presently destroy h
he refused all redress. Mo
governor of San Domingo f
to trade, confiscated the slaves
orders to his Viceroy in the We
circumstances whatsoever were E
permitted to have any dealings wit
there. He also informed Queen Eliza
the English ambassador, that if any d
permitted mischief would ensue.

The Queen, however, in spite of the a
some of her counsellors who were anxious to
Spain, had her own ideas on the matter. She sa
Philip's anger an admission that the West Ind
was his weak point, and was keen to encourage th
adventurous expeditions of her subjects who were
fighting the country's battle more or less at their
own risk and expense, particularly if she herself
stood to make a profit. Accordingly, when Hawkins
planned a second expedition on a more elaborate
scale to recoup himself at the expense of Spain, the
Queen not only took shares in the project, but was
also induced to lend him the *Jesus of Lubeck*, a man-
of-war of 700 tons.

The Earl of Pembroke, Lord Robert Dudley—
afterwards Earl of Leicester—and other courtiers
helped Hawkins and his London friends to raise the
necessary funds, and on October 18, 1564, he sailed
from Plymouth with the *Jesus*, his old *Solomon* and

chronicler of the voyage describes how some of the
natives ate their enemies, and how they filed their
teeth and tattooed their bodies "as workmanlike as
a jerkin maker with us pinketh a jerkin."

Capturing some slaves and despoiling the natives
of rice, fruit and cattle, the squadron left the island
on December 21st, and the following day the boats
were sent up a river and returned with a goodly
haul of negroes. Flushed with success Hawkins
was then persuaded by some Portuguese traders
to attack a town said to contain a great quantity
of gold and many negroes suitable as slaves. Forty
men-at-arms were landed with their weapons, and
guided by the Portuguese attacked the place. Contrary to orders, however, they split up into small
parties and began to search the houses for gold,
with the consequence that the negroes attacked them
and drove them pell-mell back to the boats, some
being cut in pieces or killed and wounded by arrows,
others drowned in the mud as they strove to embark.
Hawkins himself with a dozen men returned to the
beach to find a mob of 200 yelling natives shooting
arrows at the boats. He dispersed them and embarked with difficulty, and while not more than ten
slaves had been captured, seven Englishmen, including the captain of the *Solomon*, had been killed and
twenty-seven wounded.

Leaving the place, the smaller ships and the boats
went up a river and captured more slaves and did
a little trade. The evil climate, however, was beginning to tell upon the ships' companies, and on
January 29, 1565, the squadron left the African coast
for the long passage to the West Indies.

For nearly three weeks, crowded with seamen,
soldiers and slaves, the four ships were becalmed
in the Atlantic, though sometimes they had contrary
winds and fierce tornadoes. As was usual in those
early voyages, water became scarce and the men soon

began to suffer the torments of thirst. This "happened to us very ill," says the narrator of the expedition, "being but reasonably watered, for so great a company of negroes, and ourselves, which pinched us all." Some of the men gave up hope of ever reaching the Indies without great mortality; but eventually "Almighty God, who never suffereth his elect to perish," sent them a north-westerly breeze on February 16th. In view of the nature of their voyage it is peculiar to think of Hawkins and his men praising God for His goodness; but the words quoted above are evidence of their profound belief in the innocence and righteousness of their actions, detestable though they really were.

March 9th saw the ships off the island of Dominica, which was inhabited by "Cannybals . . . the most desperate warriors in the Indies." Here they tarried only long enough to replenish their water, and then sailed on across the Caribbean.

The most important Spanish colony in the West Indies and the largest market was in Hispaniola, or Hayti as it is now called. After what had happened subsequent to his previous voyage, however, Hawkins knew better than to go there. Instead he determined to proceed to the remoter settlements on the Spanish Main—the north coast of the South American continent—where he imagined his name would be less known and his squadron would show to greater effect than in Hispaniola.

Arriving on March 16th at Margarita, an island off the Venezuelan coast, the local authorities provided the ships with sheep and oxen. But the governor of the island would neither receive Hawkins nor permit him to trade, nor allow him to engage a pilot. Moreover, he sent a fast caravel to San Domingo to warn the Viceroy of the Indies that the dreaded "Achines de Plimua"[1] had appeared.

[1] "Achines de Plimua." Hawkins of Plymouth.

The Viceroy promptly sent word to all Spanish settlements, reiterating Philip's orders that the inhabitants were on no account to have any dealings with Englishmen, but were to resist with all the force they could.

Seeing that nothing could be done at Margarita, Hawkins sailed on to the mainland, and on arriving at Cumana went ashore in his pinnace to see what could be done in the way of trade. The settlers, however, had no money to buy slaves, but directed him to a convenient place for watering his ships. Here the casks were filled, and they traded with the natives, who brought maize-cakes, fowls, pine-apples and potatoes, which were exchanged for beads, whistles, knives and other trifles. The potatoes, not yet having been introduced into England, were a novelty—"the most delicate roots that may be eaten, and do far exceed our parsnips and carrots."

Sailing on to the westward along the coast, Hawkins came across many Carib Indians, who invited him by signs to trade with them. On hearing that they were addicted to a diet of human flesh he did not tarry, and on April 3rd brought his squadron to a Spanish settlement called Burboroata, near the present town of Puerto Cabello.

Going ashore to interview the governor, Hawkins, declaring himself to be an Englishman who came for legitimate trade, asked for the necessary licence. The Spaniard replied that his countrymen were forbidden to trade with foreigners on pain of forfeiting all their belongings, and requested him to leave. To this the Englishman retorted that he could not sail as he was in command of one of the "Queen's Armadoes of England," and that, with many troops on board, he had need of food and money. Queen Elizabeth and Philip of Spain were at peace, he went on to explain, while the English were allowed to trade with Spain and Spanish Flanders. Why should they not enjoy the same privilege in the West Indies? The local governor, rather perplexed, said he would send to the governor of the district to see what was to be done, but that, on account of the distance at which he lived, ten days must elapse before the answer could be expected. Meanwhile Hawkins might bring his ships into harbour, where they would be provided with what victuals they required.

The food was forthcoming, and Hawkins then came to the conclusion that to remain there idle for ten days was mere folly. He therefore requested a licence to sell at once certain lean and sick slaves who were likely to die upon his hands. If he could not sell them, he went on to say, he had no money to pay for the goods he had received. The local governor, in a greater dilemma than ever, eventually gave him leave to dispose of thirty negroes, but though eagerness to buy them had previously been shown, no purchasers came forward on the day of the sale itself. The Spaniards, with many excuses, were trying to beat down the price, whereupon, annoyed at the delay, Hawkins threatened to leave the place, taking his negroes with him. The Spaniards, however, very short of labour, were anxious for him to remain, and after some further parley a few slaves were actually sold.

On April 14th the governor himself appeared in person, and to him Hawkins repeated his request to trade, adding that "he was come thither driven by wind and weather," and that he had urgent need of stores and provisions, as well as money for the payment of his soldiers. He himself, he said, was quite ready to depart, but his troops were not.

Any more specious excuse than that of being driven there by stress of weather it is difficult to imagine, and well the Spaniards knew the falsity of it. It was designed, however, merely to give them a chance of clearing themselves in the eyes of their

superiors, and after some further talk Hawkins
gained his point. Sitting in council the governor
duly granted the licence, but refused any abatement
of the customs dues, which amounted to thirty
ducats on each slave. This sum, worth at that time
about £15, would be equivalent to about £225 now.
This enormous duty would entirely swallow up all
the profits, and Hawkins determined to have no
further haggling but to take the law into his own
hands. Accordingly, on April 16th he landed one
hundred men in armour armed with arquebuses,
bows, arrows and pikes, and marched them towards
the town. The governor, very alarmed, sent to ask
the meaning of this warlike display, and Hawkins
replied that the suggested duty upon the slaves was
quite unreasonable, but that he was perfectly willing
to pay the customary seven and a half per cent. If his
terms were not accepted "he would displease them."
The governor, unable to meet force with force, and
unwilling to see the town pillaged and burnt and
the inhabitants perhaps massacred or held to ransom,
had no alternative but to comply with the demands,
and was also willing to hand over hostages for the
faithful carrying out of the terms.

Remaining at Burboroata until May 4th a good
number of slaves were disposed of. The squadron
then sailed on to the island of Curaçoa, where they
established a profitable trade in hides. They were
also allowed to help themselves to as much beef,
mutton and lamb as they wanted without payment, for
the island was so overrun with cattle that the settlers
merely killed them for their skins and ate nothing
but the tongues, leaving the carcasses for the birds.

From Curaçoa Hawkins passed on to Rio de la
Hacha,[1] on the coast of what is now known as

---

[1] So called from the original Spanish settlers having given
the natives a hatchet to show them where the water might
be found.

Colombia, where, interviewing the King's Treasurer of the Indies, he showed him a certificate of good conduct signed by the governor of Burboroata, and requested permission to trade. He was told, as before, that trade was against the orders of King Philip, whereupon he repeated his old excuse of being forced to visit the place on account of stress of weather and scarcity of provisions. Realizing, however, that the Spaniards were determined not to accede to his request, he curtly informed them that with the ships and men at his disposal he would not have it said that he had been frustrated by mere words. Sooner than that he would use force; and peremptorily told the Spaniards either to give him his licence or to stand to arms to resist him. The threat succeeded and the licence was granted; but when he tried to sell the slaves he was offered half what he had received before. More than this the Spaniards would not give, so he wrote them a letter saying that they dealt too rigorously with him, but, "seeing they had sent him this to his supper, he would in the morning bring them as good a breakfast."

He was as good as his word, for early the next day, May 21st, he fired a gun to summon the town, and went ashore with a hundred armed men and with small guns mounted in his boats. The Spaniards, to the number of 150 foot soldiers with thirty horsemen, marched to the beach with drums throbbing and ensigns displayed. They made "great bragges with their cries," but on Hawkins opening fire with his two light guns the infantry first fell flat on their faces and then scampered for safety when the boats drew near. The cavalry, with their white leather shields in one hand and javelins in the other, pranced their horses up and down the beach in defiance, but also retired to a discreet distance as soon as the boats grounded. Finally, when the Spaniards had sent a flag of truce, Hawkins, in armour and unarmed, went out alone between the parties and interviewed the Treasurer. His requests were granted, hostages were given and trade was soon in full swing. The slaves were all disposed of on the English terms, three boats, with guns in their bows and filled with armed men, superintending the settling of accounts. On May 31st, their business finished, the unwelcome visitors sailed.

It is needless to describe Hawkins' subsequent wanderings to Jamaica, Cuba and Florida. He had it in mind to invest the money received for his slaves in a cargo of hides, but was unable to make any suitable port to effect the sale. Finally, in great want of water, he sailed out into the Atlantic and ranged along the coast of Florida, anchoring each night lest they should miss a watering place.

In the St. John's River they came across a colony of Huguenots which had been founded in 1562. They were practically destitute, and through starvation, wars with the Indians and fighting among themselves, their numbers had been reduced from 200 to 40. In exchange for water Hawkins gave them food and stores and also volunteered to take them home. This they refused, but purchased his little *Tiger* in which to return to Europe. One thing of interest which Hawkins' men noticed in Florida was that the natives used tobacco.

On July 28th the squadron again put to sea for its passage to England, but was delayed by contrary winds and currents to such an extent that provisions ran short. The greater number of the men were in despair of ever reaching home, "had not God of his goodness better provided for us, than our deserving. In our state of great miserie we were provoked to call upon him by fervent prayer, which moveth him to hear us, so that we had a prosperous wind."

This fair breeze brought them to the banks of Newfoundland, and here, partly by fishing, partly by barter with French fishing-boats, they obtained a great number of fresh cod.

On September 2, 1565, the squadron arrived in safety at Padstow, in Cornwall, with a loss of no more than twenty men during the entire voyage. The ships were well laden with hides, gold, silver, pearls and other jewels, and the profits to Hawkins and his friends who had financed the expedition were reckoned at 60 per cent over and above their original outlay.

Hawkins' reputation was now assured. He arrived in England to find himself the hero of the hour and in great favour with Queen Elizabeth. He had rendered good service to his country by opening up a new branch of trade, and as an honourable augmentation to his coat of arms—sable, a golden lion walking upon the waves—he was granted as a crest a demi-negro bound captive, in commemoration of his doings on the Guinea coast.

Meeting De Silva, the Spanish ambassador in England, he gave him a full account of his voyage, only omitting the manner in which he had contrived to trade in defiance of Philip's orders. The ambassador, very perturbed, promptly informed his Sovereign that the success of the voyage was encouraging others to go and do likewise, and that Hawkins himself was fitting out another expedition. With no faith in the innocent intentions of the adventurer he pointed out the necessity of preventing further voyages. "I do not believe," he wrote, "that a ship would be safe, if they were strong enough to take it."

Philip, furious at the infringement of his trade monopoly, became more anxious than ever for the safety of the great fleets of treasure-laden galleons which sailed regularly across the Atlantic to Spain from Mexico and the West Indies. They were ill protected on passage, and for a number of years French and English pirates had reaped a steady harvest by capturing Spanish merchant vessels and raiding ports in the West Indies. It was only natural that in Hawkins he should see a new and formidable recruit to the pirate ranks.

Instead, however, of making any official protest to the Queen, De Silva attempted to undermine Hawkins' loyalty by sounding him as to his willingness to use his ships in consort with the Spanish galleys for a war against the Turks. Hawkins, full of guile and quite equal to the occasion, replied that he was prepared to do so.

The ambassador, in fact, was hopelessly duped, and it was not until Hawkins was on the point of sailing that the Spaniard's eyes were opened to the fact that the squadron, as before, was bound to the coast of Guinea. Demanding an audience with Elizabeth, he proceeded to upbraid her for encouraging her subjects to break the laws of her friend and ally, Philip of Spain. The Queen expostulated, but as at the time it was not expedient for Spain to be further offended, an order was issued forbidding Hawkins to go armed "for the purpose of traffic to places privileged by the King of Spain." He was further required to execute a bond for £500 that he would not send to any Spanish possessions the ships he was fitting out for his slave-trading enterprise. Hawkins at once made up his mind not to take any part in the voyage, and though the ships sailed and returned the next year their doings are obscure. It is tolerably certain, however, that their cruise was a piratical one.

Hawkins had not given up all idea of another expedition, and in 1567, by which time the atmosphere at Court had changed, his preparations were once more in full swing. On this occasion, however, he suffered little or no hindrance, the Queen, even if she was not an actual shareholder, again lending him the *Jesus of Lubeck*, which was brought round to Plymouth.

While the squadron was fitting out at the West Country port, an incident occurred which clearly showed the state of feeling between England and Spain. A Spanish squadron from the Netherlands under the command of a Flemish admiral appeared in Plymouth Sound and, with their flags flying, bore up for the Catwater, where Hawkins' ships were lying. These ships were expected, and Elizabeth had given orders for their honourable reception at any place they might visit; but by custom of the sea they should have struck their topsails and colours on entering a foreign friendly port. This they did not do, and suspecting their intention Hawkins opened fire and did not cease until the colours came down. The next day, also, some private vessel, English or Dutch, ran alongside the Spanish flagship and rescued a number of prisoners who were being taken to Spain.

It is clear that the foreign admiral had no hostile intent, and for his action Hawkins was formally reproved by the Queen. This, however, was not enough for the Spanish ambassador, who wrote Elizabeth a furious letter. "Your mariners rob my master's subjects at sea and trade where they are forbidden to go," he said; "they attack our vessels in your very harbours, and take our prisoners from them. Your preachers insult my master from their pulpits; and when we apply for justice we are answered with threats. We have borne with these things, attributing them rather to passion or rudeness of manners than to any deliberate purpose of wrong; but seeing there is no remedy and no end, I must now refer to my Sovereign to learn what I am to do. . . . I entreat your Majesty to punish this last outrage at Plymouth and to preserve the peace between the two Nations."

But if the Queen had wished to punish Hawkins, which was unlikely, it was beyond her power to do so. Four days before the ambassador's letter was written he had sailed from Plymouth Sound, and by the time of its receipt must have been well on into the Bay of Biscay. Elizabeth herself must have smiled grimly on reading De Silva's outburst, for nearly three weeks before Hawkins had written to her saying that he proposed "to load negroes in Guinea, and sell them in the West Indies, in truck of gold, pearls and emeralds."

The squadron, which sailed from Plymouth on October 2, 1567, comprised two "great ships" of the Royal Navy, the old *Jesus of Lubeck*, commanded by Hawkins himself and carrying 180 men, and the *Minion* of 300 tons, commanded by John Hampton. There were also four merchant vessels; the *William and John*, 150 tons; *Swallow*, 150 tons; *Angel*, 32 tons; and the *Judith* of 50 tons. The last-named was commanded by Francis Drake, a kinsman of Hawkins, who though only twenty-four years of age had already made voyages to the Spanish Main.

The ships were armed, equipped and organized precisely as a naval squadron, and cannot have been manned by less than 500 officers, seamen and soldiers. Hawkins has often been depicted as a swashbuckling irresponsible pirate, but he was never that. He was a wealthy ship-owner, and in this voyage, in which he had invested some £32,000 of our money and had personal effects and furniture on board the *Jesus* valued at about £6,000, he maintained all the pomp and circumstance of one of Her Majesty's "Admirals-at-the-Sea."

The only known pictorial record of the *Jesus of Lubeck* is that contained in the Anthony Roll of about 1545, and we know little of her detail except that she had vertical clenchers, or external ribs, which were abolished in England soon afterwards. The *Jesus* was the largest ship in the squadron and would have a length of about 140 feet over all. The

*Minion* would be some twenty feet less, while the breadth of both ships on the waterline would be about one-third of their length. Both vessels had low waists amidships with castles forward and aft, that in the stern rising tier by tier, deck by deck into an enormous poop which towered high above the sea. The *Jesus*, having originally been a merchant ship, may have had a high bow of the carrack type; but as a rule at this period the bows terminated in a long beak-head overhanging the water and designed to break the force of the sea. At the extremity of the beak-head there was generally a fanciful figure-head painted and gilt. The hulls of the ships "tumbled home," which meant that the sides fell inwards until the breadth on deck was considerably less than that on the waterline. Above the waterline they were painted timber colour, while the upper-works were profusely and brilliantly decorated with squares, diamonds and scrolls, probably picked out in green and white, and red and blue and gold. Figures of saints on flags were no longer in use; but other emblems were still employed: falcons, lions, the Royal arms, and the personal badges of the senior officers. The St. George's Cross was in general use, and the flag shown on the ensign staff of most Elizabethan men-of-war was of narrow green and white horizontal stripes—the Tudor colours—superimposed with the red St. George's Cross of England. Both the *Jesus* and the *Minion* had four masts with a topgallant-sail on the main, and with great lateen sails on long slanting yards on the two mizzen-masts. They had no fore-and-aft head-sails, merely square sprit-sails set on yards beneath the bowsprit, a great spar standing up out of the bows over the beak-head at an angle not far short of forty-five degrees. With their ponderous super-structure to catch the wind and their unwieldy canvas, they must have been difficult to handle in anything approaching heavy weather. They were good sea boats, though, buoyant like corks and very short, they pitched horribly and lay over to alarming angles.

The small-arms and armour provided consisted of arquebuses, bows, arrows, pikes, bills, corslets and morions—or steel caps—while the guns then used afloat were not very inferior to those employed at Trafalgar, nearly two and a half centuries later. Culverins—seventeen pounders—and demi-culverins —nine pounders—each with a range of 2,500 paces, were the favourite ship guns, but there were also sakers, minions, falconets, robinets and bases, throwing shot weighing from five to one pound. Some of them were breechloaders, as were also the "murdering pieces," mounted on movable swivels, firing swan-shot, and used for repelling boarders.

Little is known of the internal accommodation of the vessels, though the men were herded together like cattle in the narrow ill-ventilated spaces between decks. Sanitary arrangements were conspicuous by their absence and medical attention practically unknown, and in the long voyages to unhealthy parts of the world sickness and disease claimed many victims.

The monthly wage of the common seaman was six shillings and eightpence, equivalent to about five pounds of our money, and their daily ration consisted of one pound of biscuit, one gallon of beer and two pounds of salt beef, with a quarter of a stock-fish,[1] two ounces of butter and four ounces of cheese substituted for the beef on three days of the week. This dietary sounds liberal enough, but the provisions were generally vile in quality, and the cooking arrangements primitive. In these circumstances it is little to be wondered at that mutinies at sea were not infrequent and that the punishments were very severe. A murderer was tied to the corpse

[1] Dried cod.

and thrown overboard, while a man drawing a weapon on an officer had his right hand severed at the wrist. For sleeping on watch the fourth time the delinquent was tied to the bowsprit with a biscuit, a can of beer, and a knife, and was left either to starve or to cut himself into the sea and be drowned. A thief was ducked two fathoms deep, towed ashore at the stern of a boat and dismissed. These punishments sound barbarous, but were not out of keeping with the penalties inflicted on malefactors ashore considerably later than the sixteenth century.

While still in the Bay of Biscay a great storm arose in which the fleet were scattered and the *Jesus* was damaged. For a time it was thought that the voyage would have to be abandoned, and Hawkins actually turned homeward, but on October 11th a change of wind brought better weather, and he continued on his course. Meeting at the Canary Islands, the fleet watered, and sailing thence on November 4th, arrived at Cape Verde a fortnight later.

For some time the Portuguese in Africa had done their utmost to drive off intruding rivals, building forts and maintaining galleys to protect their trade. English vessels had been attacked and captured, and once in Portuguese waters Hawkins, in return for their recent behaviour to some of his own ships, started a private war against them. There is no possible excuse for his conduct, for so far as can be ascertained he had no commission of reprisal from Queen Elizabeth. Moreover, as he refrained from mentioning these activities in his own account of the voyage it is probable that he did not regard them as above suspicion. Nevertheless, from the narrative of the gunner of the *Jesus* we learn that the *Minion* chased and captured a Portuguese caravel of 150 tons named the *Grace of God*, which was added to the squadron, with Drake temporarily in command.

The ships spent nearly two months in searching the rivers between Rio Grande and Sierra Leone, capturing several more caravels and despoiling them of their slaves. In this way they obtained 150 negroes. By January 12, 1568, however, sickness was again prevalent among the English crews, while a number of men had died from wounds inflicted by poisoned arrows. As the season was well advanced Hawkins accordingly determined to sail on to the West Indies with what negroes he had. They were on the point of departure when a negro king asked him for his help in a tribal war, promising him all the prisoners that were captured. One hundred and twenty men were accordingly landed, and on January 15th, with their negro allies, attacked a town of 8,000 inhabitants. It was strongly defended, and six of the English were killed and forty wounded before the place was captured and set on fire. Hawkins and his men took 250 prisoners, men, women and children, and the natives some 600 more. Hawkins hoped to have had his choice of these latter; but during the night the cunning negro king decamped, taking his prisoners with him.

The slaves now on board amounted to between four and five hundred; but before sailing Hawkins found seven more Portuguese caravels, which were driven ashore and destroyed after a smart action. Finally, having watered his ships and laid in a stock of wood for fuel, he sailed from the Guinea coast on February 3rd.

After a wearisome voyage of fifty-five days Dominica was sighted on March 27th, and the ships then coasted from place to place, trading with the Spanish wherever they could. It was a difficult business, for King Philip's orders against foreigners were as stringent as ever. "Notwithstanding," says Hawkins, "we had reasonable trade and courteous entertainment from the Isle of Margarita, unto

Cartagena, without anything greatly worth the noting . . . save in a town called Rio de la Hacha, from whence come all the pearles."

From other accounts, however, it is evident that Hawkins concealed the whole truth, for at Margarita, to quote one narrative, "our general, in despite the Spaniards, anchored, landed, and took in fresh victuals." At Burboroata, too, they moored their ships and stayed for two months refitting. It was before the time of copper sheathing and anti-fouling compositions, and after six months in the tropics the ships were so foul with weed that careening was necessary. It was while this work was in progress that he sent some of his men to a town called Placentia to interview a bishop; but the bishop, on hearing of their coming, "for fear forsook the town."

After a sojourn at Curaçao, where they provisioned, the ships visited Rio de la Hacha. The *Angel* and *Judith*, with Drake in command, were the first vessels to arrive. The Spanish officials were quite ready to receive him; but the garrison had been augmented by one hundred arquebusiers and the approaches to the town protected by newly erected barricades. As soon as Drake anchored he was fired upon, whereupon, after retaliating with a shot through the governor's house, he retired out of range and blockaded the port for five days. While he was doing this a Spanish despatch-boat arrived from San Domingo, and Drake, chasing her, drove her ashore and brought her off under fire. It was the act of a lawless freebooter, probably in excess of his instructions; but was the first of a long series of dare-devil exploits which made him famous in his own country and caused his name to stink in Spanish nostrils.

It is little to be wondered at that on Hawkins' arrival with the main body the Spanish officials not only forbade him to trade, but also prevented him from obtaining food and water. Seeing that argument was useless he accordingly landed with 200 men and "broke in upon their bulwarks, and entered the town with the loss only of two men, and no hurt done to the Spaniards, because after their volley of shot they fled." Once in possession of the place he had the whip hand, and before long a secret trade was opened, "partly by the Spaniards' desire of negroes, and partly by friendship of the Treasurer," the inhabitants coming down at night and buying 200 negroes.

Sailing on to the westward the ships visited other small settlements where the people were glad enough to trade. At Cartagena, however, the capital of the Spanish Main, the governor refused absolutely to have any dealings with them. Hawkins' own narrative merely says that he sailed on July 24th. From another account, however, it seems that the *Minion* fired upon the castle, while men landed and carried off some wine, leaving cloth of equal value in its stead.

Meanwhile the hurricane months of August and September were at hand, and as the voyage had been moderately successful Hawkins determined to return to England by way of the Yucatan Channel. On August 12th, however, off the western end of Cuba, the squadron was caught in a severe storm which lasted for four days. When the weather moderated the *William and John* had lost touch with her consorts,[1] while the *Jesus*, which had been bought in 1544 and was thus over twenty-four years old, was so badly strained that portions of her upperworks had had to be cut away, her rudder was sprung and she was leaking like a basket. Repairs were essential before the voyage home could be resumed, and for a fortnight or more they searched the south coast of Florida for a convenient anchorage. But the water was everywhere too shallow,

[1] She returned to England.

and after another three days of very heavy weather Hawkins was forced to shape his course for San Juan de Ulua, the port of Vera Cruz, the capital of Mexico. On the way there he captured three ships and took them on in company, in the hope that the hundred passengers found on board would be useful hostages to induce the Spanish authorities to grant him facilities for repairing damage and obtaining food and water.

San Juan de Ulua was a small anchorage protected from the northerly gales by a low, narrow island lying about half a mile from the mainland. Its inner face formed a sort of quay to which ships made fast by the bows, their sterns being secured to anchors laid out in the harbour. Arriving at this place on September 16th Hawkins' squadron was mistaken by the Spaniards for their "flota" and its escort, which were expected daily from home to embark the valuable contents of a dozen treasure-ships lying in the harbour. On going on board and perceiving their mistake the officials were naturally dismayed, for the treasure seemed entirely at Hawkins' mercy. On being told that he wanted nothing but food and facilities for repairs, however, they were so relieved that they allowed the visitors to moor at the quay and to occupy and fortify the island protecting the anchorage from seaward.

There is no real reason to believe that Hawkins had designs upon the treasure. From first to last he had always found trade a more lucrative business than piracy, and, except for his acts of aggression against the Portuguese in Africa, he never indulged in it and considered it mere folly. Probably he was anxious to effect the sale of his remaining slaves and what merchandise he had left, though on this occasion his excuse of being compelled to enter the port through stress of weather seems to have been justified. Moreover, to show he harboured no evil designs, he released all his hostages except two and caused a letter to be sent to the authorities at Vera Cruz, fifteen miles inland, informing them why he had come and requesting that steps should be taken to prevent bloodshed when the Spanish fleet arrived.

This message was sent off on the evening of his arrival, and at dawn the very next morning thirteen Spanish vessels, headed by a great galleon, were sighted to seaward. The fleet was commanded by Don Francisco de Luxan, and at least two of the ships were armed as regular men-of-war. On board the flagship, moreover, was Don Martin Enriquez, the new Viceroy of Mexico, and Hawkins must have been well aware that neither he nor de Luxan would treat him as anything but a pirate, no matter how innocent his intentions.

But he was not the man to hesitate. Securely in possession of the island, the key position, he sent word to the Spanish admiral that he would not permit him to anchor unless he guaranteed there should be peace. Having done this, however, he was in a dilemma. He probably could prevent the Spanish ships from entering, though, if he did, the first northerly gale would probably cause their shipwreck and total loss on the dangerous lee shore. They carried cargoes of treasure worth many millions of money, and he feared the "Queen's Majesty's indignation in so weighty a matter."

On the other hand, he mistrusted the Spaniards from the very first, and the harbour was so small that if they entered their ships must lie practically side by side with his own, which meant that he might be overwhelmed by sheer weight of numbers if treachery was intended. In the circumstances, therefore, there was no alternative but to permit their entry after receiving pledges for his safety, and Hawkins' sublime impudence in keeping the Viceroy and his fleet out of his own harbour was justified by the very difficult position in which he found himself.

Negotiations were opened, and for four days a wrangle continued. The Viceroy, naturally enough, maintained that "he was a Viceroy and had a thousand men, and therefore would come in"; to which Hawkins retorted with equal vigour: "I represent my Queen's person and I am Viceroy as well as he: and if he have a thousand men, my powder and shot will take the better place."

Eventually an arrangement was entered into whereby the English were to be permitted to repair and revictual and were to have licence to sell slaves and goods to pay for their requirements. The island, with the eleven brass guns that they had mounted, was also to remain in English hands and no armed Spaniards were to land there, while ten Spanish hostages of rank were to be sent on board the English ships.

On the evening of September 20th the Spanish fleet anchored just outside the port. The following morning they came into harbour, the fleets saluting each other according to custom, and for the next two days English and Spanish seamen worked in harmony in berthing their vessels in the congested space available. The ships were finally safely moored with their bows overhanging the quay and their sterns made fast to anchors; but so restricted was the space that there was a gap of only twenty yards between the *Minion* and the nearest Spaniard, while close alongside the former came the *Jesus* and then all the other English vessels in turn.

On the evening of his arrival under cover of darkness the Spanish admiral embarked a reinforcement of 120 soldiers from Vera Cruz, and spent the next two days evolving a scheme for Hawkins' punishment. Between the *Minion* and the nearest Spanish ship had been moored a large "urca," or merchant ship, and during the night of September 22nd it was discovered that she was full of men and that she had been connected by a hawser to the head-ropes of the *Jesus*. The next morning, too, the Spanish were seen to be moving weapons from ship to ship, while additional guns were being mounted, and armed parties passed to and fro.

Hawkins, his suspicions thoroughly aroused, sent to the Viceroy to remonstrate and received an answer that the word of a Viceroy was a guarantee against all treachery. Still dissatisfied, he then sent a Spanish-speaking officer with another protest, and while awaiting the reply sat down to a meal in his cabin. Ashore on the island, meanwhile, Spaniards with concealed daggers were fraternizing with the English and plying them with drink.

As a guest at Hawkins' table was one of his hostages, a Spaniard of high birth. While the meal was in progress there came the sudden screech of a trumpet and a hubbub on deck, and according to one account, an attendant in the cabin snatched a dagger from the sleeve of the Spanish hostage. Hawkins, giving hasty orders for his confinement, rushed on deck, to find that the trumpet call had been the signal for a general attack upon the English.

Already the men on the island were being struck down by the hidden weapons of those with whom they had been carousing, and soldiers, jumping ashore over the bows of the Spanish ships, were running in among the batteries, slashing right and left with their swords to send the guards flying. A few, very few, saved their lives by swimming to the *Jesus*; but soon there was not an Englishman left ashore alive, while the guns, in Spanish hands, were making ready to open fire at close range on the English ships.

Meanwhile the merchant vessel between the two squadrons was hauled alongside the *Minion* and a torrent of armed men poured on board that vessel and thence to the *Jesus*.

"God and Saint George!" Hawkins shouted. "Upon these traitrous villains and rescue the *Minion*! I trust in God the day shall be ours!"

The English seamen and soldiers swarmed from the *Jesus* into the *Minion* with a cheer, and after a fierce hand-to-hand struggle drove the enemy head-long overboard or back into their hulk with heavy loss. And before the attack could be resumed the *Minion*, casting off her head-ropes, was slowly hauled off the shore by her stern moorings and continued to pour a furious fire upon the enemy's flagships, one of which was already in flames.

The Spanish fire now became concentrated upon the *Jesus*, until her main-mast was shot through in five places, her fore-mast went overboard and her hull was riddled through and through. But she kept up a heavy fire and gave as much as she received, and, assailed again by the hulk and two other ships, repelled a desperate attempt to capture her by boarding. With heavy loss Hawkins then managed to cast off his bow-ropes and to haul off close to the *Minion*, and the two ships together maintained a furious fire.

Their weighty armaments soon had their effect. Within an hour the guns of the Spanish ships were practically silent, while their vice-flagship was burning furiously and two other ships were in a sinking condition. The first-named eventually blew up with most of her crew, and for a time the Viceroy himself was practically alone on board the flagship, and in great personal danger. But a storm of shot was now poured into the English ships by the guns on the island. The *Angel* was soon sunk and the *Swallow* so crippled that she had to be abandoned, the little handful of survivors reaching the *Jesus* in their boat.

In this desperate situation, however, Hawkins still encouraged his men to victory. In the midst of the roaring cannon and the reek of powder-smoke he called to his page for a goblet of beer, which was brought to him in a silver cup. "Drinking to all the men," runs the account, "he willed the gunners to stand by their ordnance lustily, like men. He had no sooner set the cup out of his hand but a demi-culverin struck away the cup . . . which nothing dismayed our general, for he ceased not to encourage us, saying: 'Fear nothing, for God, who hath preserved me from this shot, will also deliver us from these traitors and villains!'"

However, the rigging of the *Jesus* was so badly cut about and her hull so battered that to save her was impossible. She was therefore warped in front of the *Minion* to protect that vessel from the fire from the island, the intention being to maintain the fight until darkness fell and then to transfer to the *Minion* what stores could be salved and about £12,000[1] worth of treasure in gold, silver and other commodities that had been obtained by trading. The *Jesus* was then to be abandoned and the *Minion* to make her escape.

But at this critical time the Spaniards sent down two fireships, and the *Minion's* crew fell into a panic, cast off and started to make sail without orders. Hawkins just managed to jump on board as she slid free and a few of the flagship's men followed in a small boat. Many of the wounded, however, besides those which the boat was not able to embark, had to be left behind to the mercy of the Spaniards, which, says Hawkins, "I doubt was very little."

Those now on board the *Minion* and the crew of Drake's *Judith*, which, with her small armament, had taken little part in the engagement and had warped clear of the harbour when it had started,

[1] Worth about £180,000 at present standards.

were the only survivors. The *Jesus*, the *Swallow*, the *Angel* and the Portuguese prize *Grace of God* had been all destroyed, and the lives of over a hundred English seamen had been sacrificed to Spanish treachery. The enemy's losses amounted to 540 killed out of the 1,500 or so engaged; but the results of Hawkins' trading, the money for which he and his men had endured so much and striven so hard, was lost.

The firing died away, and darkness came down to find the *Minion* and *Judith* outside the harbour. They were in a sorry plight, the larger vessel riddled with shot and both crowded with survivors for whom there was insufficient food, clothing and bedding. Presently, as the night-breeze came stealing off the land, they set their canvas, and with the water rippling round their bows disappeared into the night, a sorry remnant of the brave little squadron that had sailed out of Plymouth Sound less than a year before.

Such was the engagement of San Juan de Ulua, the first of a long series of actions which were finally to free the seas for British maritime endeavour. Some of its details may be wrapped in mystery; but it is clear that both Don Martin Enriquez and de Luxan behaved with calculated treachery in the face of their solemn word and formal agreement. Whatever may be said of Hawkins, he had conducted himself honourably and not as a pirate, and when the Spaniards ransacked the battered *Jesus* they found every one of the hostages unharmed. By every rule of war Hawkins had a perfect right to have executed them. To his everlasting honour not a hair of their heads had been touched.

It was the affair of San Juan, more than any other incident, which stirred the indignation of the English public, earned for the Spaniards the whole-hearted hatred and contempt of the English people and brought on their heads the fiery vengeance of Drake and a score of emulators.

On the night following the action the *Minion* and *Judith* parted company, and the next day a strong northerly gale decided Drake to proceed to England alone. At the time he was severely blamed on the score of having deserted his leader; but as the *Judith* was overcrowded with survivors and short of provisions, stores and water, it would seem that his action was perfectly justified. The *Judith* arrived in Plymouth Sound on January 20, 1569.

The *Minion*, meanwhile, overburdened with men, short of provisions and water, damaged and leaking through her injuries, and with only two anchors and cables left, rode out the gale under the lee of an island. Then, for a fortnight she wandered about the Gulf of Mexico seeking a convenient place to effect repairs, some of her crew, in the meantime, wishing to surrender themselves to the Spaniards or natives. So short were the victuals that "birdes were thought very good meate, rattes, cattes, mise and dogges, none escaped that might be gotten," also "parrates and monkayes."

Driven by hunger the *Minion* reached an anchorage on October 8th, but only to find a barren and uninhabited land where about a hundred men were landed at their own request sooner than continue the voyage.[1]

Having watered and nearly been wrecked in another storm, Hawkins sailed from the coast of Mexico on October 16th, and after a month of beating about eventually passed out into the Atlantic by way of the Bahama Channel. During the passage home his men were dying continually of starvation,

[1] The terrible sufferings of these wretched men were graphically described by Miles Philips, David Ingram and Job Hortop, three of the survivors, their accounts being reprinted in Hakluyt's *Principal Navigations*.

and the survivors became so weak that they could hardly manage the ship. Foul winds, moreover, forced them into Pontevedra, in Spain, on the last day of the year, where many more died through an excess of fresh meat after their privations. After calling at Vigo, and borrowing twelve men from English ships found there, the *Minion* at last reached Mount's Bay on January 25, 1569.

Says Hawkins in concluding his account: "If all the miserie and troublesome affairs of this sorrowful voyage should be perfectly and thoroughly written, these should need a painful man with his pen, and as great a time as he had that wrote the lives and deaths of the martyrs!"

We can but agree with him. The voyage had been one of ill-luck and misadventure.

It is beyond the scope of the present narrative to describe Hawkins' subsequent career in detail; but a brief summary is desirable for the sake of completeness.

His first idea was to fit out another expedition at once to rescue his comrades left behind in Mexico and to recoup himself for his losses. But his reputation had suffered through failure. He was in disfavour at Court, for his subscribers had lost their money and the Queen her ship. Accordingly his proposed voyage was strictly forbidden.

Some Spanish treasure-ships carrying money to Antwerp for the Spanish troops had, however, been driven by Huguenot privateers into Southampton, Plymouth and Falmouth. The loan of this money had been arranged by an Italian financier in London, who is stated to have had a substantial interest in Hawkins' voyage. For fear of the privateers in the Channel the specie was landed in England under a safe-conduct with the intention that it should be forwarded to its destination by way of Dover. Then came a garbled version from Spain of the disaster at San Juan de Ulua, while it was also discovered that the money passing through the country was still the property of the Italian bankers. It was promptly confiscated, whereupon the Spanish ambassador in London at once wrote off to the Duke of Alva, in Flanders, urging him to lay an embargo upon the property of all English subjects in the Netherlands. The embargo was duly enforced.

England was in a ferment. The Spaniards, enraged at the stoppage of their money and believing that many Englishmen were discontented with the Queen's government and that the country was divided against itself, meditated an invasion for the purpose of putting Mary on the throne and converting England to Roman Catholicism. This provided Hawkins with an opportunity, for, pretending to be one of the dissatisfied malcontents, he asked the Spanish ambassador to intercede with King Philip with a view to the release of the men left behind in Mexico. The ambassador did so, suggesting to his government that it might be worth while to win Hawkins over to his side by granting his request. No reply was received; but Hawkins, still hoping to gain his end, then gave the ambassador to understand that he was willing to enter the King of Spain's service and to bring with him the pick of the English ships and sailors. A staunch adherent of the Queen's all the time, he was merely pretending to act the part of a traitor to suit his own purposes.

The ramifications of what is known as the Ridolfi plot are too subtle and complicated to be set forth here; but finally Philip's suspicions were lulled, and freeing some of the prisoners at Seville he sent Hawkins £40,000 for the equipment of the promised ships, together with a patent proclaiming him a grandee of Spain. The money thus obtained Hawkins regarded as part compensation for his loss at

San Juan, and once more the Spaniards had been hopelessly hoodwinked.

"I have sent your Lordship the copy of my pardon from the King of Spain," he subsequently wrote to Lord Burghley, the Queen's most trusted counsellor, "in the order and manner I have it, with very great titles and honours from the King, from which God deliver me. Their practices be very mischievous, and they be never idle; but God, I hope, will confound them and turn their devices on their own necks."

In 1572 Hawkins was Member of Parliament for Plymouth, and the following year became Treasurer and Comptroller of the Navy, an important office he held with distinction until the end of his life. His wide experience at sea enabled him to adopt many improvements and innovations in the building and rigging of ships, while he increased their seaworthiness by reducing the size of the castles at bow and stern, and augmented their speed by constructing them on finer lines. He also introduced chain-pumps, boarding nettings and various other devices, some of them of his own invention. It was alleged at one time that he made a considerable profit for himself by juggling with the stores and materials intended for Her Majesty's ships and converting things to his own use. There is no proof that these statements were entirely unfounded; but bribery and peculation were rife in official circles, and in contrast with previous administrations Hawkins' hands were clean. At any rate, by the time the English fleet was called upon to defend the country on the advent of the Spanish Armada in 1588, it was ready and efficient.

The war with Spain opened in 1585, and during the battles against the Armada Hawkins was captain of the *Victory*, rear-admiral third-in-command of the fleet and a trusted member of the Council of War.

He took an active part in the various actions, particularly in that off the Isle of Wight on July 25th, and on the evening of that day, in company with Frobisher, Lord Thomas Howard and others, was knighted for his gallant services on the deck of the *Ark Royal* by Lord Howard of Effingham, the Lord High Admiral.

It was soon after the defeat of the Armada that Hawkins and Drake between them are supposed to have instituted the "Chatham Chest" as a fund for the benefit of disabled seamen; while early in 1590 the former was associated with Frobisher in an expedition to Portugal for the annoyance of the King of Spain. The voyage was not a success, for after five months' cruising the fleet came home with so few prizes that they did not pay for the fitting out of the ships. Queen Elizabeth, loud in her indignation, said exactly what she thought and Hawkins tendered an effusive apology in writing. "Paul might plant, and Apollos might water," he said in concluding, "but it was God only who gave the increase."

The masterful lady who was his mistress was not appeased. "God's death!" she exclaimed. "This fool went out a soldier, and is come back a divine!"

For the next five years he was ashore, but in 1595, at the age of sixty-three, sailed as second-in-command to Drake in a new voyage to the West Indies. The expedition, designed to attack Panama, was unsuccessful, for everywhere the Spaniards were forewarned and prepared. Hawkins, however, did not live to see its failure, while his death was followed soon afterwards by that of Drake himself.

The old seaman's constitution had been weakened by former hardships and successive attacks of fever and ague. He was depressed at the bad news of his only son, Richard, who in 1593 had sailed in command of a squadron to the Pacific and had been captured by the Spanish. Already long past his prime, the deadly West Indian climate had its effect, and on November 13, 1595, his strength having been ebbing for days, the gallant old sea-dog passed away, his body being committed to the deep within sound of the enemy's guns.

An epitaph to Hawkins and Drake was indited by Richard Barnfield in 1598. "The bravest voyages in the world have been made for gold," he wrote. "For it men have ventured to the furthest parts of the earth. In the pursuit thereof, England's Nestor and Neptune (Hawkins and Drake) lost their lives. Upon the deaths of which two, of the first I write thus:

The waters were his Winding Sheete, the Sea was made his Toombe;
Yet for his fame the Ocean Sea was not Sufficient roome."

# SIR MARTIN FROBISHER

## HIS THREE VOYAGES IN SEARCH OF THE
## NORTH-WEST PASSAGE, 1576–1578

MARTIN FROBISHER came of an old Welsh family which settled in Normanton in York-shire in the fourteenth century. He was born in or about the year 1535, his father died during his infancy, and as a boy he was sent to London to Sir John Yorke, a relative, to receive his education. In 1554, perceiving Frobisher to be of great spirit and courage and natural hardness of body, his relation sent him on a voyage to Guinea in a ship belonging to a fleet sent thither by some London merchants. This was one of the first of the voyages in which Englishmen sailed on the African coast in the wake of the Portuguese navigators, and the expedition, visiting the Gold Coast, started a prosperous trade in gold and elephants' teeth before returning to England in the summer of 1555.

For the next eleven years nothing is known of Frobisher, though it is probable that he took part in further voyages to Africa and the Levant, in the course of which he acquired a knowledge of sea-manship and navigation. In any case, he was com-manding his own vessel by 1566, for in the summer of that year he was examined by the Queen's Council on suspicion of having fitted out a ship as a pirate, with what result we do not know.

For another five years after this date his doings are again wrapped in mystery. It seems likely, however, that he was still at sea as a sailor and trader; possibly also as a pirate, piracy in those days not being looked upon as a crime against

4

humanity, but being punished or rewarded according to its value or inconvenience to the State.

In 1571 a ship was being built for Frobisher at Portsmouth, and for the next two or three years he seems to have been employed more or less officially to assist in quelling rebellion in Ireland. This work brought him into touch with Queen Elizabeth and various influential people at Court, including Sir Humphrey Gilbert, who in 1566 had written his well-known *Discourse to prove a passage to the North West*, to demonstrate that it was practicable to voyage to the wondrous lands of Cathay (China) and India round the north of America.

The primitive charts of the period all show a broad waterway, known as the "Straits of Anian," running east and west and connecting the northern portions of the Atlantic and Pacific Oceans. By this passage, Sir Humphrey explained, Englishmen might sail to divers very rich countries beyond the jurisdiction of Spain and Portugal, "where there is to be found great abundance of gold, silver, and precious stones, cloth of gold, silks, all manner of spices, grocery-wares, and other kinds of merchandise of inestimable value, which both the Spaniard and the Portuguese, through the length of their journey, cannot well attain thereto."

In 1574, thanks to Frobisher's association with the Court, Queen Elizabeth sent him with a letter to the Muscovy Company,[1] reminding them that they had been incorporated for the express purpose

---

[1] In 1552 had been formed a "Mystery Company of Merchant Adventurers for the discovery of regions, dominions, islands and places unknown," which sent out an expedition to discover a north-eastern route to Cathay round the north of Europe and Asia. The main object failed; but trade was opened up with Russia by way of the White Sea. In 1555, arising out of this, was formed the "Muscovy Company," which nearly every year dispatched expeditions to northern Russia for trade and exploration.

of finding a new passage to Cathay, and that it was twenty years since they had sent out their last expedition. She called upon them either to continue the search or else to transfer this privilege to someone else. The company, already finding the Russian trade very lucrative, demurred to the Queen's suggestion, whereupon in 1575 a licence was granted to Master Martin Frobisher and certain other gentlemen to undertake the work. Out of this grew Frobisher's three voyages in search of the North-West Passage.

For the next sixteen months Frobisher and his friends were busily preparing for the expedition, the first consideration being the collection of the necessary funds. By the summer of 1575 no more than £875 had been subscribed, which, though it must be multiplied by nine or ten to get its modern equivalent, was still insufficient.

Finally, in May 1576, and owing in no small measure to the good offices of the Earl of Warwick, the expedition was ready to start. Frobisher received a commission as "Captayne Generall," and on the morning of June 7th the *Gabriel* and *Michael*, stout little barques of twenty-five tons, together with a ten-ton pinnace, dropped down the Thames from their anchorage near Old London Bridge. The three ships were manned by about forty officers and men.

It was not until a week later, however, that the expedition really sailed, for on passing Greenwich the ships fired a salute in honour of their Sovereign. Queen Elizabeth watched them from a window in the palace and waved her hand, and sending a message of encouragement to the adventurers, desired Frobisher to come ashore and take his leave of her. The leave-takings were not finally completed until June 12th.

On getting to sea foul winds caused the ships to put into Harwich and Yarmouth; but sailing on up the North Sea past the Shetlands and Faroe Islands, they stood away to the westward. From June 30th until July 8th they had very stormy weather and could carry no sail, while the little pinnace foundered with her crew of three men.

Battling on when the weather moderated, the inhospitable coast of Greenland was in sight by July 11th. Frobisher wished to land, but was prevented from doing so by masses of drift-ice and many icebergs lying off the shore. The land, says one who took part in the voyage, was "marvellous high, and full of ragged high rocks all along the coast, and some of the islands of ice near it of such height that the clouds hanged about the top of them."

Troubled by fog and incessant bad weather the *Gabriel* and *Michael* struggled on. Another storm arose between Greenland and the coast of Labrador, during which the *Michael* lost her consort. After trying to rejoin without success, her captain sailed on to the westward and sighted Labrador, but found it so studded with icebergs that he dared not approach. Thereupon, supposing Frobisher to have been wrecked, the *Michael* shaped course for England, arriving at Bristol on September 1st.

The *Gabriel*, meanwhile, on July 13th was cast over on to her beam-ends by the storm, and filling with water, lay wallowing like a half-tide rock in the angry sea. The men gave themselves up for lost; but eventually, after losing the fore-yard and cutting away the mizzen-mast, the ship righted, and, still full of water, drove off before the tempest. They pumped her dry and for a day and a night scudded before the wind, damaging the main-mast. At last the storm subsided, and Frobisher, with a crippled ship manned by eighteen mariners and gentlemen, continued his voyage alone.

On July 20th they sighted land at the southern end of the Davis Straits near what is now known as Frobisher Bay, in Baffin Island. The spot first seen was christened "Queen Elizabeth's Foreland" in honour of the Queen, and sailing on, Frobisher sought for a landing-place and a convenient harbour wherein to refit his battered little ship. The coast, however, was encircled by icebergs, and several days passed before they found an anchorage at Hall Island, so named after the *Gabriel's* master, who was the first to land upon it. Here the ship was repaired to the best of their ability.

Sailing again, Frobisher sighted another cape with a great sheet of water dividing, as it were, two great continents. He sailed on, baffled by contrary winds and beset by ice with land on either side of him, firmly convinced that he had discovered the route to Cathay, and that the land to the left was America and that to the right, Asia. Accordingly he christened the channel "Frobisher's Streytes." It was, in point of fact, what is now known as Frobisher Bay.

In this, his first voyage, he only explored a portion of the coast and a few of the islands; but on landing found many things that were then considered strange and wonderful. "He saw mighty deer which seemed to be mankind," says one of the voyagers, "which ran at him, and hardly he escaped with his life in a narrow way, where he was fain to use defence and policy to save his life." In the same place that the "Captayne Generall" was pursued by the reindeer they also came across traces of human habitation, while on climbing a hill Frobisher saw a number of small things floating in the sea, which at first he imagined to be seals or porpoises, or some other kind of strange fish. They were really Esquimaux in their little "kyaks" of sealskin stretched over a thin framework, who, immediately on their arrival, tried to steal Frobisher's boat. The captain was forced to flourish his halberd to dissuade them.

Friendly relations were soon established with the natives, who came with salmon and raw seal-meat and fish and greedily devoured the same, much to the astonishment of the Englishmen. Presently, when they came to know each other better, there was a brisk interchange of food and seal- and bearskins for bells, mirrors and "tryfles of haberdash." But not all the Esquimaux were so friendly. In another place Frobisher met some "of a nature given to fierceness and rapine," and in general none of the *Gabriel's* men seem to have been particularly enamoured of the natives. "Their manner of life and food is very beastly," said one of them. "They be like Tartars, with long black hair, broad faces and flat noses, and tawny in colour, wearing sealskins; and so do the women, not differing in fashion; but the women are marked in the face with blue streaks down the cheeks and round about the eyes."

On August 20th five of the *Gabriel's* crew, anxious to do a little exploring on their own account, left the ship with a native in the only boat carried, and rowed out of sight. They did not return, and for four days Frobisher searched for them, sailing along close to the shore, sounding a trumpet and firing guns. Then, convinced that the missing men had been murdered by the natives, bereft of his only small boat, and realizing the utter impossibility of continuing the voyage with only thirteen men and boys, he unwillingly came to the conclusion that he must abandon the work for the season and return to England.

But before he sailed, "desirous to bring some token of his being there," and being firmly convinced that his plans for further exploration had been ruined by the treachery of the natives, he decided to abduct one of them and carry him off to England, as was then the cruel practice. Enticing a kyak alongside by offering its occupant a bell, he caught hold of the Esquimau and dragged him on board by main force, kyak and all. The native, finding himself in captivity, "for very choller and disdain, he bit his tongue in twain within his mouth." One can well understand the angry terror of the poor wretch at thus being plucked away from his country and family, and though he lived until the *Gabriel* arrived in England, he died not long afterwards of a cold caught during the passage.

On August 26th the *Gabriel* weighed her anchor and sailed for home, and passing by Greenland and Iceland, arrived at Harwich on October 2nd. They had bad weather during the voyage, and a man, falling overboard in a gust of wind, caught hold of the fore-sheet and was trailed in the water alongside. Frobisher plucked him out of the sea with the same strong arm that had captured the Esquimau, and both incidents give some idea of the *Gabriel's* absurdly low freeboard.

The explorers had been absent for rather less than four months, and though they had examined coasts considerably to the northward of the point reached by other travellers, had done comparatively little towards finding the sought-after passage to the land of Cathay. Nevertheless, having been given up for lost on the strength of the *Michael's* report, they were received with much popular acclamation, the miserable Esquimau and his boat receiving their fair share of attention.

One of the seamen had brought back with him a piece of black stone rather like coal, which he had seen glittering in the ground. He had shown it to Frobisher, who, being busy at the time, thought nothing of it. The man, however, had kept his curio, and showing it to some of his friends in England, they had it tested. It was stated to contain the purest gold, unalloyed with any other metal.

Another version of the same story says that

Frobisher himself brought home the stone, and that, on his return, he broke it into pieces which he gave to his friends as mementoes. A lady into whose hands one of the pieces fell threw it by mistake into the fire, where, in burning, it glittered like metal. The precious fragment was rescued, and, on being assayed, was stated to contain gold.

In sober truth it was not gold at all, though some assayers said that it was. But it was a credulous age. The doubters were disbelieved, and the word was passed from mouth to mouth that Frobisher had discovered a country where gold could be had by the handful.

The effect can be imagined. Courtiers and merchants, scientists and seamen, clamoured for another voyage to a land of such promise, saying that the discovery of a route to Cathay was of minor importance if gold could be obtained nearer at hand. Queen Elizabeth and Lord Burghley, her most trusted counsellor, were both anxious for another expedition, and finally, after a petition tendered by Frobisher and some of his influential friends, a company was formed to further the project. This was the Company of Cathay, endowed with all the rights and privileges of the older Muscovy Company, and in the new concern, at a fixed yearly stipend, Martin Frobisher was appointed "Captain-General by sea and Admiral of the ships and navy of the Company."

The false report of gold having been found was to be the ruin of Frobisher's subsequent voyages; but the truth did not become generally known until after the conclusion of his third expedition in 1578.

Money soon poured in for the new venture, the Queen herself subscribing £100. The company's formal charter was issued in March 1577; but some months previously the work of preparation had begun. The expedition was to consist of three ships—the old *Gabriel* and *Michael*, manned between them by twenty seamen and five soldiers, and the *Aid*, a "talle shippe" or man-of-war belonging to the Queen, a vessel of 200 tons with a crew of sixty-five seamen and twenty-five soldiers. Among the men, it may be mentioned, were ten convicts, ex-highwaymen, who were sent to sea, according to the custom of the time, to retrieve their characters. It was men of this stamp who were ringleaders in the frequent mutinies at sea, though on this occasion Frobisher landed his undesirable shipmates before sailing.

The three ships left Blackwall on May 26th, instructions for their guidance having been drawn up by the Queen, who addressed Frobisher as her "loving friend." In these orders it was stated that the finding of the passage to Cathay was to be regarded as secondary to the discovery of gold-producing lands in the north of America and their conversion into an English colony, Frobisher being told to leave the *Aid* at a suitable anchorage and to use the smaller ships in the search for gold. If successful he was to found a colony and leave the *Aid* and her soldiers to protect it; if unsuccessful the *Aid* was to return to England. In any case, the *Gabriel* and *Michael* alone were to be used for finding the passage to Cathay, if, indeed, the search should seem desirable. Frobisher was further enjoined to capture eight or ten Esquimaux, both young and old, "whom we mind shall not return again thither, and therefore ye shall have great care how ye do take them, for avoiding of offence towards them and their country."

After tarrying a day at Gravesend, where the crew were prepared for their dangerous mission by the administration of the Sacrament, the ships sailed out of the Thames. They were delayed at Harwich for three days by foul winds, Frobisher taking the opportunity of embarking provisions and weeding out the unsatisfactory members of his company; but finally sailed on up the North Sea. Arriving in the Orkney Islands they found the inhabitants almost as barbarous as the Esquimaux, for they fled from their cottages, thinking that the visitors were pirates. By and by, however, the English made friends with them and visited their houses.

"The goodman, wife, children and others of the family," says one of the voyagers, "eat and sleep on the one side of the house, and the cattle on the other; very beastly and rudely, in respect of civility. . . . They dress their meat very filthily, and eat it without salt. Their apparel is after the rudest sort in Scotland."

Leaving again on June 8th the three ships sailed on for twenty-six days without sight of land, suffering much from heavy seas and foul winds. They met icebergs, but thanks to the high latitude and the almost complete absence of darkness were able to avoid them.

Greenland was sighted on July 4th, but though for four days Frobisher sought an anchorage, they were unable either to anchor or to land because of the dangerous coast, wrapped in mist, and the masses of ice. They were somewhat surprised to find that most of the ice was fresh to the taste.

Between Greenland and Frobisher Bay there came a great storm, during which the little *Michael* lost her topmasts and had her steering-gear damaged, besides losing touch with the others. They all met again on July 17th, when Frobisher tried to push his way into the "straits" which bore his name. He was unsuccessful on account of the ice, and after searching in vain for a harbour eventually returned to Hall Island, where the ships came to an anchor.

Sometimes with the whole fleet, sometimes with

the two small ships, but more often in the boats, Frobisher and his men spent the next few weeks in scouring the adjacent coasts, islands and waters, their main object being the discovery of the gold-bearing ore. They found a good deal of it in some of the islands, and in the course of their wanderings had many adventures with the natives, who were sometimes friendly and sometimes distinctly hostile.

On one occasion the Esquimaux waved a flag and made a great noise, "with cries like the mowing of bulls." Frobisher and his followers imitated them and sounded the trumpets, whereat the natives "seemed greatly to rejoice, skipping, laughing and dancing for joy." Talking in dumb-show the Englishmen exchanged pins and other trifles for what the natives could spare, and on returning to the shore towards the boats the explorers were followed by the Esquimaux with every sign of friendship.

Then occurred an unjustifiable and very ill-advised proceeding on the part of Frobisher himself. Anxious to take some of the natives back to the ship, he enticed a couple of them to the beach with gifts and tried to force them into a boat. They escaped and ran back for their bows and arrows, and presently the arrows were whistling round Frobisher and his companion, who seem to have been separated from the others and carried no weapons. There was nothing for it but flight, Frobisher being wounded by an arrow in the lower part of his back as they ran towards the boats. The pursuers were finally put to flight by a soldier in one of the boats firing his caliver, but one of them was overtaken by a Cornishman, "a good wrastler," who showed the wretched Esquimau "such a Cornishe tricke, that he made his sides ache against the ground for a month after." This man was carried on board as a prisoner; but in the circumstances we cannot help feeling a secret satisfaction that, for a day or two at any rate, sitting down must have been something of a penance to the Captain-General.

The explorers had many adventures ashore and afloat which we cannot stop to describe in detail. The *Aid* was set on fire and narrowly escaped disaster by the negligence of the cook in overheating the galley fire. On another occasion the fleet was beset by a violent storm, which, breaking up the ice, brought such an army of icebergs surging down upon them that they barely avoided destruction. They were only saved by good seamanship, clawing this way and that in a gale of wind to avoid collision, now and then being scraped by a great berg as they flashed past under shortened sail. God, said an eye-witness, was their best steersman.

The violent weather cleared some of the ice from Frobisher Bay, and standing into it, often anchoring, the ships penetrated it for a distance of about a hundred miles. Exploring the southern shore, which they thought to be the mainland of America, they collected considerable quantities of what they imagined to be the gold ore, and also came upon a great dead fish about twelve feet long having a horn two yards long "wreathed and straight, like in fashion to a taper made of wax" growing out of its snout. The horn they sawed off and took home to the Queen, who put it among her curiosities. Finally, they took possession of the country under the name of "Meta Incognita," marching with ensigns displayed and building cairns on mountains and other high places as signs of ownership.

This done the explorers crossed over to the northern shore of the bay, which they thought was the mainland of Asia, and examined it, finally anchoring in an inlet near the entrance which they named the Countess of Warwick's Sound. In this locality they found much of the fancied gold.

Those who were present describe in faithful

detail the characteristics and habits of the wandering tribes of Esquimaux, their dress and appearance, their rude weapons, their dogs and sledges and peculiar underground habitations. At one place the English were saluted on landing with a volley of darts and arrows, to which they replied with flights of arrows and a volley from their fire-arms, hoping to frighten the natives away. But the Esquimaux were nothing if not brave. They fought manfully so long as their arrows lasted, even plucking English arrows from their wounded bodies and shooting them back. In this encounter five or six of the natives were killed and one Englishman was dangerously wounded. A native woman was also taken prisoner, being taken on board the ship as a companion for the man captured some time before.

About two hundred tons of the ore were embarked, but by the middle of August the cold weather was beginning to set in and the ships were gradually becoming hemmed in with ice as the sea froze. Frobisher saw it was impossible to do much more that year, and on August 23rd, having previously lit a great bonfire and marched his men round it with flags flying and trumpets sounding while the ships fired a salute, he weighed anchor and stood out to sea.

They had more stormy weather during the passage home, in the course of which a man was washed overboard and drowned. Except for another man who was ill when he embarked and had since died, this was the only death during the entire expedition, which is all the more surprising when we consider the primitive sanitary arrangements of the period, the miserable accommodation, bad food and the general prevalence of scurvy. It is true they had been absent for no more than three months; but in Anson's voyage, over a century and a half later, scurvy made its appearance within a month of leaving England.

The food supplied for Frobisher's voyages consisted of biscuit, meal, beer, wine, salt beef and pork, peas, salted stock-fish, butter, cheese, oatmeal, rice, raisins, almonds, liquorice. This sounds a liberal dietary; but the quality of the provisions left much to be desired.

The ships were separated by a tempest on September 1st; but by the 23rd of the same month had all reached home in safety. The adventurers were received in England with much public rejoicing, the news that they had brought home two hundred tons of the rich ore filling the people with joyous excitement. Frobisher himself was summoned to Windsor and there gratefully thanked for his services and entertained by the Queen, while the supposed treasure was deposited, some in the Tower of London, some in Bristol Castle, the Queen herself sending down a message that four locks were to be placed upon the doors.

The ore was finally delivered to the best gold refiners that could be found, and when one method of smelting failed they tried another. But nothing could be done with it. It was a long time, however, before people could be induced to believe that the ore contained no gold at all, and in December 1577 Sir William Winter, in charge of the experiments at Bristol, wrote to say that they could not get a furnace hot enough for the work.

Finally, it was admitted that the ore was "poor in respect of that brought last year, and of that which we know may be brought the next year." With this opinion the members of the Cathay Company, the Court and the general public had to console themselves, while those responsible hurried on the preparations for a third and much larger expedition to be sent out early the following year.

In the spring of 1578 full instructions were delivered to Frobisher for his third voyage. The

expedition this time was to consist of fifteen ships—
the *Aid*, *Gabriel* and *Michael* as before, and the
*Thomas Allen*, *Ann Frances*, *Judith*, *Hopewell*, *Bear*,
the *Thomas* of Ipswich, *Emanuel* of Exeter, *Frances*
of Fowey, *Emma* of Bridgewater, *Solomon* of Weymouth, the *Moon* and the barque *Dennis*.

Cathay was entirely forgotten, Frobisher being
ordered not to pursue his discoveries for more than
two hundred leagues, but to concentrate his energy
upon acquiring the supposed wealth of Meta Incognita. The fleet was to be manned by 130 seamen,
160 pioneers and 60 soldiers, besides the requisite
number of miners, gold-refiners, gunners, bakers,
shipwrights, carpenters and surgeons, together
with "a minister or two, to administer divine service
and the Sacrament according to the Church of
England."

A colony of one hundred men was to be established
ashore, and for their accommodation one of the
vessels carried "a strong fort or house of timber,
artificially framed . . . whereby those men that
were appointed there to winter and make the
abode for the whole year, might as well be defended
from the danger of the falling snow and cold air,
as also to be fortified from the force or offence"
of the Esquimaux.

Frobisher's own orders for the conduct of his
fleet at sea are not without interest. Swearing,
dice and card-playing and filthy communication
were prohibited, and divine service was to be held
twice daily. The flagship would carry a light at
night, when no ship was to pass ahead of her, while
at all times the other vessels were to remain within
a mile. It was before the days of signalling with
flags, and gun signals were laid down for use in fog
or distress, or on sighting land, heaving-to and
tacking, while at seven o'clock every evening the
ships were to "come uppe and speak with the

Admirall" to receive orders for the night. If a vessel found herself close to another during the night and did not know who she was, the watchword was, "Before the world was God," to which the reply was, "After God, came Christ, His Son." During fog the ships were to make a "reasonable noise" with trumpets and drums, while a rendezvous was given in case of separation.

The expedition assembled at Harwich on May 27th, whence Frobisher and his captains were summoned to Greenwich to take leave of the Queen, from whom they received gracious encouragement in their enterprise. Frobisher himself was presented with "a fair chain of gold," a mark of distinction, and equivalent to a modern decoration.

Sailing from Harwich on the 31st the fleet took a new route, passing through the English Channel, calling at Plymouth, and then proceeding along the south coast of Ireland. On June 6th, off Cape Clear, they fell in with a Bristol merchant barque which had been attacked by French pirates who had "slain many of them, and left the rest so sore wounded that they were like to perish in the sea, having neither hand nor foot whole . . . nor victuals to sustain their hungry bodies . . . some of them having neither eat nor drink more than olives and stinking water in many days before." These unfortunate mariners had their wounds attended to and were given a supply of food and water and put on their course for England.

With a fair wind the fleet then sailed on to the north-westward, sighting Greenland on June 20th. On this occasion Frobisher succeeded in finding a suitable harbour, and going ashore took possession of the country in the name of the Queen, and called it "West England." The inhabitants fled when the explorers landed, but entering their rude tents the Englishmen found a box of small nails and other evidences of comparative civilization, and leaving behind them bells, looking-glasses and toys, brought away two dogs in exchange.

They left again on June 23rd, and the last cliff they sighted before the coast faded away in the mist they called "Charing Cross," because of "a certain similitude." Steering to the southward because of the thick mists, icebergs and floating ice, they encountered, on June 30th, a large school of whales. One of the ships, the *Solomon*, struck one of these creatures end on under full sail, so that the vessel stood still. The whale made "a great and ugly noise," flung up its flukes and disappeared. Two days later they came across a dead whale floating on the surface and supposed it to be the one collided with.

On July 2nd the fleet was in sight of the coast of Meta Incognita, and, closing in upon the land, endeavoured to reach the Countess of Warwick's Sound, the final anchorage during the previous voyage. But the entrance of Frobisher Bay was so choked with thick ice that the ships could make no progress. Time and time again they were forced to sail stem on into huge blocks of ice, trying, as they said, to drive their way through great mountains of it. Sometimes they found open passages in the frozen surface and made their perilous way through them; but were ever in danger of being nipped and seriously damaged. At the first attempt only the *Michael* and *Judith* reached the anchorage.

The *Dennis*, a barque of one hundred tons, was struck by a great berg and sank in sight of the whole fleet. Her men were all saved; but the greater portion of the fort for the accommodation of the colonists was lost in her.

While the fleet were thus working their weary way through the ice-fields which surrounded them on all sides, the wind started to blow from the east.

It speedily freshened to a full gale, and in the midst of a sea of bergs and ice-floes, some large, some a few yards in diameter, rolling, grinding and crashing together in all directions, the entrapped vessels were soon in the gravest danger of being squeezed and battered to pieces. They could not retrace their course towards the open sea, for the ice had closed behind them. Some hove-to, some drifted, and others moored themselves to bergs, all ships strengthening their sides as best they could with cables, mattresses, spare masts and planks to withstand the terrible blows. For a day and a night the ships' companies, with pikes and poles, bore off the great floes which threatened to sink their vessels; but it was only by the mercy of God that they were saved.

When the tempest subsided the fleet fought their way back to the open sea and tried to find their old anchorage at Hall Island; but in the fog and snow and darkness they could not tell icebergs from rocks and solid land. They wandered about until July 10th, keeping together with the greatest difficulty, and on that day found themselves, more by good luck than by management, opposite an opening in the coast. Frobisher thought it to be the entrance to the "straits" bearing his name. Captain Hall, his chief pilot, was of a different opinion, and after a quarrel with his leader left the *Aid* in a spirit of mutiny, went to the *Thomas Allen*, whose captain was second-in-command of the expedition, and with three other vessels stood out to sea.

Hall's supposition, as it afterwards turned out, was quite correct, and eventually, after finding the real entrance to Frobisher Bay and rescuing two or three vessels which were wandering aimlessly up and down, not knowing where they were, he and his ships arrived in the Countess of Warwick's

Sound on August 2nd, to find Frobisher and the main body already anchored there.

Frobisher, meanwhile, had discovered the great channel afterwards known as Hudson's Straits, and thinking that at last he had found the route to Cathay, sailed along it for a distance of three hundred miles. His men started to murmur, though at first he managed to quiet them by telling them "they were in the right course and known straits." But the murmurings soon grew into discontent, and discontent into virtual mutiny, and at last, much to his disgust, he was forced to turn back.

Retracing their course to the eastward they again had vile weather accompanied by much fog. Groping their way among the rocks and islands off a treacherous coast, beset by erratic currents, they were in constant peril of shipwreck, so that the ships' companies, thinking their last moments had come, recommended themselves to death and prayed, "Lord, now help us or never; now, Lord, look down from heaven and save us sinners, or else our safety cometh too late!"

On July 23rd Frobisher fought his way clear of the corner of Meta Incognita, and the seamen, believing they had been saved only by a dispensation of Providence on their especial behalf, and unwilling to trust themselves further, proposed an immediate return to England, leaving their missing companions to their fate. The ships were leaking and badly damaged by frequent contact with the ice, and the men weary after constant labour at the pumps, "five hundred strokes . . . in less than half a watch, being scarce two hours." It is not altogether to be wondered at that mutiny was in the air.

Frobisher, however, succeeded in mastering them. Then came another storm with heavy snow, in which the men could "scarce see one another for the same, nor open our eyes to handle our ropes and sails, the snow being half a foot deep upon the hatches of our ship, which did so wet our poor mariners' clothes, that he that had five or six shifts of apparel, had scarce one dry thread to his back, which kind of wet and coldness, together with the overlabouring of the poor men amidst the ice, bred no small sickness." However, on July 31st they reached the Sound to find the *Michael* and *Judith* already there. Two days later, moreover, Hall and his detachment also appeared.

A special prayer of thanksgiving was offered up for the happy meeting, and the mutinous conduct of Hall and the men overlooked and forgiven. Nevertheless, mutiny was still in the wind, Hall openly declaring that he had lost Frobisher's confidence and could be of no further use to the expedition, while more than half the seamen showed their sympathy with him. Altogether, things were not turning out at all well. Many of the men were ill, while a whole month had been lost in finding the anchorage, and another month was needed to make good the damage sustained by the ships. Frobisher was discouraged, as were also many of those under his command. Moreover, he could not forget the new straits he had found, and keen on another Cathayan quest by the new route, made up his mind to a speedy return to England. This, indeed, was highly necessary unless he wished to stay in the Arctic throughout the fast-approaching winter.

They spent the month of August effecting repairs, in further exploration of Frobisher Bay and in collecting and embarking as much of the ore as they could find. The month passed; as it drew to a close preparations were made for the homeward voyage. The intended colonists, naturally enough, were unwilling to spend the winter in the inhospitable climate, particularly as most of the materials for their fort had been lost. What remained, however, was taken ashore and piled together in a heap and covered with lime and stone, for use in another expedition which it was supposed would be sent out the following year.[1]

On August 30th, having embarked several hundred tons of the ore, the fleet left its anchorage, and on September 2nd stood out to sea. Hardly had they done so when another violent storm dispersed the ships and wrought severe damage. Heavy weather and contrary winds prevailed throughout the entire passage to England, where, however, one or two at a time and at various ports, they all arrived in safety at about the beginning of October. The total loss of life during the expedition had amounted to about forty men, a number which was not considered excessive.

As before, the voyagers received a hearty welcome from their countrymen, and great were the expectations of profit from the large quantity of ore brought home. But before very long people were to be disappointed. During the voyage the gold-refiners at home had been working at the ore brought back from the second expedition, and not one ounce of gold could they find in it. Moreover, the third

---

[1] Englishmen did not return to Meta Incognita for many years. It is interesting to note, however, that in 1861–1862 Captain Hall, the American explorer, visited the scene of Frobisher's activities 283 years before. On questioning the Esquimaux he heard of a tradition passed down from generation to generation that, a long, long time before, white men had visited the neighbourhood and had masted a ship. The natives had also come upon pieces of wood, coal and brick. Captain Hall searched the islands in the Countess of Warwick's Sound and himself found bits of coal, fragments of iron, tiles, glass and pottery, besides the ruins of stone houses, a musket bullet, an excavation supposed to have been one of Frobisher's gold-mines, and an inclined trench which had obviously been used for the building of a small ship. There is little doubt that these were all relics of Frobisher's three voyages.

consignment was soon discovered to be equally worthless. It was nothing more nor less than iron pyrites.

Public rejoicing soon turned into open discontent, and there ensued a series of quarrels in which Frobisher's officers and men, as well as those who had risked their money in the venture, gave vent to their displeasure in no uncertain terms. Frobisher was accused of being arrogant, obstinate, insolent and prodigal, "full of vain talk, impudent of tongue, and perchance the most unprofitable of all that have served the Company," while it was also alleged that the non-success of the expedition was due to his wilful neglect of duty. None of these accusations was true; but always a man of hasty temper and not given to mincing matters, Frobisher retaliated by hurling abuse at his detractors, even going so far as to offer personal violence.

It is unnecessary to follow the course of these unsavoury disputes; but by the discovery of what was thought to be gold in the first voyage, any hope of finding a passage to Cathay vanished. Moreover, on the real nature of the ore being found out, the Cathay Company was ruined, and Frobisher was prevented from following up his discovery of the great channel now named on our maps the Hudson Straits.

Frobisher had regained favour at Court by 1580, in which year he was employed as captain of one of the Queen's ships, the *Foresight*, in preventing the Spaniards from giving assistance to the Irish rebels in Munster. At about the same time he received an official appointment as "Clerk of Her Majesty's Shippes," though it is not clear if he ever entered upon his duties as such.

That he was a poor man and in need of paid employment is evident from a letter written by his wife, who styled herself "the most miserable poor woman in the world," to Sir Francis Walsingham in 1578. She stated "in her most lamentable manner," that though she and her children had been left well-off by her former husband, Thomas Riggat, Frobisher—"whom God forgive!"—had spent all her money and "put them to the wide world to shift." She and her family were starving in a garret at Hampstead, and she asked Walsingham to help her to recover a debt of £4 due to her husband to keep them from starvation until Frobisher returned.

Whether or not her appeal was successful there is no record. It seems unlikely, however, that Frobisher, on coming home, was able to do much towards returning the money borrowed from his wife, more particularly as the salary due to him by the Cathay Company remained unpaid when the ore was found to be worthless.

In this short account, treating primarily of Frobisher's three voyages to the north-west, we cannot deal at length with his subsequent career. It seems probable that at times, between 1578 and 1585, he indulged in a certain amount of piracy; but in the last-named year he sailed as vice-admiral in the *Primrose* in an expedition commanded by Sir Francis Drake, sent out to the West Indies to annoy the King of Spain, San Domingo, Cartagena, Santiago, and other towns being attacked and captured and booty to the amount of £60,000 in money being brought home.

In 1588 Frobisher was in the *Triumph* as vice-admiral in command of a squadron during the battles against the Spanish Armada. He greatly distinguished himself, and for his services was knighted at sea by Lord Howard of Effingham, the Lord High Admiral. In the same year, and again in 1589, he was employed in command of a squadron of six ships ordered to scour the Narrow

Seas, while in 1590 we find him as vice-admiral to Sir John Hawkins in an expedition of twelve or fourteen vessels sent to ravage the coasts of Spain and to intercept a fleet of Portuguese carracks with rich cargoes homeward-bound from India.

In the summer of 1591 Frobisher was living in Yorkshire, where he married his second wife, and in May the following year was once more sent out to annoy the Spaniards off the coast of Spain returning with a large Biscayan ship with a cargo of iron worth £7,000.

In 1593 he paid his last visit to his Yorkshire home, and in the autumn of 1594, in command of a squadron, co-operated with Sir John Norris in relieving Brest and the neighbouring fort of Crozon, both in the hands of the Spanish. In the last fight, when the garrison surrendered and were put to the sword and their fort razed to the ground, Frobisher, at the head of his men, was wounded by a musket bullet in the hip. The bullet was removed, but thanks to the unskilful surgery of the time a piece of the wadding was left in the wound. Mortification set in, which led to the death of the gallant old seaman through septic poisoning a few days after the return of his squadron to Plymouth. His entrails were buried in the church of St. Andrew at Plymouth, while the corpse was sent up to London and interred in St. Giles', Cripplegate, on January 14, 1595.

Frobisher, though a gentleman by birth, was no great scholar, as his letters most clearly show. Trained in a rough school, he was also harsh and possessed of a violent temper. But both in his voyages to the frozen north and subsequently in many fights against the hated Spaniards, he showed himself a man of undaunted courage, with all the qualities of a great commander.

# DRAKE'S VOYAGE OF CIRCUMNAVIGATION

IN the Bodleian Library at Oxford is preserved an oaken chair fashioned from the timbers of a ship. It is one of the few relics that now remain of the famous *Golden Hind* (previously the *Pelican*), in which Francis Drake, one of the most romantic figures in English history and one of the greatest seamen and navigators our country has produced, circumnavigated the world in 1577–1580.

On December 13, 1577, after one abortive start the previous month, a squadron of five vessels sailed out of Plymouth Sound. They were the *Pelican*, of one hundred tons, on board of which was Francis Drake, Captain-General of the expedition; the *Elizabeth*, eighty tons, Captain John Wynter; the *Marigold*, a barque of thirty tons; the *Swan*, a provision ship of fifty tons, and the *Christopher*, a little pinnace of fifteen tons. The last-named was commanded by Thomas Moone, who had been Drake's carpenter in previous expeditions to the Spanish Main.

Francis Drake was born at Crowndale, near Tavistock, in 1542 or 1543, and was thus in his 35th or 36th year. He had married, in 1569, at Budeaux, near Plymouth, Mary Newman, of whom little is known except that she was a native of London. Drake, we are told, was a short, burly man of great strength, with massive limbs and chest. In a miniature painted shortly before his departure and still treasured by his descendants, he is shown as a young-looking man of pleasing expression, with brown wavy hair, slight moustache, grey-blue eyes, and the curiously arched eyebrows so noticeable in all his portraits. The familiar reddish beard shown in all his later representations seems to have been grown during the voyage.

He had been a seaman since boyhood; but, unlike many of the rough old sailors of his day, came of a good family, had refined and cultivated tastes and was a competent Spanish linguist. Of masterful temper, intolerant of opposition and impatient of advice, he had the force of character to make himself obeyed, and, fiercely ambitious, was as fearless of responsibility as of an enemy. A hard taskmaster, he was a born leader of men; but possessed a kindliness of disposition which made him loved and respected by his subordinates. He was courteous and generous, even to his enemies, and was never known to take life unnecessarily.

An expert seaman and navigator and an intrepid fighter, he had already established a reputation by his daring forays against the hated Spaniards in the West Indies. From the modern point of view some of his exploits seem little better than piracy, for England and Spain were nominally at peace. But there was no peace beyond the line— the line drawn by the Pope, after the discoveries of Columbus, dividing the rich, newly found territories of the world between Spain and Portugal. There was no international law in the sixteenth century. Means of communication were slow, and in the eyes of Drake and most of his countrymen his attacks were just and honourable reprisals for the wrongs inflicted by the Spaniards.

In his various expeditions Drake had captured and looted many vessels, had ravished more than one town, and for a time had paralysed the coasting trade in the Spanish Main, besides diverting the steady flow of precious metals and jewels from Peru to the coffers of Spain. Time and time again he had been within an ace of irreparable disaster; but as often his fertile readiness of resource and seamanship converted almost inevitable disaster into startling success. Essentially a man of action and restless energy, he was a master in the art of surprise. His blows fell like lightning where they were least expected, and Philip of Spain, smarting at the indignity of the buffets and the disorganization of his trade, complained bitterly of the depredations of this latest reincarnation of the Evil One, and demanded his condign punishment.

The invariable policy of Queen Elizabeth, meanwhile, was to keep the peace. She possibly foresaw a future war with Spain; but as yet she was unprepared and did not wish to provoke a conflict. So, while frowning in public upon her unruly seamen, and disclaiming all responsibility for their misdeeds, she was secretly sympathetic to their efforts. Indeed, she even lent her ships and money for filibustering expeditions, and was not averse to sharing in the profits.

After Drake's voyage to the West Indies in 1573, however, during which he sighted the Pacific Ocean from the isthmus of Darien, and vowed that with God's help he would sail upon that sea in an English ship, he came home to find the atmosphere changed. Politicians, fearful lest maritime adventures in Spanish waters should plunge the country into war, so influenced the Queen that she discountenanced further expeditions. Advisers at Court considered rivalry with Spain as madness, and were quite content if England maintained the position of a second-rate Power and picked up a precarious subsistence in those parts of the world that were not required by Spain. At one time there was even the possibility of Drake being arrested and punished as a pirate.

The daring seaman was therefore not permitted to put into practice the scheme for which his heart was yearning, and for a time was forced to content himself with assisting the Earl of Essex in trying to subdue a rebellion in Ireland fostered by the Spaniards. In this work he greatly distinguished himself, returning with a glowing letter of recommendation to Walsingham, the Secretary of State, himself a consistent supporter of the war policy.

Again the atmosphere at Court had changed. For various reasons war was being seriously considered, and in January 1576 came news that an English ship had been seized in a Spanish port and her crew flung into the dungeons of the Inquisition. The Queen was furious at this fresh insult and the country was thoroughly roused, Parliament being summoned to vote the necessary money for hostilities.

War did not come; but the Queen, pining for revenge, sent for Drake. His adventures, his daring and resource, were all passports to the Royal favour, and with all the attraction she so strongly exercised over the sturdy manhood of her time, she appealed to his chivalry as some distressed damsel to a knight-errant. She had been evilly wronged by her cousin, Philip of Spain, and, with all the subtle persuasion of her sex, claimed Drake's service.

Drake had been present with his uncle, John Hawkins, when their small squadron was treacherously attacked by the Spaniards at San Juan de Ulua in 1568, and ever since his heart also had been burning for revenge. Some of the English survivors of that disaster had been tortured and burnt at the stake, and this injury to his friends, coupled with the loss of his own property, fixed in him that indelible hatred which caused him to consider war with Spain as a crusade in defence of truth and humanity, no less a personal than a national duty. It

was his ardent desire to penetrate to the South Sea
—the Pacific—and as an accompaniment to a mission
of revenge, he conceived the exploration of the
Pacific coast of America, with a view to taking
possession of new lands beyond the limits of Spanish
occupation. His mind was filled with great schemes
for the aggrandizement of his country by oversea
colonization, the spread of the Protestant faith and
the extension of British trade. The actual circumnavigation of the globe may or may not have been
in his mind when he set out; but from the evidence
it appears as if it was his original intention to
return home by a passage which he imagined to
exist round the north of America.

For once his ambitious schemes fitted in with
the wayward moods of his Sovereign, and with
his heart full of hope he set forth at once to make
preparations for the voyage. But within two
months Elizabeth had again changed her fickle
mind and obstinately convinced herself that Philip
meant peace.

How the perverse lady was eventually persuaded
it is impossible to say; but Thomas Doughty,
with whom Drake was on terms of great friendship,
had become secretary to Sir Christopher Hatton,
one of the gentlemen of the Queen's privy chamber,
the captain of the Royal bodyguard, and her prime
favourite. Doughty probably turned Hatton's head
with the dazzling prospect that the venture promised, and the Queen in turn was influenced by her
favourite. Walsingham's genius for management,
moreover, also seems to have shown him in Drake a
convenient instrument to force Elizabeth into war
with Spain.

Finally the Queen yielded and informed Drake
that she was prepared to subscribe a thousand crowns
towards the expenses of the expedition; but only on
condition that the enterprise was kept a dead secret,

and that, above all things, Lord Burghley, the Lord High Treasurer and her most trusted counsellor, should not be told what was afoot. That astute statesman, however, was fully aware what was happening. He said nothing; but seems quietly to have gone to work to prevent, by underhand means, the prank which his Royal mistress had set her mind to. His tool was Thomas Doughty, who accompanied Drake as a gentleman adventurer and nominally as captain of the land soldiers.

The project was very popular. Courtiers and merchants took shares freely, and cadets of the best West Country families offered their services as volunteers. The objects of the voyage had been carefully concealed lest the Spaniards should be forewarned, and it had been given out that the expedition was destined for Egypt. The Spaniards, however, aware through their agents that something was in the wind, thought a stroke was again intended for the West Indies. But the secret seems to have been well kept, for it was not until the ships reached the Cape Verde Islands that the rank and file of the expedition learnt that they were bound to the coast of Brazil, and thence to the River Plate and beyond.

By the time Drake sailed, war with Spain again loomed large upon the political horizon, and there is considerable evidence which proves that the voyage was undertaken with the full consent of the Queen, and that the original commission for innocent trade and exploration was supplemented by secret orders for a regular war of reprisal. It is stated by some authorities that the *Pelican* belonged to the Queen, while Spanish prisoners stated that Drake carried the Royal arms of England during his voyage. Prior to his departure Elizabeth also presented him with a sword and sundry furnishings for his cabin. A gold embroidered sea-cap, and a green silk scarf edged with gold lace and embroidered at each end in fine gold thread with the words, "The Almighty be your guide and your protector to the ende," were also bestowed by the Queen, and are still in the possession of the Drake family. Some authorities state that they were given after the great voyage; but from the wording on the scarf it would appear equally likely that they were given before sailing. In any case, it is improbable in the extreme that marks of Royal approval and encouragement would have been bestowed upon an unlicensed adventurer.

According to modern ideas the five ships comprising the expedition, the largest of which was the flagship of one hundred tons, seem absurdly small for an ocean voyage of unknown duration. But it was the age of small ships, and before the days of a regular system of ship measurement according to the amount they could carry. The *Pelican*, then accounted a sizable vessel, was probably about the dimensions of a coasting schooner of the present day, though with considerably more freeboard and superstructure. Subsequently renamed the *Golden Hind* by Drake, the *Pelican* must not be confused with Flemyng's vessel which discovered the Spanish Armada. The only pictorial evidence of Drake's famous ship is contained in the Hondius chart of the voyage of circumnavigation, which shows her to have had the features to be expected in so small a craft. She had no fourth, or bonaventure-mizzen, mast and no quarter or stern galleries.

The vessels were manned by 150 men and 14 boys, which number included men of science as well as gentlemen volunteers and mariners. They were amply stored and provisioned for their hazardous voyage, and carried on board four pinnaces in sections, ready to be put together when required. A rich man through his successes on the Spanish Main, Drake spared no expense in fitting out.

Arms and munitions were of the best, expert musicians were provided, and the table furniture in Drake's cabin, itself redolent at times with perfumes given by the Queen, were of silver, richly gilt and engraved with the family arms. There were also, according to Francis Fletcher, the chaplain, who wrote an account of the voyage, "divers shows of curious workmanship, whereby the civility and magnificence of his native country might, among all nations whithersoever he should come, be the more admired."

Drake was generally a man of simple tastes. But he realized the value of display before strangers, and in setting forth on his voyage he surrounded himself with all the pomp and luxury possible.

With a fair wind and smooth water the little fleet ran down across the Bay of Biscay, and finally arrived at Mogador, on the coast of Morocco, on December 25th. Here they set up one of the pinnaces and obtained some provisions and merchandise, sailing again to the southward on the last day of the year. On the way they captured three Spanish fishing-boats and three caravels, and with them arrived at Cape Blanco on January 16, 1578. Five days were spent in cleaning the ships, trading with the miserable inhabitants and laying in provisions, and all but two of the prizes were released, for one of which, a stout vessel of forty tons, the little *Christopher* was given in exchange. On the 21st the squadron sailed from Cape Blanco, and with a fair north-easterly breeze shaped course for the Cape Verde Islands, where Drake meant to water and victual, preparatory to the long stretch across the open ocean to Brazil.

In the Cape Verde Islands he had anything but a friendly reception. Hawkins and other slave-traders had made hateful the name of Englishmen, and on the arrival of the squadron the inhabitants fled, after filling their wells with salt and doing everything in their power to prevent provisions from being obtained. It was at the island of Maio that Doughty started to sow the seed of dissension which finally lost him his head, for on being landed with a party of musketeers he began secretly to tamper with the men.

Off St. Iago they captured a Portuguese ship on her way to Brazil. She carried various passengers and was laden with a rich cargo of wine, silk, cloth, and various stores useful to the fleet. Doughty was placed in command of the captured vessel, and the fleet passed on to the island of Brava, where they provisioned and watered. Here Drake went on board the prize, to find that Doughty was accused of pilfering the cargo. There was a serious quarrel, which resulted, justly or otherwise, in the offender being sent on board the *Pelican*.

The Brazil ship was so suitable a vessel that Drake attached her to the expedition, setting all the prisoners at liberty without ransom, and providing them with a pinnace for their return to St. Iago, acts of clemency which much surprised them. One man Drake retained, and he, a Genoese pilot for the Brazils, named Nunez da Silva, volunteered to serve in the expedition as soon as he heard that it was intended to pass into the Pacific by the route discovered by Magellan, but since abandoned as too hazardous. On February 2nd the fleet sailed on its long passage, Drake himself transferring to the prize, which was renamed the *Mary*.

Fifteen days later the squadron crossed the equator, where for three weeks they were becalmed in the doldrums and made little or no progress. Mr. Fletcher finds time to admire the bonito, the flying-fish and sea-birds, but "being in the bosome of the burning zone," he says, "we felt the effects of sultring heat, not without the affrights of flashings, lightnings, and terrifyings of often claps of thunder; yet still with the admixture of many comforts."

The ships had not been able properly to fill their water-casks since leaving England, and Mr. Fletcher's "comforts" were that between February 10th and 27th "there was not one day went over us but we received some raine, whereby our want of water was much supplied." Scarcity of water was one of the chief terrors of early seamen, and with no distilling plants to replenish their stock in mid-ocean we can well understand their gratitude for the blessings of Providence.

They were out of sight of land for sixty-three days before sighting the coast of Brazil in the vicinity of the Rio Grande on April 5th, and during the long ocean voyage Doughty's behaviour again gave cause for complaint. He was not a seaman by profession, merely a gentleman adventurer, and had been put on board the *Pelican* more or less under reprimand. But once there he had endeavoured to take command, giving the crew to understand that he was Drake's deputy, and that, as such, he had the powers of life and death conferred by the leader's commission.

The whole root of the trouble lay in the fact that the relative status of the gentlemen adventurers and sea officers had never been properly defined, and in fomenting jealousy between them and consequent insubordination, Doughty possibly saw formidable weapons for carrying out Burghley's instructions and jeopardizing the success of the expedition. In the Spanish Navy it was the custom for the professional seamen of the ship to be subordinate to the soldier in command, a habit which accounted largely for its inefficiency. Drake, however, wished it otherwise. He was determined that the sailor should command at sea, and Doughty's assumption of authority incited his wrath. It was the last straw when Drake's trumpeter, who had been sent on board the *Pelican* with a message, was subjected to a cobbing at the hands of Doughty and his men. The leader regarded the incident as a deliberate insult and insubordination, and without permitting the offender to say a word in defence, sent him on board the victualler in disgrace.

Coasting along the land to the southward, the fleet experienced bad weather and contrary winds, during which the *Christopher*, as the Spanish fishing-boat captured off Cape Blanco had been named, lost touch with her consorts. But finally they all reassembled again in the River Plate, their predetermined rendezvous, anchoring in various bays from April 14th until the 27th. Considerably to their surprise they found fresh water alongside, and spent the time refilling their casks, refitting the ships and killing a quantity of seals for food.

On sailing the little fleet stood on to the south; but again had ill-luck, for the weather was very bad and the victualler *Swan*, on board of which was Thomas Doughty, parted company. Gale succeeded gale as Drake crept slowly on to find an anchorage. The *Mary*, commanded by his brother, Thomas Drake, lost touch. The ships were constantly separated, and though from time to time they anchored off the coast, it was only to be driven out to sea again by bad weather. Drake had determined to reduce the number of his vessels so that they might more easily keep company, and, by concentrating the men, facilitate the supply and issue of provisions. But for several weary weeks the search for a suitable port continued, and so bad was the weather that Drake, superstitious like other seamen of his day, came to the conclusion that the malcontents in his fleet were responsible for it by sorcery and black magic. Thomas Doughty had a considerable following among the gentlemen adventurers, including John Doughty, his brother, and never had they ceased their efforts to undermine Drake's authority.

On May 18th, when the rest of the fleet lay at anchor at Port Desire, some 300 miles north of Magellan's passage, the *Swan* with Doughty on board reappeared. She was unladen and broken up for firewood, her ironwork and other necessaries being preserved. But her master had an unsavoury tale to tell. Doughty, it would seem, had never ceased to disparage Drake and to question his authority, and when reminded of the fate of Magellan's mutinous captains, had laughed and said that gallows were for dogs, not gentlemen. Drake seems to have overlooked it, for he took the offender back on board the *Pelican*. But still Doughty continued to preach mutiny. A violent quarrel took place, the upshot of which was that the offender found himself ignominiously punished by being lashed to the mast. He was presently released, and, with his brother, was ordered on board the *Christopher*. They refused to obey, whereupon Drake directed tackle to be rigged to hoist them on board.

On June 3rd the four ships still in company sailed on. Once more the weather was tempestuous, and the *Christopher* lost touch. She was found again, and, to make the squadron still more compact, was broken up. The Doughtys, in disgrace, were put on board the *Elizabeth*, Captain Wynter, with strict orders that nobody should talk to them. Their fare and lodging were of the roughest, and for giving them the use of a cabin the boatswain of the *Elizabeth* was summarily disrated.

As the expedition moved slowly south the weather got worse. It was summer-time as they knew it; but every mile they travelled the skies became more wintry, the weather colder and the sea heavier and more threatening. The *Mary*, commanded by Thomas

Drake, was eventually found, and on June 20th the squadron entered Port St. Julian to refit and to make preparations for the desperate attempt to pass through the Straits of Magellan and out into the Pacific. It was the very port where Magellan had anchored over half a century before, and the first thing they set eyes on in that lonely wilderness was the remains of a gibbet. Buried at its foot they found two skeletons, those of Magellan's mutineers.

At Port St. Julian Drake lost two of his best men in an encounter with Patagonians; but the place was the scene of a greater and more memorable tragedy, the trial and execution of Thomas Doughty. It is no part of our business here to discuss the rights and wrongs of that unhappy affair; but a jury was formed with Wynter as its foreman and the prisoner was solemnly tried for mutiny and treason. He was found guilty of mutiny, and in the course of the trial is said to have admitted betraying the object of the expedition to Lord Burghley. The prisoner was given the choice of execution on the spot, of being sent back to England, there to answer the charges against him, or of being marooned. He chose death, and on July 2nd, having been present at a farewell banquet with Drake, after which they received the Sacrament together, was beheaded. He died with great fortitude.

But there were other malcontents in the fleet, and as the work of refitting progressed there were further quarrels between the gentlemen and the seamen. It was more than Drake could stand. He saw that the constant bickerings were jeopardizing success, and ordering the ships' companies ashore, he addressed them. The speech is so little known and the words were so much to the point that they are worth quoting at some length.

"I am a bad orator," he said. "My bringing up hath not been in learning, but what so I shall here speak . . . I will answer it in England, yea, and before Her Majesty.

"We are very far from our country and friends. We are compassed in on every side with our enemies. . . . We must have these mutinies and discords that are grown among us redressed, for by the life of God it doth take my wits from me to think on it; here is such controversy between the sailors and gentlemen, and such stomaching between the gentlemen and sailors, that it doth make me even mad to hear it. . . . I must have the gentlemen to haul and draw with the mariners, and the mariners with the gentlemen. . . . Let us show ourselves to be of a company, and let us not give occasion to the enemy to rejoice at our decay and overthrow.

"I would know him that would refuse to set his hand to a rope," he went on. "But I know there is not any such here; and as gentlemen are very necessary for government's sake in the voyage, so have I shipped them for that, and to some farther intent, and yet though I know sailors to be the most envious people in the world, and so unruly without government, yet may I not be without them."

He proceeded by offering the *Marigold* to any who wished to return to England—"but," he added, "let them take heed that they go homeward, for if I find them in my way I will surely sink them."

This strange mixture of cajolery, compliments and defiance went straight to the hearts of his hearers, and one and all they consented to sail on, leaving the matter of wages to him. But he had not done with them yet. He proceeded to dismiss Wynter from the command of the *Elizabeth* and all the other officers from their posts. He was asked why. "Is there any reason why I should not do so?" he demanded.

He went on to explain how Doughty had betrayed the expedition to Burghley, and charged various other members of the company by name with treachery. Thereupon they humbled themselves before him, and he continued by telling them that the Queen had sent them out on the expedition, and warned them that if the voyage were a failure they would not only be objects of derision to their enemies, but also a great blot on their country for ever. He concluded by restoring every officer to his original rank and station in the squadron, and told them they served Her Majesty the Queen, not himself.

At Port St. Julian the Portuguese prize *Mary*, being leaky, was unladen and broken up, and on August 17th the fleet, now reduced to the *Pelican*, *Elizabeth* and *Marigold*, sailed to the southward. Three days later they came to the entrance to the Straits of Magellan, where Drake, in homage to the Queen, caused the ships to salute by striking their topsails upon the bunt. The *Christopher* had been broken up, and Sir Christopher Hatton, through Doughty's execution, now had no visible connection with the expedition. Drake accordingly placed Hatton's crest of a golden hind on the poop of his flagship and renamed her the *Golden Hind*. It was a shrewd stroke of policy, for Drake was well aware of Hatton's influence with the Queen, and knew how useful he could be in shielding him from the possible wrath of Burghley at Doughty's execution.

Drake was the second navigator to accomplish the passage of the Straits. For the greater part of its length it is tortuous and narrow, a place of fierce, irregular tides, studded with dangerous rocks and shoals. There were no accurate charts, and on all sides the ships were hemmed in by steep, iron-bound cliffs rising inland to huge snow-covered peaks. On one side lay an active volcano, which, with fires lit by the natives, encouraged the superstitious credulity of the seamen. The biting wind came down the glacier-filled valleys in fierce gusts which buffeted the ships this way and that. Unable to anchor on account of the depth of the water, they were carried hither and thither by the strong currents. Not once, but many times, they were nearly cast ashore. The passage was difficult enough to appal the stoutest seaman. Even in these days it is regarded as hazardous enough for a sailing vessel. But Drake's cumbrous little ships struggled on, and in sixteen days he brought his fleet out in triumph into the Pacific.

Not far from the western outlet of the Straits they came to three islands which appeared large and fruitful. The crew slaughtered many penguins for food and found in them "a very good and wholesome victual," while Drake, landing upon the largest island, named it Elizabeth Island in honour of the Queen.

On September 6th they entered the Pacific; but at once the great ocean belied its name. It proved rather to be a "Mare furiosum," says Fletcher, for it was the stormiest sea they had ever sailed upon.

A furious westerly gale hurled the ship 600 miles back to the south-east of Cape Horn. The sky was darkened with masses of piled-up cloud, and, says Mr. Fletcher, "the winds were such as if the bowels of the earth had set them all at liberty. The seas were rolled up from the depths, and being aloft were carried as feathers or drifts of snow by the violence of the winds. Our anchors gave over their holdfast, committing the distressed ships and helpless men to the uncertain and rolling seas, which tossed them like a ball in a racket."

After three weeks' incessant struggle the *Marigold* went down with all hands. The *Elizabeth* also parted company with the flagship and fought her way back into Magellan's Straits. Here Wynter, her captain, lit

fires nightly to tell Drake where he was. But no
Drake appeared. It had been agreed that in the event
of separation the fleet should rendezvous off the
coast near Valparaiso; but Wynter lost heart. After
three weeks he set sail for England, arriving on
June 2, 1579, with the report that all the ships were
lost except the *Golden Hind* and that she probably
had perished also.

It had hitherto been thought that Tierra del
Fuego was the northern extremity of a vast continent
stretching to the South Pole, and that the Straits of
Magellan provided the only means of communication
between the Atlantic and Pacific. But Drake, by
being driven far to the southward by the storm,
proved that Tierra del Fuego was merely an island.
October 28th, when the storm ceased, found him
anchored among islands in the neighbourhood of
Cape Horn. He was southward of anything known
to geographers or seamen, and before him the
Pacific and Atlantic mingled in mighty turmoil.
The discovery was of vast importance in the progress
of geographical knowledge, and landing on the
farthest island with his instruments, Drake fell to
his knees and embraced the southernmost point of
the known world.

The *Golden Hind*, now alone, tarried awhile, to
refresh and recuperate her crew, and on October
30th sailed for the rendezvous appointed for the
squadron near Valparaiso. The weather became fine
and sunny, and sailing on up the coast west of
South America she stopped at various anchorages,
where they had intercourse with the natives and
replenished with food and water. At one place,
however, they were attacked by Indians, two men
being killed and many others being wounded.
Drake himself was shot in the face by an arrow,
and received another wound in the head.

On December 5th they arrived at Valparaiso.

Here there were no traces of the *Elizabeth* or *Marigold*, but in their stead a great Spanish galleon—*The Grand Captain of the South*—lay at anchor in the harbour. Laden with gold and wine, she was waiting for a fair wind to take her to Panama, and her crew, taking the *Golden Hind* for a Spaniard, hoisted their colours and beat their drums. They were soon disabused. Drake took his little ship alongside and boarded with his men, and in a few minutes all the Spaniards who had not jumped overboard and swum ashore were safe under hatches. Not a life was taken.

For three days the *Golden Hind* remained in harbour, relieving the galleon of 400 lb. weight of gold and other valuables. Landing, they rifled the church, finding a chalice, two cruets and an altar-cloth, which were given to the chaplain to improve his Communion furniture, and provided themselves with a quantity of provisions in the shape of wine, bread and bacon.

Drake's next anxiety was to collect his squadron for attacks upon Lima and Panama. He explored many a little creek and bay: but not a trace of his countrymen could he discover. On December 19th he entered a bay near a Spanish town called Cyppo, where on landing his men were instantly attacked by Spaniards. One man, in a spirit of foolish bravado, refused to retreat to the boats. He was killed, his corpse being dragged in brutal triumph to the shore, where his head and hands were cut off, his heart torn out, and his body shot full of arrows by the Indians.

The next day they found a better harbour to the north-east, where they remained for a month, thoroughly refitting the ship and setting up one of the pinnaces. Their next place of call was Tarapaca, where, while looking for water, they came upon a Spaniard asleep who had lying by him thirteen bars of silver to the value of 4,000 ducats, or about £1,400. "We would not (could we have chosen) have awakened him of his nap," the Reverend Mr. Fletcher states, "but seeing we, against our wills, did him that injury, we freed him of his charge, which otherwise perhaps would have kept him waking, and so left him to take out (if it pleased him) the other part of his sleep in more security."

A little later they came across a Spaniard driving eight Peruvian sheep, or llamas, carrying 800 lb. of silver. This they possessed themselves of. On January 26, 1579, Drake anchored at Mormorena, where he obtained supplies from the Spaniards. "We found them (more from fear than love) somewhat tractable," says the chaplain.

On February 7th the *Golden Hind* arrived at Arica, the spot where the wealth of the Potosi mines of Peru was shipped for Panama. In two small ships they found some forty bars of silver weighing 800 lb., "of which we took the burden on ourselves to ease them." At Ariquipa they were disappointed of booty, but on the passage up the coast they encountered another barque laden with linen, "some of which we thought might stand us in some stead, and therefore took it with us."

The other ships not having been found, Drake had now come to realize that he was entirely alone, and had only himself and his crew to depend upon. On February 15th, at dead of night, the *Golden Hind* entered Lima. There were thirty ships in the harbour. All were ransacked, but nothing was found except a few chests of small coin and some bales of silk and linen. But here it was learnt that the galleon *Our Lady of the Conception*, nicknamed *Cacafuego*, or *Spitfire*, had sailed fourteen days before for Panama with the whole produce of the Lima mines for the season. She was ballasted with silver, with a cargo of gold and jewels. It was enough for Drake.

Leaving Lima on February 16th, he set sail in chase. He crossed the equator on February 28th, and on the way fell in with a brigantine which they despoiled of eighty pounds' weight of gold and a great gold crucifix said to be set with emeralds as large as pigeons' eggs.

The Viceroy of Peru, meanwhile, had dispatched ships in pursuit of the raider, but the *Golden Hind*, staggering northward under all the sail she could carry, rapidly overhauled her quarry. Drake had offered a golden chain to the man who should first sight her unmistakable sails, and at last, on the afternoon of March 1st, off Cape St. Francis, his nephew John Drake claimed the reward.

The *Cacafuego* was sailing lazily along close by the shore, and thinking she was being followed by some heavily laden trader and glad of company in her long voyage, shortened sail. The sun was still well above the horizon, however, and Drake was well aware that if the galleon suspected his true character she would run in upon the land. He had no desire to capture her before night, when there would be an off-shore breeze, and filling empty wine-skins with water, he trailed them astern to check his way.

At last the sun sank in the west, and the rosy after-glow faded from the snowy peaks of the Andes. Then, when darkness came, the wine-skins were hauled in and the water rippled round the *Golden Hind's* forefoot as she drove ahead in the freshening breeze. She rapidly overhauled the galleon, crossed her bows and came alongside her starboard side.

San Juan de Anton, the *Cacafuego's* captain, looked over the side of his ship; but already the English were grappling her and shouting: "Englishmen! Strike sail!"

"What England is this which orders me to strike sail?" the Spaniard replied, accustomed to the

Spanish monopoly of the Pacific and hardly able to believe his ears. "Come on board and strike the sails for yourselves!"

A whistle blew on board the *Golden Hind*. A trumpet screeched. It was followed by a flight of arrows and a volley from many arquebuses. A gun roared, and the shot carried away the galleon's mizzen-mast and sent it overboard with its sail and lateen yard. Another gun blazed out, and forty archers from the pinnace, which had been sent round to her port side, boarded the galleon and were soon in possession.

Seizing San Juan, they took him to Drake, who was removing his fighting helmet and coat of mail. Drake embraced him, saying, "Have patience, for such is the usage of war," and ordered him to be locked up in the poop cabin under guard.

For three days the two ships in company sailed to the north-westward, and another three were spent in transferring the booty from the *Cacafuego* to the *Golden Hind* by means of the pinnace. It was a rich haul—a quantity of pearls, emeralds and diamonds, eighty pounds of gold, thirteen chests of coined silver, twenty-six tons of uncoined silver, and besides fruit, conserves, sugar, meal and other victuals, "two very fair silver-gilt drinking-bowls and other trifles." The whole capture was subsequently valued by the Spanish ambassador at a million and a half ducats, or roughly £750,000. One may readily believe that the great silver and gilt cup now preserved among the Drake relics at Nutwell Court is one of those captured from the *Cacafuego*.

The Spanish captain remained a week on board the *Golden Hind*, during which he was well treated and cared for. Then, putting the hapless Spaniards on board their plundered vessel with a little linen and the like in exchange for the commodities taken from them, and signing his name in the ship's log as a receipt for all the treasure, which had been entered as freight, Drake permitted them to depart. He had also given San Juan a safe-conduct in case he should be molested by any other English ship, and thinking, no doubt, of his kinsmen and friends who had been tortured and burnt at the stake by the Inquisition, had said to him, "I know the Viceroy will send for thee to inform himself of your proceedings. Thou must tell him that he shall do well to put no more Englishmen to death, and to spare those four that he hath in his hands, for if he do execute them they shall cost the lives of two thousand Spaniards, whom I will hang and send him their heads."

Drake's only desire was now to get home. To attempt to capture Panama single-handed was sheer folly, for the whole coast of New Spain was in a fever of apprehension, troops were being collected, and ships were being fitted out and armed. From England various navigators were seeking the fabled Strait of Anian, which was supposed to connect the Atlantic and Pacific round the north of America, and having already established the non-existence of the great continent to the southward of Tierra del Fuego and mapped out the western coast of South America, Drake made up his mind to add to his reputation by going home by this north-west passage. His resolve completely outwitted the Spaniards who had been sent to intercept him, for he was sought off Panama and the Straits of Magellan with no success.

Three weeks after dismissing the *Cacafuego*, Drake fell in with another Spanish vessel from which he helped himself to some linen, cloth, porcelain dishes, silk, and a falcon wrought in pure gold, with a great emerald set in its breast. After taking out the pilot he allowed the ship to proceed. Don Francisco de Zarate, the captain of this vessel, gives an intimate picture of Drake—"a man of some five-and-thirty years, small of stature, and red-bearded, one of the greatest sailors on the seas, both from skill and power of commanding. His ship carries about 400 tons, is swift of sail, and of a hundred men, all skilled and in their prime, and—much experienced in warfare. Each one in particular takes great pains to keep his arms clean; he treats them with affection, and they treat him with respect; he brings with him nine or ten gentlemen. . . . These are his council. . . . None of these gentlemen sits down or puts on his hat in his presence without repeated permission. He dines and sups to the music of violins. When our vessel was plundered, none dare take anything without his leave; he was very gracious to them but punished the smallest fault. He carries also painters who paint him the coast in its own colour!"

Drake refitted his ship at Canoas Bay, in California, careening her, setting up a forge and repairing and re-rigging her from stem to stern. On April 15th, running into the port of Guatulco for water and provisions, he found a Spanish court sitting for the trial of a batch of negroes. An English boat's crew appeared, tied the judges hand and foot, and carried them off to the *Golden Hind* as hostages, making them send an order to all the inhabitants to leave the town. They laid in a stock of water and provisions from the Spanish storehouses, and did not forget, according to Mr. Fletcher, "to take with us also a certain pot—full of ryalls of plate—together with a chain of gold, and some other jewels, which we entreated a Spanish gentleman to leave behind him as he was flying out of the town!"

Remaining only for a day, the *Golden Hind* sailed again on April 16th, and off the coast of Nicaragua had the happy fortune to fall in with a galleon carrying a new governor to the Philippines. The official was dispossessed of his valuables, but, what was more important, Drake obtained charts showing the course of the rich Spanish trade across the Pacific.

Between April 16th and June 3rd the *Golden Hind* sailed 1,400 leagues to the northward and arrived in about the latitude of Vancouver. Here, though it was summer, the weather was very severe, the very ropes of the ship being frozen stiff and the men half-paralysed with cold. They endured bitter tempests and "most vile, stinking fogs," and the men, willing enough in ordinary circumstances, began to complain. Further progress to the northward was impossible, and here it was that Drake probably made up his mind to return to England round the Cape of Good Hope.

Running south, he brought the *Golden Hind* to a natural harbour near San Francisco on June 17th. Here they remained until July 24th, being received with great friendliness by the natives, who are said first to have worshipped the strangers as gods, and then, when convinced they were human, to have crowned Drake as king. Here Drake set up a brass plate announcing the annexation of the territory to the realm of Queen Elizabeth, and named the country "New Albion," because its cliffs were white like those of England.

Towards the end of July the *Golden Hind* finally left the west coast of America for her long passage across the Pacific. She steered straight for the Moluccas, and was out of sight of land for sixty-eight days, until, on September 30th, she came to what are now known as the Pellew Islands, but christened by Drake the "Islands of Thieves," for the predatory habits of the people.

It is unnecessary here to describe Drake's subsequent wanderings to Mindanao, the southern island of the Philippine group, and his run south through the Molucca passage to Ternate, where he visited, and was visited by, the native king, and was supplied with all his requirements, together with a small quantity of cloves. In great friendliness he negotiated a commercial treaty with the king, which for some time afterwards was of no small value to British diplomats in their wrangles with the Dutch and Portuguese on the subject of the East India trade. He seems to have created a most favourable impression, for half a century later the king's son, who had succeeded his father, wrote to King James to say how eagerly he had looked forward to Drake's return. "I have lived in the same hope," he writes, "till I was the father of eleven children." He then adds that, disappointed at English indifference, he had been obliged to call in the Dutch to help expel their enemies, the Portuguese. It was at Ternate, also, that Drake met an influential Chinaman, who begged him to visit China, an invitation which was not accepted.

Leaving Ternate the *Golden Hind* passed on to an island southward of the Celebes, where she remained for twenty-six days and was careened, watered and victualled. Sailing again on December 12th she tried to beat northward into the Straits of Macassar, but was forced to turn south again on account of the many shoals and small islands. With no accurate charts and imperfect navigational instruments, they were beset by constant danger of grounding, and on January 9, 1580, at eight o'clock in the evening, while running before a light breeze with all her sail set and drawing, the ship ran hard and fast upon a reef. Expecting instant destruction and death, they prayed to the Almighty for help. The prayer concluded, Drake encouraged his men to bestir themselves, and to their joy they found the ship was not holed. The water round the shoal was so deep that anchors could not be laid out for kedging off, and they jettisoned four guns and some of the less valuable cargo. Still she remained fast. Then, providentially, the wind lulled and started to blow from the opposite direction. The tide rose, and at four o'clock the next afternoon, having been ashore for twenty hours, the *Golden Hind* heeled over and slid bodily off into deep water. It was a merciful escape, the greatest danger they had encountered throughout the entire voyage.

For nearly a month more they struggled to the westward through the dangerous rocks and shoals of the Flores and Java Seas, until, in the middle of March, they came to a port in southern Java, where they had friendly intercourse with the natives, cleaned and refitted their ship, and were supplied with everything they wanted.

Drake had fulfilled his purpose of carrying the English flag into the Pacific. He had outwitted the Spaniards, had crossed from end to end a lonely ocean hitherto regarded as the property of Spain and Portugal, and had made important geographical discoveries. On March 26th the little *Golden Hind*, her work done and her hold crammed with Spanish treasure, set her white wings to the favouring breeze and shaped her course direct for the Cape of Good Hope.

Little remains to be told. On May 21st they sighted Africa, coasting along it to the southward until June 18th, when, in fair weather and a south-easterly breeze, they rounded the Cape of Good Hope so closely that their guns might have shot to the land.

On July 22nd they came to Sierra Leone, where they watered and obtained lemons and oysters. On September 26, 1580, "after two years, ten months and some odd days besides, in seeing the wonders of the Lord in the deep, in discovering so many admirable things, in going through with so many strange adventures, in escaping out of so many dangers, and overcoming so many difficulties," the little *Golden Hind*, battered and weather-worn, her silken flags and pennons fluttering bravely in the breeze and her trumpeters playing a fanfare, sailed again into Plymouth Sound.

Beyond a vague rumour that Drake had been hanged by the Spaniards as a pirate, nothing had been heard of him in England for some time. Wynter, returning in June 1579, had brought home the news of the great storm in which the *Golden Hind* had vanished; but two months later Mendoza, the Spanish ambassador in London, hurled a bombshell into the political arena by springing upon the Queen the startling intelligence of Drake's depredations in the eastern Pacific, news of which had been received from the Viceroy of Mexico. The peace party were horrified; but Walsingham could well afford to congratulate himself, for there seemed no alternative but war.

The Queen, however, pacified the Spanish ambassador by disclaiming all responsibility—declaring that Drake was a mere private adventurer, and that, if already executed, she would not object, while, if he ever came home, she would see that he was severely dealt by.

At the time of the *Golden Hind's* return, indeed, the peace party was predominant at Court, and though Drake was enthusiastically received by the inhabitants of Plymouth, friends warned him of possible trouble brewing in London. He sent a message to announce his arrival; but with characteristic resource warped his ship behind St. Nicholas, or Drake's Island, in Plymouth Sound, and remained on board with his wife.

Before long he was summoned to Court to give an account of himself, and took the precaution of taking the best part of the booty with him. The

spicuous service to his country against the hated
Spaniards at sea. But we cannot here follow his
fortunes until, on that fateful January 28, 1596, he
passed away on board the *Defiance* within sight of
Nombre de Dios, and his mortal remains, enclosed
in a leaden casket, were committed to the ocean
that he knew and loved so well.

Still treasured by Sir Francis Drake's descendants
is the great drum bearing his arms which is said
to have accompanied him round the world in
the *Golden Hind*, and may have been beaten in the
final salute when his body was committed to the
sea. A legend immortalized by Sir Henry Newbolt
in his stirring poem, "Drake's Drum," says that
by beating this drum the great seaman can still be
summoned when his country is in danger:

> Take my drum to England, hang et by the shore,
>   Strike et when your powder's runnin' low;
> If the Dons sight Devon, I'll quit the port o' Heaven,
>   An' drum them up the Channel as we drumm'd them
>         long ago.

# WILLIAM DAMPIER

## 1652–1715

WILLIAM DAMPIER, buccaneer, pirate, circumnavigator, and captain in the Navy, was born at East Coker, near Yeovil, in 1652. The son of a farmer who died in 1654, he was originally intended for a commercial life, and for some time was educated at a classical school, where he acquired a knowledge of Latin. Very early, however, he had evinced an overwhelming desire to travel and to see something of the world, and in 1669, the year after his mother's death, having first been instructed in writing and arithmetic, he was apprenticed by his guardians to the master of a vessel trading out of Weymouth. In this ship he made a short journey to France, following it, the next year, at the age of eighteen, with a voyage across the Atlantic to Newfoundland. The experience did not please him. In this voyage, as he says, "I spent one summer; but so pinched with the rigours of that cold climate, that upon my return I was absolutely against going to those parts of the world, but went home again to my friends."

When we picture the sort of vessel in which young Dampier probably went to sea, his remarks are not surprising. The sea-going ships of his day were about the size of a Thames barge; but with a length no more than about three times the breadth, with great bluff bows, and in the stern, tall, upstanding poops, which caught the wind and made them unmanageable in heavy weather. Cumbrously rigged with square-sails only, they were deplorably slow and could not beat to windward; but could only sail with the wind on or abaft the beam. Reliable charts were lacking and methods of preserving provisions primitive, and besides the perils of storm and tempest and the terrors of unknown shoals and hidden rocks, navigators had to face the pangs of famine and the ravages of pestilence.

The use of the magnetic compass had already been applied to navigation; but there were no chronometers for the exact measurement of longitude. This could only be obtained by estimating the day's run in miles, and it was the habit of sea captains first to sail to the latitude of the place they wished to reach and then east or west along the parallel of latitude. The altitude of the sun, and hence the latitude, could be obtained by means of the rough and ready cross-staff and by the astrolabe, which, invented in 1485, was the forerunner of the modern sextant. The latitude thus obtained might be as much as sixty miles in error; though, even so, it was more accurate than the longitude, which was a mere matter of guesswork.

Moreover, the conditions of life at sea were appalling, men being vilely fed and herded together like sheep in a pen. Sanitation was practically unknown and medical supervision non-existent, so that scurvy and other diseases claimed many victims. Water was stowed in casks and soon became putrid and unpalatable. There were no means of distilling at sea, no method of replenishing the supply except by catching the rain which fell from the sky. In these circumstances it is little to be wondered at that seafaring required courage of the highest order.

Dampier's determination to see the world, however, was too strong to be resisted, and soon after his return from Newfoundland he heard of a "warm" voyage about to be made to Java by an East Indiaman sailing from London. He entered himself on board as an able seaman, and in an absence of little more than a year gained some knowledge of navigation, and learnt of the trade and activities of the Dutch in the East. As yet, however, he had not begun to keep a journal.

The outbreak of the second Dutch War in 1672 caused him to remain at home with his brother in Somersetshire; but the following year, weary of the shore, he joined the *Royal Prince*, Sir Edward Spragge's flagship, and in that vessel took part in two battles against the Dutch. Falling ill, he was eventually landed at Harwich, whence he returned again to his native county.

On recovering his health the old wanderlust returned with redoubled strength. Jamaica had been captured by the English in 1655, and in 1674, at the age of twenty-two, Dampier accepted the submanagership of a plantation in that island, working his passage out before the mast. The humdrum monotony of life ashore, however, did not suit his disposition, and engaging himself on board a sloop he made several coasting voyages and became well acquainted with the ports, anchorages and general resources of the island. During these short cruises he must have met seamen who had sailed farther afield among the islands of the Spanish Main and to the coasts of central America, and, possessed of an insatiable thirst for travel, the tales of what they had seen probably fired his ambition to follow in their footsteps.

In August 1675 he accordingly shipped as a seaman on board a small trading ketch bound for the bay of Campeche, not far from Yucatan, with a cargo of rum and sugar to be exchanged for logwood. The wood-cutters, a party of about 250 ex-privateersmen, mostly English, lived in rude huts on the shores of the creeks and were a wild and unruly lot, with their old piratical instincts well to the fore. The labour of felling the trees, some of which measured six feet in circumference, and sawing the wood into convenient lengths to be carried on men's backs to the coast through dense forest and virgin jungle, was very heavy, and on the arrival of a vessel the cutters invariably flocked on board and celebrated the occasion in bouts of heavy drinking.

"We were but six men and a boy in the ship," says Dampier, "and all little to entertain them; for besides what rum we sold by the gallon or firkin, we sold it made into punch, wherewith they grew frolicksome. We had none but small-arms to fire at their drinking healths," he continues, referring to the practice of discharging guns when toasts were drunk, "and therefore the noise was not very great at a distance; but on board the vessels we were loud enough until all our liquor was spent."

Having embarked the cargo, the ketch sailed again for Jamaica, the passage being protracted to thirteen weeks through the incompetence of the master and the sluggish sailing qualities of the ship. A short, stoutly built little vessel with great round bows and the general shape of a barrel, she would not beat to windward, and in a head sea plunged and staggered so that every wave brought her up all standing. They were closely pursued by two Spanish vessels who regarded all English vessels as pirates, and afterwards blundered ashore, being saved from destruction only by the ship's stout construction. The provisions ran out, and but for two barrels of beef which had been intended for barter, but the contents of which were so rotten that nobody would buy them, they would probably have perished of starvation. Every day, says Dampier, they boiled two pieces of the meat, and cutting it again into smaller pieces, boiled them afresh with flour and ate it with spoons as a kind of broth. Altogether, it was a troublesome voyage. "I think never any vessel before or since made such traverses in coming out of the Bay as we did," he observes. "In these rambles we got as much experience as if we had been sent out on a design."

Dampier seems to have been fascinated with the free and easy life of the logwood-cutters, and early in 1676, having provided himself with the necessary implements, he made the best of his way back to join them. For over two years he remained there, enduring the greatest hardships, and alternating log cutting with hunting the wild "beeves" with which the country abounded. For some portion of the time he and his companions, thrown out of their employment by a great flood and driven by dire necessity, became pirates or buccaneers—"privateers," Dampier politely terms them—taking to their small ships and ravaging and plundering the villages on the neighbouring coast.

In the autumn of 1678, having saved some money and acquired a thorough knowledge of the logwood business, Dampier returned to England with a view to procuring everything necessary to develop a regular trade in the wood. His stay in England was very short, but whilst at home he was married to a lady of whom little is known except that her Christian name was Judith and that she came "out of the family" of the Duchess of Grafton. Leaving his wife at Arlington House, the Duchess of Grafton's residence, he sailed again for Jamaica early in 1679, intending to join the logwood-cutters in the forests of Yucatan. On arrival, however, he changed his mind, and remained in the island engaged in business until the end of the year. On the point of returning to England he was asked by a Mr. Hobby to take part in a short cruise to the Mosquito coast, an invitation he accepted as the expedition promised to be profitable. Logwood cutting, moreover, was becoming more and more hazardous on account of the activities of the Spanish in rooting out the intruders who were filching their property from under their very noses. The dissolute habits of the cutters, indeed, brought about their undoing, for many of Dampier's old companions, found by the Spaniards in a drunken stupor in their huts, were either killed outright or else carried off in captivity and sold as slaves.

On putting into Negril Bay, Jamaica, in Mr. Hobby's vessel, they found there a number of "privateers" mustered in great force. Tempted by the splendid prospects of loot held out by the adventurers, the entire crew of Mr. Hobby's ship joined them, and three or four days later, leaving the unfortunate Mr. Hobby in the lurch, Dampier himself followed suit. His motive, however, does not appear to have been the mere acquisition of a fortune. The pirates, for such they really were, were planning a descent upon the coast of Darien, and intended following it up by crossing the isthmus and preying upon the Spanish trade and coast towns in the little-known "South Sea," or, as we now know it, the Pacific Ocean. To Dampier, obsessed with a fervid longing for travel and new experiences, the opportunity of visiting this lonely ocean was too tempting to be missed.

Before dealing with Dampier's life as a pirate it is as well to give some idea of the man himself. Too frequently he is remembered merely as a buccaneer, though the instinct which led him to join these desperadoes in their lawless war against Spain was due neither to any fundamental defect in his character nor to any great desire to grow rich. Indeed, his portrait by Thomas Murray, painted in 1707, and now in the National Gallery, shows a man with the grave refined features of a thinker and scientist rather than those of a vicious, swashbuckling corsair.

A born naturalist, a botanist of no mean capability, he was possessed of an insatiable curiosity and appetite for new experiences. Moreover, he was an expert navigator and hydrographer, and practically throughout his entire career, except during his service with the pirates, which he hardly touches upon at all, he kept journals remarkable alike for their accuracy and wealth of information. With a power of vivid description he recorded in detail not only the habits and customs of the natives, and the strange birds and beasts and fishes which he came across in his wanderings, but also the scenery, trees, plants and resources of places he visited, together with much valuable hydrographical information as to anchorages, channel, winds, currents, weather and the like. The list of contents printed in quaint old English before each chapter in one edition of his writings published in 1729 shows that nothing escaped his notice. To select a few subjects at random, he deals with "The Flamingo, and its remarkable nest," "The coast of Guinea, the commodities and negroes there," "Small red lobsters," "The Dildoe-tree," "A wild vine of great virtue for sores."

He was born too early to take part as a scientist in any of the great voyages of discovery and exploration, and beset with the burning desire to travel and to see the world for himself, he joined the pirates, because, at the end of the seventeenth century, they were the people who travelled the most. He became a pirate by accident, as it were, and through the age in which he lived.

It must be remembered, moreover, that piracy was not then regarded as a crime. The Spaniards, for all their sweeping claims, were bad seamen and poor fighters. Ever since the days of Drake and the Spanish Armada they had regarded the English as devils incarnate, and on Jamaica falling into English hands in 1655 the island had at once become a base for swarms of "privateers" who existed entirely upon plunder filched from Spain. By Dampier's time these free-booters had become a numerous and well-organized band who sacked and ravaged the Spanish coast towns, and captured, looted or burned their ships wherever found. It mattered not at all if England and Spain were nominally at peace. Beyond "the line" there was no peace at all. Every ship went armed and prepared to fight, and Europeans, not Spaniards, even though their nations might be at loggerheads, united together as "Brethren of the Coast," and waged a ceaseless war of reprisal against their common enemy. Among them it was regarded rather in the light of a crusade against an intolerant people—a crusade, however, in which there was ever the possibility of reaping a golden harvest.

From his desertion of Mr. Hobby in 1679 until April 1681, Dampier dismisses his adventures in a couple of pages written a long time afterwards. One Ringrose, however, has given us a very full account of the expedition, in which Dampier apparently served at first as a forecastle hand on board a ship of eight guns and ninety-seven men commanded by a man named Coxon.

Their first attack was directed at Portobello, which they duly sacked and plundered, each man's share of the booty amounting to 160 pieces of eight.[1] Emboldened by their success, the pirate fleet of seven sail next assembled off the coast of Darien, where, in April 1680, leaving sufficient men on board to guard the vessels, they landed a party of over three hundred well-armed men, each carrying four cakes of bread, known as "dough-boys," and toys and implements for barter with the natives. They marched in companies, each with its distinguishing banner, and we may imagine this band of burly, bearded pirates, dressed in tattered finery and spurred on by the greed of gold, plodding

[1] Piece of eight, i.e. the Spanish silver dollar.

wearily along under the broiling tropic sun over mountains and across rivers, through the jungles and forests and fever-laden swamps of a hostile, unknown country.

Accompanied by native guides they fell upon the town of Santa Maria after a march of nine days, and captured it easily, though the Spaniards, having wind of their coming, had removed most of the valuables. Not an Englishman was lost; but, possibly in revenge for the absence of booty, many Spaniards were killed, some being butchered in the woods by the natives, their hereditary enemies. After a stay of three days to refresh themselves the corsairs embarked in boats and canoes and rowed down the river and across the gulf to Panama. No sooner were they seen from the shore than three armed ships came out to meet them, two of which were captured by boarding, while the third fled. It was a bloodthirsty fight, with, as usual, no quarter on either side, and though many Spaniards perished the pirates lost forty-eight killed and wounded.

But Panama, encircled by a wall surmounted by many cannon and garrisoned by 300 regular troop and 1,100 armed militia, was too tough a nut to be cracked. Moreover, lingering in their ships after the initial success, the pirates gave the Spaniards time to perfect their scheme of defence. Then, pretending a sentimental interest in the natives, the pirate leader sent word to the Spanish governor that if he would grant the Indians their full liberty, and send the rovers 500 pieces of eight for each man and one thousand for each leader, they would desist from further hostilities.

This impudent demand evoked a polite reply, the governor asking from whom the marauders had received their commission. Captain Sawkins, who had been elected leader, answered in a spirit of truculent bravado that as yet he had not collected all his men; but that, before long, he would pay Panama a visit "and bring our commissions on the muzzles of our guns," when the governor could read them "as plain as the flame of gunpowder can make them." But it was a mere idle threat. The capture and sack of the golden city of Panama was impossible, and already the pirates were beset by famine, while mutiny was in the air.

On May 23rd Sawkins was killed during an attack upon Puebla Nova, and the command devolved upon one Sharp, who, disheartened at their ill-success, ordered a retreat. The defeat caused the smouldering fire of discontent to burst into the flame of open mutiny, and when the captain called his men together and proposed a cruise against the Spanish in the Pacific and then to sail home round Cape Horn, guaranteeing that each man should be worth a thousand pounds by the time he returned to England, sixty-three men deserted. Dampier, however, elected to remain.

On June 6, 1680, Sharp and his men sailed to the southward, and, sacking and plundering the coast towns, looting and burning Spanish ships, finally arrived at the island of Juan Fernandez on Christmas Day. Here Sharp, who had never been popular, was formally deposed according to the usual custom of voting and Captain Watling was elected leader in his stead. He attempted to introduce some order and discipline in his lawless band, and on January 9, 1681, the Sabbath was observed for the first time since the death of Sawkins, who, it is said, once threw the dice overboard on finding them in use on a Sunday. This strange admixture of piety and cold-blooded piracy is a little difficult to understand.

At the end of January the pirates attacked the town of Arica, in Chile, but were repulsed with severe loss. Watling was killed and the freebooters then retired to an island to the northward off the coast of Columbia, capturing a few more ships and raiding towns on their way. Seething with discontent and quarrelling among themselves, some men wanted Sharp re-elected as their leader, while others, including Dampier, strenuously opposed it. As a result of the ballot Sharp was reinstated and took over the command, while Dampier and forty-six men who objected were allowed to take the longboat and a couple of canoes with the idea of sailing to the isthmus of Darien, recrossing it on foot and so returning to civilization.

They had their arms with them, and were provisioned with about a quarter of a hundredweight of chocolate rubbed up with sugar and as much flour as they could conveniently carry. On April 17th, having previously made a compact that if any man faltered on the way across the isthmus he should be shot by his comrades to prevent the Spanish from gaining information as to their strength, the adventurous party left the ship for their long boat journey of six hundred miles.

After a difficult passage in bad weather Dampier and his men managed to elude the Spaniards, who kept a constant look-out along the coast, and landed in safety in the Bay of St. Michael, in the Gulf of Panama, where, after removing their belongings, they sank their boats. Space will not permit a detailed description of their arduous march of twenty-three days across the isthmus in torrential rain, during which they had to negotiate trackless forests and rivers, torrents and precipitous mountains. But in spite of the difficult country, the bad weather, and their own fatigue and hunger, they hurried on, for they were in enemy territory, and there was every chance of meeting Spanish patrols.

They had many adventures. On the evening of the second day, tired out and dispirited and having lost their way, they inquired the route of a native;

but though they used every artifice to placate him, offering him axes, knives, beads and money, he replied angrily and refused to help them. It was a critical moment, for they began to suspect that the man intended handing them over to the Spaniards, and it was only at the last moment that the situation was saved by one of the sailors, who pulled a sky-blue petticoat out of his bag and threw it over the head of the lady of the house. It so delighted her that she talked her husband round and prevailed upon him to provide a guide.

The gunpowder carried by the "chyrurgeon" was set on fire by a careless fellow passing by with his pipe alight, and, blowing up, severely scorched his knee, so that he could not march. He was too valuable a man to be left behind, and providing him with a slave to carry his belongings, the famished men, their feet blistered and their thighs skinned by wading through so many rivers, plodded wearily on. Another man, carrying his fortune of 300 dollars, was swept away and drowned while crossing a river; but in spite of all these anxieties and vicissitudes Dampier still found time to write his journal; preserving his manuscripts from the wet by placing them in a hollow bamboo sealed at both ends with wax.

At length, procuring canoes to carry them down a river, they were eventually taken on board a French privateer near Point San Blas, the ship sailing two days later to join a fleet of English, French and Dutch privateers lying in the vicinity. As the other vessels were already overcrowded Dampier and his men were transferred to another French privateer commanded by a Captain Archembo, but speedily took a dislike to their new shipmates, who, says Dampier, "were the saddest creatures I was ever among." Even in bad weather, when all hands were required aloft and on deck, they "never stirred out of their hammocks except to eat."

Accordingly they prevailed upon a Captain Wright to fit and arm a small prize for their use, and in this ship cruised for a time in search of provisions, being so badly off that they were forced to depend upon manatees, or sea-cows, parrots, gulls, boobies, monkeys, and other strange "deer," all duly described by Dampier.

For over a year he remained with the pirates cruising on the Spanish Main and off the coasts of Brazil. The results, however, were disappointing, for though they captured sundry vessels they yielded little more than some tons of sugar, marmalade, cocoa, hides and earthenware. It was during this cruise that Dampier met a French man-of-war to whom he sold ten tons of sugar. "I was on board twice or thrice," he remarks, "and was very kindly welcomed by the captain and his lieutenant; and they both offered me great encouragement in France if I would go with them." It is to Dampier's credit that the offer was refused.

Not being able to dispose of their cargoes the freebooters eventually decided to divide the spoils and to separate, and Dampier and nineteen companions took a captured barque and sailed to Virginia, where they arrived in July 1682. There he remained for thirteen months, but, as he says, "that country is so well known to our nation that I shall say nothing of it, nor shall I detain the reader with the story of my affairs and the trouble that befel me."

In August 1683, glad of the opportunity, Dampier engaged himself to a Captain Cook, "a sensible man who had been for some time a privateer," who had been shipmates with Dampier in the previous expedition to the "South Seas," and, with him, had returned across the isthmus of Darien. Cook, in a prize ship of eighteen guns which he had named the *Revenge*, had planned a cruise round Cape Horn to prey on Spanish towns and shipping on the coasts

Indies and so home. It was a project, says Dampier, "very agreeable to my inclination," though some of the men in their ignorance thought that Swan would carry them over the edge of the world.

After an unsuccessful attack on Santa Pecaque, in Mexico, Swan careened and refitted his ship, and on March 31, 1686, left the American coast on his lonely voyage to the westward across an ocean still practically unknown to Englishmen.

During the passage they endured the greatest privation through lack of provisions. Dampier mentions salted jew-fish, which one would imagine a most unpalatable article of diet in the blazing heat of the tropics, and ten spoonfuls of maize per man per day—there seems to have been little else. The crew were soon bubbling over with mutiny, and in the midst of their hardships one of their number was found guilty of theft, and was condemned, according to the usual custom, to receive three blows on the bare back with a rope's end from every man on board.

Guam, one of the Ladrone Islands, was reached after a voyage of fifty days with only three days' provisions left. It was just as well, for, as Dampier observes, "the men had contrived, first to kill Captain Swan and eat him when the victuals was gone, and after him all of us who were accessory in promoting the undertaking of the voyage. This made Captain Swan say to me after our arrival at Guam—'Ah, Dampier, you would have made them but a poor meal!' for I was as lean as the captain was lusty and fleshy."

It is pleasing to know, however, that in spite of their privations the men still cared for their pets, for the two dogs and two cats on board all received a daily share of the scanty food. Moreover, when the captain gave away one of the dogs in return for some civility the crew were highly indignant.

Friendly relations were established with the Spanish governor, who, though he well knew the character of his visitors, was as unable to withstand an attack as they, in their enfeebled condition, were unwilling to make one. While a brisk trade was being carried on with the shore the galleon from Acapulco, which sailed each year across the Pacific to Manila with money for the Spanish colonies, hove in sight off the island. She was a strong, well-armed ship; but had not the governor sent out a native craft to warn her of the danger, Swan and his men would certainly have attacked her.

After a stay of twelve days at Guam the buccaneers sailed on to Mindanao, the southern island of the Philippine group, arriving on June 21st. Here they were soon on excellent terms with the natives, who wished them to settle in the island. Dampier regretted they did not accept the invitation, for he thought, and rightly, that a colony in the Spice Islands would be of great benefit to England, while among the buccaneers there were sawyers, carpenters, joiners, bricklayers, shoemakers, tailors, and men of other useful trades. Mindanao had many attractions, and Captain Swan and many of the men soon took to living ashore. Those who had saved their money found ample opportunity for spending it in riotous living, sixteen of them dying of over-indulgence. The crew, however, soon divided into two parties, those with money, and those with none—the latter, drunken and quarrelsome, first selling the ship's stores for drink, and then insisting upon going to sea to look for more prizes, while the rest were equally determined to stay ashore and enjoy themselves.

The sojourn lengthened into six months; but then came the inevitable mutiny. Swan, though he had excellent qualities, was a man of irresolution, bad temper, and "small courage," incapable of keeping his wild rascals in order. One day, when he was ashore, some of the crew found his private journal, wherein he had noted for future punishment the names of several men who had misconducted themselves. This brought matters to a head, and on January 14, 1687, the mutineers seized the ship and sailed off, leaving the captain and forty-four men behind. Dampier, who denies all knowledge of the plot, and, according to his own account, did his utmost to persuade his shipmates to return for the captain, sailed in the ship. Swan, it may be mentioned, after helping the local rajah in his wars, was subsequently killed by the natives.

The mutineers, after cruising off Manila and capturing a couple of prizes, proceeded from port to port and island to island, sometimes rioting in luxury, but more often reduced to virtual starvation. Eventually they headed southward past the Celebes, sailed out into the Indian Ocean by way of Timor, and presently arrived off the coast of "New Holland," or, as we now know it, Western Australia, which had already been discovered by Dutch navigators. At this time, it must be remembered, Dampier was still serving as a sailor, and though his journal was meticulously kept and faithfully describes the new country and its natives, he evidently had no idea of the true character and extent of it, though he was certain, he says, "that it joins neither to Africa, Asia, or America."

Leaving the coast again on March 12, 1688, the *Cygnet* arrived at the Nicobar Islands on May 5th. For some time Dampier had been very anxious to leave the "mad crew," who had become utterly unruly and capricious; but the captain, fearful of anyone leaving the vessel lest they should inform against him, resisted all his efforts to escape. However, on arriving at Nicobar there was more trouble, and after much quarrelling Dampier and seven other men were put ashore with all their effects.

At midnight on May 6th the ship sailed and left them to their fate.

The captain of the *Cygnet* thought it impossible for any one to leave the island; but the next day the castaways purchased a small canoe about the size of a wherry. She carried a matting sail and outriggers to prevent her from capsizing, and was so thin and flimsy that when empty four men could carry her. They victualled this crazy craft with "mellory," a sort of bread-fruit, coconuts and water, and on May 15th started off for Sumatra, a distance of about 180 miles, with no better appliances than a small pocket compass and a few navigational notes in Dampier's pocket-book.

Sometimes they rowed and sometimes sailed, and on May 18th, at dusk, they were beset by a great storm. Says Dampier: "The sky looked very black, being covered with dark cloud, the wind blew very hard, and the seas ran very high. The sea was already roaring in a white foam about us; a dark night coming on and no land in sight to shelter us, and our little ark in danger to be swallowed by every wave; and what was worse for us all, none of us thought ourselves prepared for another world. I had a lingering view of approaching death, and little or no hopes of escaping it; and I must confess that my courage, which I had hitherto kept up, failed me here; and I made very sad reflection on my former life; and looked back with horror and detestation on actions which before I disliked, but now I trembled at the remembrance of."

However, thanks to Dampier's good seamanship, they successfully weathered the tempest and reached Sumatra after a terrible passage lasting five days. Stricken by fever they were too weak to stand upright on landing, but luckily fell into the hands of friendly natives who cared for them.

On recovering his health Dampier made a trading

voyage to Tonkin, during which he assiduously kept up his journal, and for a time left his ship and wandered about the country acquiring information. At one place he came across a friendly French priest who inquired if any of the English ships would sell him some gunpowder. Dampier answered that they had none to spare, whereupon the holy father asked if he could manufacture it. On Dampier replying in the affirmative he produced sulphur and saltpetre and asked him to try his hand. The experiment was a success, and there is something not a little whimsical in this picture of a buccaneer solemnly assisting a missionary to make gunpowder to help him in propagating the gospel among the mustard-coloured heathen of Tonkin.

We need hardly weary the reader with a full account of Dampier's wanderings before he returned to England. In March 1689 he went again to Sumatra, and three months later became mate of a Dutch sloop which made a voyage to Malacca. In January 1690 he sailed in command of the same little vessel to Madras with a cargo of pepper. He stayed for some months, and here obtained a tattooed prince called Jeoly, hailing from an island east of the Philippines, with whom, in April, he returned to Sumatra. Dampier next obtained a berth as gunner to an English factory at Bencoolen, but soon, dissatisfied with the governor, anxious to get home, and thinking that his "painted prince" would bring him a fortune if exhibited in England, he was clamouring to be off. The governor, however, was averse to losing him; but on January 2, 1691, Dampier and Jeoly secreted themselves on board an English vessel lying in the roads. Except for a bad outbreak which carried off thirty men, the voyage home was uneventful, and on September 16th the ship anchored in the Downs.

In this, his first circumnavigation of the world,

Dampier had spent eight years since sailing from Virginia, and twelve years since leaving England in 1679. But his voyage had benefited him little. Beyond acquiring much information, duly noted in his journals, he was practically penniless, his only asset being the "amiable savage," whom, however, he was presently forced to sell. As for Jeoly, he was carried about on show for a time and finally died of the small-pox at Oxford.

Of Dampier's life for the next six and a half years, which he seems to have spent in England, there is no written account. In 1697, however, he published his journal of the voyage round the world, dedicating it to Charles Montague, afterwards Earl of Halifax, the president of the Royal Society and one of the most influential politicians of his time. The book had a great vogue, running into four editions in two years. In a second volume, which appeared in 1699, Dampier described his voyages from Sumatra to Tonkin and Madras, and gave an account of his early adventures with the logwood-cutters at Campeche together with "A Discourse of Winds," one of the most valuable early contributions to meteorological geography.

The president of the Royal Society seems to have introduced him to the Earl of Orford, First Lord of the Admiralty, to whom his second volume is dedicated, and in 1697 Dampier was directed to draw up proposals for a voyage of exploration to New Holland. As previously described he had already visited that country in the *Cygnet*, and had found it barren and desolate; but did not accept what little he had seen as a fair sample of "this large and hitherto almost unknown tract of land situated so advantageously in the richest climates in the world."

"In coasting round it," Dampier says, "I could not but hope to meet with some fruitful lands, continents, or islands, or both, productive of any of the rich fruits, drugs, or spices (perhaps minerals also) that there are in other parts of the torrid zone. . . . I meant also to make as diligent a survey as I could of the several smaller islands, shores, capes, bays, creeks, and harbours, fit as well for shelter or defence . . . and of rocks and shoals, the soundings, tides and currents, winds and weather variation; whatever might be beneficial for navigation, trade, and settlement. . . ." In short, it was hoped that exploration of the new territory would eventually lead to its becoming the scene of an English spice trade as lucrative as that of the Dutch in the East Indies.

Dampier's training had well qualified him to serve in such a voyage, for his curiosity was unbounded, and he possessed a naturally scientific mind seasoned by ample experience. Moreover, he was a skilful seaman, pilot and navigator. On the other hand, he lacked those qualities necessary to make him a successful leader of men, being a stranger to discipline and quite unused to the habit of command.

However, on January 14, 1699, having been appointed to the command of His Majesty's ship *Roebuck*, a vessel of 290 tons and twelve guns, manned by fifty unseasoned men and boys, he sailed from the Downs. The *Roebuck*, a fifth-rate of 292 tons, had been built at Wapping in 1690, and was originally designed to carry [1] 26 guns and 115 men. Both armament and crew, however, were reduced for Dampier's voyage. Reefs had come in again during the century in place of "bonnets" laced to the foot of a sail. The bowsprit was also fitted with the small sprit-sail topmast shown in pictures of ships from the reign of James I to that of George I. Very early in the voyage there was trouble with his crew. They were an incompetent and mutinous lot, "almost heartless in the pursuit of the voyage," and

[1] At this period wooden quakers were often mounted in ships to enhance their apparent strength.

the captain, whenever he went ashore, was in constant dread lest they should cut or slip the cables and return to England. In his journal he mentions being forced to "keep myself all the way upon my guard, and to lie with my officers, such as I could trust, with small-arms upon the quarter-deck; it scarce being safe for me to lie in my cabin, by reason of the discontents among the men."

Some of the crew of the *Roebuck* were even too lazy to change their clothes when drenched to the skin by the heavy tropical rains, for the heat made them careless. The poor wretches—one cannot help sympathizing—would "lye down in their hammocks with their wet clothes, so when they turn'd out they caus'd an ill smell where ever they came, and their hammocks would stink sufficiently." It was this unpromising material that Dampier, the ex-buccaneer with no knowledge of discipline, had undertaken to keep in order for a lengthy voyage.

Even with his officers Dampier could not agree, for his lieutenant, George Fisher, was sent ashore in irons at Bahia, in Brazil. The upshot of this particular quarrel will be mentioned later.

However, after touching at the Canaries, the Cape Verde Islands and Bahia, all of which are described in great detail in her captain's journal, the *Roebuck* rounded the Cape of Good Hope without calling, and, on July 31st, made the coast of New Holland, or Western Australia. Sailing northward to discover a harbour where they could anchor and refresh themselves after their journey, they eventually came to in Shark's Bay, where, however, on digging wells, they could find no water. They caught sharks, which were eaten "very favourily," together with turtle, sea-fowl, and what Dampier calls "raccoons."

But scurvy was making itself manifest among the men, and after ranging for about 900 miles along the inhospitable coast without finding any good fresh water or any convenient place to clean the ship, Dampier, on September 1st, set sail for the island of Timor, where there were Dutch and Portuguese settlements. The Dampier Archipelago, off the coast of Queensland, together with Roebuck Bay and a range of hills called Roebuck Downs, both in the district of Dampier in Western Australia, still bear their names in commemoration of the explorer and his vessel.

On December 12th, having careened and cleaned his ship, refreshed his men and laid in a stock of water and provisions, the *Roebuck* sailed again from Timor, and on New Year's Day, 1700, sighted the coast of New Guinea. She proceeded to round its western extremity by what is now known as the Dampier Straits, and then sailed on to the eastward. Here Dampier discovered that the eastern portion of New Guinea was really an island and called it "Nova Britannia," and the strait dividing it from New Guinea "Dampier's Passage" or Strait.

He had meant to continue his voyage by rounding the eastern end of New Guinea and then sailing down the unknown eastern coast of New Holland. But the sorry state of his ship and the mutinous condition of the men made it impossible; and turning back to the westward he made for Batavia, arriving on July 4th. Here, in comparative civilization and by the good graces of the Dutch, he remained until October 17th following, repairing leaks, embarking stores and provisions, and generally preparing for the voyage home to England.

Sailing on the date mentioned the *Roebuck* arrived at the Cape of Good Hope on December 30th, leaving again on January 11, 1701. From the 2nd until the 13th of February she was at St. Helena, and on the 21st of the same month sighted the island of Ascension and stood in towards it.

The *Roebuck*, however, was never to see England

again. She was utterly worn out, and on the 22nd sprung a bad leak. Twenty-four hours' unremitting work at the pumps failed to keep the water under, while the planking, "so rotten that it broke away like dirt," could not be repaired with the means available. The ship was hauled in towards the shore, and eventually foundered with the loss of many of Dampier's books and documents, officers and men establishing themselves ashore in tents made from the sails. There was ample fresh water, and turtle, goats, land-crabs and boobies in abundance for food, so that the castaways could have existed for some considerable time without difficulty; but on April 12th three English men-of-war and an East Indiaman arrived and anchored, and Dampier and his men were rescued. They were landed at Barbados, whence Dampier and his officers eventually proceeded to England in the East Indiaman *Canterbury*.

George Fisher, who had been Dampier's lieutenant on first leaving England, had, as already mentioned, been sent ashore at Bahia under arrest on the voyage out. He had been clapped by the Portuguese governor into the common gaol, but eventually arrived in England by way of Lisbon. An old officer who resented being put under the orders of an ex-buccaneer, he accused Dampier, on reaching home, of being a bad navigator and ill-treating his officers and crew. Dampier, in his turn, accused his subordinate of calling him "Old Rogue," "Old Dog" and "Old Cheat," and so inciting the men to mutiny. There is no doubt that Dampier had been unduly harsh and cruel, and at a court-martial held on June 8, 1702, the members of which included Sir George Rooke and Sir Cloudesley Shovel, he was found guilty and adjudged to be "fined all his pay to the Chest at Chatham."[1] The court further pro-

---

[1] In the reign of Queen Elizabeth an act was passed whereby every parish was assessed at a weekly sum for the maintenance

nounced their opinion that "the said Captain Dampier is not a fit person to be employed as commander of any of His Majesty's ships."

Dampier, though he had added comparatively little to the knowledge of the world, had achieved much in carrying out a voyage in little-known waters in circumstances of considerable difficulty and danger. His reputation as a navigator and a hydrographer was enhanced; but once again, dogged by ill-fortune and in his fiftieth year, the old buccaneer found himself bereft of his employment and cast adrift with hardly a penny in his pocket. In spite of his faults we cannot but feel a certain sympathy.

It does not seem that the finding of the courtmartial was taken very seriously. In 1702 war again broke out with France and Spain, and a syndicate of merchants was formed, as in the days of Queen Elizabeth, to fit out privateers to earn large dividends by preying upon hostile shipping. Dampier was chosen to command two vessels destined to cruise for this purpose in the Pacific, the *St. George*, of 26 guns and 120 men, and the *Cinque Ports*, a galley of 16 guns and 63 men. As was usual in these privateering expeditions, officers and men were engaged upon the "no prey, no pay" system, while the captain, though he had a commission from the Lord High Admiral, had no real disciplinary power over his officers and crew.

On April 18, 1703, the *London Gazette* announced that Captain Dampier, "being prepared to depart on another voyage to the West Indies, had the

of disabled seamen and soldiers. This was the origin of the "Chatham Chest Fund," the resources of which were afterwards augmented by the compulsory stoppage of sixpence a month from the wages of each seaman in the Navy. The original chest, an iron box, is, or used to be, preserved in the museum of the Royal Naval College at Greenwich, where it was deposited by the Admiralty in 1845.

honour to kiss Her Majesty's hand . . . being introduced by His Royal Highness, the Lord High Admiral."

The two ships finally sailed from Kinsale on September 11th, though their destination was not as stated in the *Gazette*. They were first to proceed to the River Plate, to seize two or three Spanish galleons expected to be found there, returning home if the plunder amounted to £600,000. If unsuccessful in this they were to enter the Pacific and prey upon the ships which carried gold from Valdivia, in Chile, to Lima, in Peru. If this project failed they were then to raid such towns as Dampier might select, and finally to close the Mexican coast with a view to capturing the galleon which, laden with treasure, sailed annually across the Pacific from Manila to Acapulco.

Dampier gives us no account of this voyage, but a description of it was written by one Funnel, whom Dampier calls a steward.

Having touched at Madeira the privateers stood on for the Cape Verde Islands, and on October 7th arrived at St. Iago, where, after some disagreement, Dampier put his first lieutenant ashore at midnight with nothing but his chest and clothes. Sailing on again after a week they arrived in October off the coast of Brazil, where the captain of the *Cinque Ports* died and was succeeded by Thomas Stradling, of whom more will be heard later. Here, also, took place a violent quarrel between Dampier and Barnaby, his new lieutenant, which resulted in that officer and eight seamen deserting the ship.

Dampier subsequently denied wrangling with his officers; but there is little doubt that, soured by disappointment and unaccustomed to command, he habitually used foul and abusive language, and treated those under his orders with cruelty. The officers and men, for their part, were a mutinous, turbulent set of men, possessing all the vices of buccaneers without their hardy courage and experience.

On December 8th the *St. George* and *Cinque Ports* sailed from the coast of Brazil. Early in the New Year, 1704, they were off Cape Horn, where they had the usual stormy weather. By February 10th, short of water and provisions, and their men suffering from scurvy, both ships were at the island of Juan Fernandez.

It was here that Stradling, a violent and dissolute fellow, quarrelled with his men, forty-two of whom went ashore and refused to serve with him. The matter was patched up somehow and they were induced to return to their duty, and hardly had the reconciliation taken place when, on February 29th, a sail appeared off the island. The privateers were refitting, watering and provisioning their ships; but hurrying on board they slipped the cables and stood off in chase. The stranger proved to be a Frenchman of 400 tons and 30 guns, crowded with men, and after a brief encounter in which the *St. George* lost ten killed and wounded, Dampier broke off the engagement and returned to Juan Fernandez.

Before very long two more French ships hove in sight and were suffered to sail off unmolested, and leaving behind them in the island some men, their boats, ground-tackle and stores, the *St. George* and her consort sailed off to the coast of Peru. Off Lima they encountered one of the Frenchmen already seen, but Dampier, much to the disgust of his men, refused to engage. A few days later, however, they captured a couple of small prizes laden with general cargoes, which were released after having been robbed of their boats and sundry stores. On April 28th the privateers in their boats attacked the rich town of Santa Maria in the Bay of Panama. The enterprise was a ghastly failure, and on May 6th, almost at their wits' end for want of provisions and with the men in a state of mutiny, the marauders rejoined their ships. At midnight on the day of their return, by the greatest stroke of fortune, a Spanish ship arrived at the place where they were anchored. She was laden with flour, sugar, wine, brandy, salt and marmalade, besides linen and woollen cloths, and was promptly captured, looted and released, after which the privateers proceeded to an anchorage in the Bay of Panama.

Here, after a violent quarrel between Dampier and Stradling, the two ships parted company, the *St. George* steering southward for the coast of Peru and the *Cinque Ports* returning to Juan Fernandez.

Alexander Selkirk was Stradling's mate, and, for very good reasons, cordially detested his captain. At Juan Fernandez he elected to leave him and go ashore, and here, for over four years, he eked out the precarious existence described by Defoe in *Robinson Crusoe*. The *Cinque Ports*, it may be said, eventually became so leaky that her crew ran her ashore on the coast of Peru and surrendered themselves to the Spaniards, whence, after several years of captivity, Stradling found his way back to London.

Dampier, meanwhile, cruising in the *St. George*, was capturing a few small prizes, though nothing rich enough to satisfy his crew, who were mainly out for specie, not merchandise. Indeed, by refraining to attack and neglecting his opportunities, he had certainly displayed a want of enterprise, if not actual cowardice.

It had become necessary to careen and repair the ship, whose bottom "was in many places eaten like a honeycomb, insomuch that the firm planks were no thicker than an old sixpence; nay, in some places in the hold, we could thrust our thumbs quite through with ease."

She was therefore laid aground in a convenient harbour for repairs, while a prize, fitted up as a tender, cruised outside. The *Little Dragon*, as they had called this vessel, soon came in with a forty-ton barque laden with wines, spirits and sugar; but on September 2nd, while the *St. George* was still hove down, with all her powder and shot, some of the guns, and a quantity of provisions on board the new prize for safe keeping, Dampier had another fracas, and this time with Clipperton, his mate. The latter promptly seized the barque and sailed off with twenty-two men, after restoring as much of the ammunition as he did not require.

On September 23rd the *St. George* and *Little Dragon*, their crews now numbering no more than sixty-four men and boys, sailed together in quest of the galleon from Manila. Several small vessels were taken and a Spanish settlement near Acapulco raided, while, on December 6th, the galleon herself hove in sight.

She was a great, wall-sided ship heavily manned and bristling with eighteen and twenty-four pounders, while the *St. George's* guns threw a shot of only five pounds. The privateers, however, their appetites whetted by disappointment and weary of a cruise which had brought them little booty, were in high fettle for a fight, desperately anxious to capture a prize which, reputed to be worth sixteen million pieces of eight, would fill their pockets with gold and then permit them to sail straight away for home.

But it was not to be. Bearing down upon the galleon the *St. George* poured in several broadsides before she was recognized as hostile, so that, flung into utter confusion, the Spaniards tumbled over each other in their anxiety to defend themselves. Had Dampier closed in and boarded at once there is little doubt that the rich prize would have been his. But he had none of the courage of Drake. Either through over-caution or sheer cowardice he hesitated. The galleon was given time to bring her guns into action, the broadsides driving in huge pieces of her adversary's rotten timbers. Dampier was finally forced to haul off to save his ship from sinking, and the Spaniard escaped unharmed.

It was a bitter blow and not very creditable to the captain, and the crew, mutinous in their disappointment, clamoured to return home. Dampier parleyed with them, but on February 1, 1705, Funnel and thirty-two men, in spite of protests, helped themselves to what they required and sailed off in the *Little Dragon* with the intention of making their way to the East Indies.

Dampier, left with no more than twenty-eight men and boys, proceeded to refit the crazy *St. George*, the shot-holes being filled with tallow and charcoal as the planking was too rotten to take nails. The sails were patched and the rigging refitted, and having plundered the town of Puna, in Ecuador, and captured a small prize, the two ships sailed in company to an island off the coast of Mexico. Here, after a council of war, the old *St. George* was left to founder at her moorings, and having removed everything likely to be of use, Dampier and his men embarked in the little prize and sailed off to the westward across the Pacific to the East Indies.

Little is known of the voyage, but on arriving at the Dutch settlements the authorities seized the ship and her cargo, detaining Dampier for some time as a prisoner. He eventually found his way back to England towards the end of 1707, returning, as says one writer, "naked to his owners, with a melancholy relation of his and their misfortunes, occasioned chiefly by his own odd temper, which made him so self-sufficient and overbearing that few or none of his officers could bear him." His failure did not, however, prevent him from being introduced to the Queen, whose hand he again kissed, and to whom he gave "some account of the dangers he had been through." Moreover, he was well received by some of the leading members of the Royal Society, one of whom, Sir Hans Sloane, caused to be painted the portrait now in the National Gallery.

The war with Spain was still in progress, and previous to Dampier's return some Bristol merchants had arranged for two armed ships, the *Duke* and *Duchess*, to be sent out to prey on Spanish trade in the South Pacific. Dampier, though undoubtedly a bad captain and unable to handle men, had as good a reputation as a navigator as any one living, and Woodes Rogers, the captain of the *Duke*, took him as his pilot.

The expedition finally sailed from Cork on August 28, 1708, and after capturing a few prizes and various outbreaks of mutiny, quelled only by the firm hand and good sense of Rogers, stood on to the southward round Cape Horn. One third of the crews went down with scurvy and all hands were perished with cold; but on February 1, 1709, they arrived at Juan Fernandez.

Here, on sending a boat ashore, it returned and "brought abundance of crayfish, and a man clothed in goatskins, who looked wilder than the first owners of them." It was Alexander Selkirk, who had lived alone in the island ever since leaving Stradling four years and four months before. As he was a prime seaman he was immediately taken on board the *Duke* as mate.

Sailing on after refitting and provisioning, the privateers captured many prizes in Peruvian waters, and at Guayaquil, which they raided, obtained plunder to the value of £21,000, and 27,000 dollars as a ransom for not burning the town. To determined men the Spanish merchantmen were easy victims. Utterly worthless as seamen, and with no heart for fighting, their ships were crowded with priests, seasick women and merchants, who increased the confusion by lamentations and wild invocations of all the saints in their calendar on the appearance of a privateer.

In December, off the coast of California, after a brisk action, they captured an armed ship from Manila, the *Nuestra Señora del Encarnaçion*, richly laden with merchandise and carrying gold and silver worth £12,000. From the prisoners they heard of the proximity of the Manila galleon herself, and on Christmas Day she was in sight. A great vessel of 900 tons, she was powerfully armed and well manned; but the buccaneers promptly sailed in to the attack. After two days' fighting, however, in which the English lost thirty-eight men killed and wounded, the privateers were compelled to haul off. Their small six-pounders had no effect on the solid upper-works of the Spanish ship, and there were insufficient men to carry her by boarding.

The cruise, though thus foiled in its chief object, had not been unsuccessful, and on January 10, 1710, having manned the *Encarnaçion* and renamed her the *Bachelor*, the buccaneers sailed off with their three ships to the westward across the Pacific. Provisions were very scarce, the livestock consisting of four hens, while there were barely a dozen bottles of wine and spirits. The daily rations, we are told, were limited to a pound and a half of flour and a small piece of meat for each mess of five men, together with three pints of water a man for all purposes.

Arriving at Guam on March 10th they procured all the food and water they needed, and, after calling at one or two islands, finally arrived at Batavia on June 17th. The crews, stricken with famine and rotten with scurvy, were so rejoiced at the sight of the town that they hugged and shook each other by the hand, vowing there was never such a paradise in all the world; "and this," says Rogers, "because they had arrack at eightpence a gallon and sugar at a penny the pound."

Leaving Batavia in October they sailed direct to the Cape of Good Hope, whence they proceeded home in company with a convoy of Dutchmen, arriving in the Texel in July 1711. On October 14th the *Duke*, *Duchess* and *Bachelor* finally assembled off Erith, and thus ended one of the most memorable and profitable voyages ever undertaken by English buccaneers.

Rogers had all the qualities of leadership and decision that Dampier lacked, and the cargoes and treasure captured were valued at between £300,000 and £400,000, money then being worth considerably more than it is now. After deducting all expenses, such as cost of convoy, agency, lawsuits and the like, there was a gross profit of £170,000 on the voyage. Half of this went to the officers and men, and the other half to the owners, whose outlay did not exceed £14,500.

Dampier was never to enjoy the fruits of his labour, for the prize money was not distributed until 1719, and on March 15, 1715, in his sixty-third year, he died in London.

In spite of his failings, Dampier was no ordinary man. He is known neither as a great explorer nor as a leader of men. His sobriety, honesty and courage were all called in question from time to time, and, brought up in the school of the old buccaneers, his only ideas of discipline were harshness and severity and calling his subordinates rogues and rascals and other names that we cannot mention.

But as a practical navigator, a student and a writer, his age knew no equal. His writings, immensely popular, revealed a new and a strange world to people at home in England and stirred their imaginations. Further, they diverted the thoughts of scientists, geographers, merchant princes and the general public to the wonder and romance of the "South Sea," and caused Englishmen to consider the possibility of competing with the Dutch for the trade and wealth of the Spice Islands in the fragrant East.

William Dampier knew little happiness. His portrait shows a face full of sorrow and disappointment. From his boyhood almost up till the end of his life he was at sea, leading the hardest of lives in ill-found ships in the most unhealthy climates in the world, eking out an existence on food that would have been spurned by a pampered dog. The comforts of home life he had none, and save for the fact of his marriage in 1678, nothing is known of his wife. His story is bitter, one long tale of disappointment and trouble and penury, until, as says one author, he vanished "like a puff of tobacco smoke."

Yet three times he circumnavigated the globe in circumstances of great danger and hardship at a time when the knowledge of geography was still imperfect. He weathered the storms and tempests of little-known seas, braved the perils of shoals and rocks and strange coasts in ill-found, crazy vessels the size of a present-day topsail schooner, though far less seaworthy. In the face of these achievements, whatever his faults, we cannot but admire him as one of the Sea Venturers of Britain.

# ANSON AND THE *CENTURION*

AT Shugborough, in Staffordshire, is preserved the carved representation of portion of the leg of a lion. The relic has a curious history, for it is all that now remains of a great wooden lion rampant, sixteen feet high, which was once the figurehead of the *Centurion*, in which, between 1740 and 1744, Lord Anson made his celebrated voyage round the world.

The *Centurion*, thirty-seven years old, was broken up at Chatham in 1769, when her figurehead was presented to the Duke of Richmond by George III, and served for a time as the sign for a public-house at Goodwood. Here it was seen and admired by William IV, who acquired it as a staircase ornament for Windsor Castle. It was afterwards sent to Greenwich Hospital with orders from the King that it was to be placed in one of the wards, which was to be named the "Anson Ward." There it remained until 1871, when it was set up in the playground at the Naval School. It finally fell to pieces and the remains were put in an outhouse, whence the portion now preserved was recovered by Captain W. V. Anson, R.N., a descendant of the celebrated admiral.

At one period the pedestal upon which the lion stood bore the following words:

> Stay, traveller, awhile and view
> One who has travelled more than you.
> Quite round the globe, through each degree,
> Anson and I have ploughed the sea;
> Torrid and frigid zones have passed,
> And, safe ashore arrived at last,
> In ease, with dignity appear
> He in the House of Lords, I here.

George Anson was born at Shugborough, in the parish of Colwich, Staffordshire, in 1697. He joined the Navy in 1712, to become a lieutenant four years later. In 1722 he obtained his first command, and in 1724 was promoted to captain. His rapid advancement and success, though largely due to merit, was undoubtedly attributable also to the fact that he was the nephew of Thomas Parker, afterwards Lord Parker and Earl of Macclesfield, who was created Lord Chancellor in 1718.

It is through his expedition round the world in the *Centurion* that Lord Anson is best known. He was the fifth Englishman to circumnavigate the globe and added comparatively little to geographical knowledge; but the voyage was carried out with such success in the face of such extraordinary difficulties that it has long been a subject of popular interest.

A skilful navigator and seaman, Anson had unbounded energy, pluck and dogged determination. Calm and placid in temperament, unostentatious and simple in his manners, painstaking and thoughtful in all he did, he was a man of singularly accurate judgment and sound common sense. Essentially reserved and inclined to be undemonstrative, he was a strict disciplinarian. He was subject to none of those sudden flashes of genius and bursts of warm-hearted affection which characterized Nelson; but, generous and benevolent by nature, he took a fatherly interest in his men and was a firm friend to those who served him well. No less than seven of the junior officers who served with him in the *Centurion* rose to distinction as senior officers in the Navy.

As an organizer and administrator at the Admiralty later on he showed great ability and did much for the efficiency of the Service and the welfare of its officers and men. He won promotion to flag rank for his voyage round the world, and was created a peer for his defeat of the French fleet off Finisterre in 1747. Though in no sense a great or a brilliant victory, for the enemy was completely outmatched, it was nevertheless a serious blow to the French arms. Moreover, it came at a time when a naval success was much to be desired, and was received, perhaps, with greater enthusiasm than it really merited.

Anson was a lucky man. Influence and merit combined carried him forward. His career was one of steady and continuous promotion, and at his death in 1762, at the age of 65, he was an admiral of the fleet, a peer, a privy councillor, one of the richest men in the country through prize money, and for many years had served at the summit of his profession as First Lord of the Admiralty.

Appointed to the *Centurion* in 1737, Anson served in her on the west coast of Africa for the protection of trade. He afterwards sailed in the same ship to the West Indies; but was recalled to England on the outbreak of war with Spain in 1739, it being the intention to give him the command of one of two squadrons which were to be sent out to harass the Spanish in the Pacific. But naval affairs at the time were at a very low ebb, and eventually, through lack of money and heavy commitments else-where, it was found necessary to send one expedition only, of which Anson was given command with the nominal rank of commodore.

He received his commission in January 1740, and his official instructions the following June. His squadron was to consist of the *Centurion*, a fourth rate of 1,005 tons and sixty guns; the fifty-gun ships *Severn* and *Gloucester*; the *Pearl*, *Wager* and *Tryal* of forty, twenty-eight and eight guns respectively, and two victuallers. Thanks to other naval needs, and to maladministration and jobbery among the responsible officials, the equipment, manning and dispatch of the ships were much delayed.

Men-of-war in the middle of the eighteenth century were short, full-bodied, high-sterned craft, with bluff, rounded bows and low decks. Jibs, or fore-and-aft head-sails, came into use; but their jib-booms also carried square sprit-sails. They were heavy and practically unsinkable; but were unsuited for beating to windward. Ill-ventilated, they soon became full of vermin, while the food was unspeakably foul, the pay small and the treatment of the men cruel. Large crews were carried, and hundreds of men were crowded on the dark, fetid gun-decks, where privacy, peace and cleanliness were alike unknown. One of the few attractions that the Navy offered was the chance of making large sums in prize money; nevertheless few men volunteered as seamen. The untrained portions of the crews were composed of men gathered by press-gangs ashore and by offenders sent to sea instead of to prison. The best seamen were pressed from homeward-bound merchantmen, a cruel practice by which trained seamen, after a two or three years' voyage, were dragged willy-nilly from their ships within sight of home to serve in the Navy for another long period. The *Centurion* obtained seventy-three men in this way by sending a tender to the Downs. Nineteen of these, risking execution for so doing, promptly deserted at Portsmouth.

Defects in the ships themselves were constantly coming to light. A rotten cavity, eleven inches deep, was discovered in the *Centurion's* fore-mast after that spar had been passed as serviceable by officials of Portsmouth dockyard. And the food was no better. Forty-two out of the *Gloucester's* seventy-two puncheons of beef were found to be stinking and unfit for use before she left home. Biscuit was sometimes so worm-eaten that it was little better than dust when broken; peas and oatmeal were decayed when put on board. And so it was with stores and provisions throughout the Navy. That ships at sea were endangered and the lives of men forfeited signified nothing to a tribe of corrupt officials ashore who made comfortable incomes through peculation, and fed not only their families, but also their pigs and poultry, upon provisions intended for the seamen.

In June 1740 Anson's squadron was still short of 300 able seamen. Only 175 were sent to make up the deficiency, of whom 32 were from hospital and 98 were raw marines. It had also been intended that a complete regiment of foot and three independent companies of one hundred men each should be embarked as land forces. The men that were actually provided consisted of 500 out-pensioners from Chelsea Hospital, men who, from their age, wounds and infirmities, were incapable of service in marching regiments.

On hearing of this unwelcome reinforcement, Anson, being fully aware what the expedition would have to face in the way of dangers, hardship and privation, protested through the Admiralty. To his expostulation came back the curt reply that persons who were supposed to be better judges of soldiers than Lords of the Admiralty and Commodores considered the men in every way suited to the service in hand. The unhappy veterans joined the squadron in August; but instead of 500 no more than 259 actually came on board, all those who had limbs and strength to use them deserting at Portsmouth. Most of the decrepit band who did join were over sixty years of age, some upwards of seventy, while one poor creature had been badly wounded at the Battle of the Boyne half a century before. To make up the numbers 210 new recruits who were scarcely able to handle fire-arms were sent on board as marines. To anticipate, it may here be said that within a year all but three or four of the Chelsea

Hospital contingent had perished miserably from scurvy and privation. Not one of them saw England again.

The squadron finally sailed from St. Helen's, Isle of Wight, on September 18, 1740, manned by a total of 1,872 souls. Anson's orders were to proceed to the west coast of South America and there to sink, burn or destroy any Spanish vessels he came across, and to harass the Spaniards generally by raiding or capturing towns or other possessions. He was also told to look out for, and capture if possible, the galleon which sailed each year from Acapulco across the Pacific to Manila with a valuable cargo. Much was left to his own judgment, particularly in regard to the places he visited and the period of his absence, while he was at liberty to return to England either by way of China or round Cape Horn, as he thought fit.

Owing to baffling winds Madeira was not reached until October 25th, a passage of thirty-seven days. Even in this short time illness had made itself apparent, for in the squadron fourteen men had died and there were 122 sick. At Madeira Anson stayed for a week, watering and provisioning, and during his visit was informed by the friendly Portuguese governor that a Spanish squadron of six ships had been sighted cruising to the westward of the island. They were under the command of Don José Pizarro, and had been sent out to intercept Anson on his passage to Cape Horn, for, thanks to the delay in equipping and sailing, full particulars of his strength and destination had reached even the Spanish settlements on the west coast of America before he sailed from England. Don José, however, for reasons best known to himself, sailed on to South America without attempting to bring Anson to action.

On November 3rd the expedition sailed for its next rendezvous, the Portuguese island of Santa

Catharina off the coast of Brazil. During the passage one of the victuallers was emptied and sent away, while on November 20th the captains reported the excessive sickliness of their ships' companies. It was fever and the beginnings of that dreadful disease scurvy, the bane of all the earlier voyagers, and was brought on by wet decks, crowded, ill-ventilated living accommodation, unsuitable clothing and abominable food. Orders were given for six air scuttles to be cut in each ship; but even this did little to alleviate matters. No less than eighty sick were landed from the *Centurion* and housed in tents ashore on her arrival at Santa Catharina on December 21st, while her decks had to be scraped fore and aft, the ship thoroughly cleaned, and living spaces fumigated and washed with vinegar to rid her of the noisome stench that prevailed.

At Santa Catharina all the vessels were watered and provisioned. They also laid in stocks of wood for cooking purposes, and were caulked and refitted aloft in readiness for the tempestuous voyage round the Horn. The little sloop *Tryal* was in particularly bad order, her main-mast being sprung and her fore-mast unfit for use. The squadron put to sea again on January 18, 1741; but during the visit of about a month the flagship buried no less than twenty-eight of her men, while the number of her sick, after allowing for the deaths, leapt from eighty to ninety-six. In the entire squadron there had been 160 deaths since leaving England, and 450 on the sick list.

No sooner had they left for the next rendezvous, Port St. Julian, about 250 miles north of Magellan's Straits, than they ran into bad weather, with fogs and much rain. The *Tryal* lost her main-mast and had to be taken in tow. The *Pearl* lost touch, rejoining on February 17th after an absence of nearly a month to report that she had fallen in with Pizarro's squadron at sea a week earlier, and had narrowly escaped capture.

The Spaniards, indeed, had received news of Anson's arrival at Santa Catharina and left Maldonado, in the River Plate, in great haste four days before Anson sailed from Santa Catharina. It was their idea to reach the Pacific before the English, and during their passage the two squadrons must have been very close. Owing to the proximity of the enemy Anson would not have delayed had it not been for the bad condition of the *Tryal*. To repair her, however, was essential, and the squadron anchored at Port St. Julian on February 19th.

Sailing again after eight days there was little wind until they came in sight of the land at the eastern end of the Straits of Magellan on March 4th. Running on down the coast of Tierra del Fuego they passed through the Straits of Le Maire three days later in fine weather and a brisk breeze; but immediately on leaving them behind the elements seemed to break loose.

Gale after gale, assisted by a strong current flowing round Cape Horn, drove the ships to the eastward. In the huge seas the violent rolling of the ships caused many casualties, and though at times vessels set their topsails or double-reefed courses when the wind lulled, it was only to have them blown into streamers when the tempest suddenly returned. At this period it was customary in bad weather to house the topgallant-masts and even the jib-boom, the introduction of which was practically coeval with the decline of the sprit-sail topmast.

Sometimes, for days together, they lay under reefed mizzens, sometimes drove under bare poles. It became bitterly cold, with fierce storms of snow and sleet, so that sails and rigging became frozen stiff and the men badly frost-bitten. By continual labouring in the mountainous seas the *Centurion* became so loose in her upper-works that water squirted in at every roll and scarcely any of her officers ever lay in dry beds. Sails were split to ribbons, rigging was carried away, masts and yards were damaged again and again. In the lulls they did their best to effect repairs; but as often as not the work was rendered useless by the fury of the storm. For fifty-eight days on end the *Centurion* had her courses reefed.

The ships were still in company, but had been carried far to the eastward. On the night of April 14th, when they imagined themselves to be round Cape Horn, the moon shone out and the mist cleared to disclose the rock-bound coast of Tierra del Fuego two miles dead ahead. They were only saved from running bodily ashore by the merciful clearing of the murk and a providential shift of wind from south-west to west-north-west.

Meanwhile, in every ship, scurvy raged. Until she was up to the Horn the *Centurion* lost one or two men a week; but then the mortality suddenly increased. By the end of April there were few men on board who were not afflicted with the dreadful disease, and in that month no less than forty-three of her men died of it. In May nearly double that number were lost, 200 of her crew having perished since leaving England, so that there were not more than six sound seamen in each watch.

Now, with scurvy practically unknown, it is well-nigh impossible to imagine the horrible conditions of the disease. Men became dejected and as weak as tiny children, weeping, fainting, and sometimes dying if they made the least exertion. They suffered from large discoloured spots all over their bodies, their limbs swelled hideously, and they developed loathsome ulcers. Bones and flesh rotted away. Gums swelled and teeth dropped out. Limbs that had been fractured years before and had mended parted again, the joins dissolving into fluid. The wounds of the veteran of the Boyne, fifty years before, reopened and bled as though just inflicted.

In the second attempt to round Cape Horn the squadron was scattered. The *Severn* and *Pearl*, badly damaged and their crews diminishing daily, were driven eastward, eventually returning to Rio de Janeiro and thence to England. The *Wager* went ashore in the Gulf of Penas, on the coast of Chile, and became a total loss, her survivors suffering incredible hardships before reaching home. The *Gloucester*, *Tryal* and the *Anna*, the victualler, lost touch. The *Centurion*, quite alone, rounded the Horn in tempestuous weather, eventually arriving on May 8th off the island of Socoro, in Patagonia, the next rendezvous.

For a fortnight she cruised on and off the land waiting for her consorts; but at length, seeing nothing of them, sailed on towards Juan Fernandez, the next meeting-place. The bad weather continued, sails being constantly blown into ribbons, rigging damaged and masts endangered. The ship was nearly driven ashore on the island of Chiloe; but, managing to escape disaster, struggled on to the northward. The weather became finer; but deaths on board were increasing to a dreadful extent and water was running short. Moreover, through uncertainty in their longitude, they missed Juan Fernandez and spent no less than twelve days in finding it, thereby losing seventy or eighty more men whose lives might have been saved if they could have been put ashore in time.

At last, on June 10th, the *Centurion* crept wearily in towards her anchorage at Juan Fernandez. Of her original company of 506, including invalids and soldiers, little more than 200 remained, most of the survivors being so ravaged by disease that only two quartermasters and six seamen could be mustered for trimming sails. So weak were the crew that officers, servants and boys all lent a willing hand in bringing the ship to an anchor.

Soon after the flagship's arrival the sloop *Tryal* appeared, thirty-four out of her eighty men having died, and the remainder being so ill that only two officers and three men were available for duty.

The expedition, so far, had been a ghastly holocaust.

Juan Fernandez is a small island of volcanic origin some 400 miles from the coast of Chile, and owes its name to a Spaniard who discovered and attempted to cultivate it before the time of Drake. Before Anson's visit it had served as a base for the buccaneers and privateers who haunted the southern Pacific, and from 1704 to 1709, as mentioned before, had been inhabited by Alexander Selkirk, possibly the original of Defoe's *Robinson Crusoe*. The island is very fertile and well wooded, and in Anson's time provided quantities of vegetables, including turnips, radishes and wild sorrel. The sea was well stocked with fish, seals and sea-lions, while the higher slopes were infested by numbers of wild goats, some of which, of aged and venerable aspect, had been ear-marked by Selkirk 32 years before. Juan Fernandez, indeed, was a veritable little paradise to the scurvy-stricken crews who had endured the awful rigours of a long and tempestuous voyage.

At once all available men were employed in erecting tents ashore for the reception of the sick, and between June 16th and 18th all the ailing were landed. Two hundred and sixty-seven were taken ashore, the greater number being so ill that they had to be hoisted into the boats in their hammocks and carried to their tents over a rough and stony beach, work in which the commodore and all his officers assisted. Fourteen men died in the boats on their way ashore, and for the first ten or twelve days rarely less than six were buried each day. Thanks, however, to the bountiful supplies of fresh meat and vegetables that the island provided the disease gradually abated and the invalids began to recover.

On June 21st a ship was sighted by the look-outs, but presently faded away in the mist. On the 26th, however, she hove in sight again, and this time was recognized as the *Gloucester*. From her small canvas it was concluded she was in dire straits, and the commodore at once sent his boat to her laden with water, fish and vegetables. She was, indeed, in desperate condition. Two-thirds of her crew were already dead, and of those who remained alive scarcely any except the officers and their servants were fit for duty. A pint of water to each man was the daily allowance, and had it not been for the fresh supply they must soon have died of thirst.

The unhappy ship came within three miles of the island; but could come no nearer on account of contrary winds and currents. The next day she was still in sight, and Anson again sent off a boatload of water and food. The *Gloucester's* captain retained both boats' crews to assist him in working his ship; but for eighteen days she hovered off the island without being able to fetch the anchorage. At length, on July 9th, she disappeared to the eastward and was lost sight of for a week. She reappeared on the 16th, but with the wind still in her teeth could not make the anchorage. Signals of distress were made and again a boat was sent off to her. But for this last supply of water all on board must have died. Numbers of her men were expiring daily, and as she had now been nearly a month striving to make the anchorage, the survivors, losing heart, were in despair of ever reaching it.

Again she vanished from view; but hove in sight again on July 23rd, and what boats were available were sent to tow her to the anchorage. Her crew had been reduced to eighty souls, and it is difficult to imagine any torture more prolonged or heart-breaking than their thirty-two days of ineffectual attempts to reach their haven of refuge.

Anson was not unnaturally anxious as to Pizarro's movements, for if he were caught at Juan Fernandez with the greater number of his men ill ashore, and his ships dismantled and refitting, the results might have been serious. He was not to know until later that the Spanish squadron, in trying to round the Horn, had suffered even greater misfortunes than himself. Pizarro's ships were scattered in the stormy weather; two were lost, and after enduring the pangs of famine and the loss of the greater portion of their crews, the battered remnant were hurled back to the River Plate, never to penetrate to the Pacific. On board the *Asia*, Pizarro's flagship, a rat at one time had sold for four dollars, while one of the seamen lay for four days in the same hammock with the corpse of his brother in order that he might receive his allowance of provisions.

Meanwhile, at Juan Fernandez, the work of caring for the many invalids, cleaning the ships, refitting, wooding and watering continued. There was much to be done, and besides these necessary occupations men were employed in making oil from the blubber of sea-lions for use in lamps and also, mixed with pitch and wood-ashes, as composition for treating the ships' sides and waterlines. They also set up a bakery ashore, and laid in a supply of cod, which they salted for future use.

On August 16th the *Anna*, the victualler, arrived and anchored. She had spent nearly two months at an anchorage on the mainland repairing damages and recruiting the health of her crew, and as she carried provisions for the squadron, was a very welcome arrival. On unloading her, however, it was found that a great proportion of her cargo was decayed and utterly unfit for use.

The *Tryal*, which was sent off to the neighbouring island of Masafuera lest any of the missing vessels should have gone there, returned without news of them, and towards the end of August the *Anna*, which was rotten and unseaworthy, was purchased and broken up, her men being sent to the *Gloucester*.

By the beginning of September the deaths from scurvy had ceased and most of the invalids were back at work. The mortality, however, had been appalling, for since leaving St. Helen's the *Centurion* had lost 292 men out of 506 on board; the *Gloucester* 292 out of 374, and the *Tryal* 42 out of 81. The three ships had thus left England with 961 men, of whom 626, or sixty-five per cent, had perished. Only 335 men and boys, a number insufficient for the proper manning of the *Centurion* alone, were left for three vessels. A less persistent man than Anson might well have been tempted to return to England with the remains of the expedition, and nobody could have blamed him. But the commodore was not the type to flinch in the face of adversity, and determined to see the voyage through, come what might.

On September 8th a sail was sighted off the island, and the *Centurion*, hastily setting up her rigging, swaying her yards aloft and bending her sails, soon got away in chase. The stranger was lost sight of during the night, but steering the same course Anson came up with her again at daylight on the 12th. She was captured without fighting, proving to be the *Nuestra Señora del Monte Carmelo*, bound from Callao to Valparaiso with a cargo of sugar and cloth, some trunks of wrought plate and over a ton of silver dollars. From this prize Anson learnt of the fate of Pizarro's squadron, and also heard that a Spanish vessel had been stationed off Juan Fernandez to intercept him until January 6th, when, convinced that the English had been destroyed or driven back by the storm off Cape Horn, she returned to Callao. Indeed, so certain were the Spaniards that there were no British in the Pacific that they had removed the embargo on their Pacific trade and once more allowed the galleons to come and go as they chose.

It was good news, and encouraged by this first success and at the prospect of further easy captures, the men showed redoubled energy in completing the ships with water and making all preparations for leaving Juan Fernandez. The small guns from the *Anna* were mounted on board the Spanish prize, the *Gloucester* and *Tryal* were ordered to cruise off Paita and Valparaiso respectively, and on September 19th the *Centurion*, in company with the *Carmelo*, left the island.

On the evening of the 23rd the *Tryal* was fallen in with. She had a prize with her, a large merchantman named the *Arranzazu*, with a cargo of cloth and sugar and £5,000 worth of silver. The *Tryal*, however, had sprung her main-mast, and had generally become so unseaworthy that the commodore, with no means of repairing her, ordered her destruction, her crew, guns and stores being transferred to the *Tryal's* prize, which was duly commissioned as a man-of-war.

The three ships then sailed to the northward to join the *Gloucester* off Valparaiso, and on the way the *Centurion* captured the *Santa Teresa de Jesus*, a small merchantman with a mixed cargo and a limited quantity of specie. On November 11th, near Paita, the *Nuestra Señora del Carmin* was also taken, having on board a rich mixed cargo; but which, in the circumstances, was of little value to the captors. From the prisoners, however, Anson learnt that there was a considerable amount of treasure in the town of Paita, so he made up his mind to attack it.

The assault was carried out at night by three

boats and fifty-eight men under the command of Lieutenant Brett of the *Centurion*. It was a complete success, for though the alarm was raised before they landed they reached the shore in safety, and, shouting and yelling at the pitch of their voices, soon possessed themselves of the town square. Terrified at the hubbub and the beating of drums which the seamen had brought ashore with them, the Spaniards thought they were assailed by an army, and after firing one ineffectual volley quitted the town with all possible speed. Indeed, within a quarter of an hour, with a loss of one man killed and two wounded, Brett was in possession. He proceeded to place sentries guarding the approaches, seized the custom house, and scoured the town for inhabitants in case further precautions might be necessary. But the greater number of people had already fled in their night attire, the governor himself, not the last to seek safety, escaping half-naked and leaving behind him in bed his wife, a young woman of seventeen, to whom he had been married three or four days before.

Confining what remained of the inhabitants in one of the churches and using some stout negroes as transport, the happy raiders busied themselves in carrying the treasure from the custom house and other places to the small fort. The sailors, meanwhile, amused themselves by doing a little private looting, and emerged from the houses wearing embroidered jackets and trousers and laced hats over their own clothes. Once started, there was no stopping the entire detachment from imitating the idea, and when masculine attire ran out the unlucky ones had perforce to dress themselves in frilled petticoats and other feminine garments of an unmentionable but intimate nature. The grotesque spectacle of armed seamen ashore in a hostile country attired in such peculiar dress can be more easily imagined than described. The incident shows that the sailor's love of dressing up is not confined to the present century.

By daylight the next morning the *Centurion* and her consorts came close inshore, anchoring during the course of the afternoon. The first boat came off laden to the gunwale with dollars and church plate. A body of Spanish horsemen appeared on the hills "sounding their military musick," but doing little else, and reinforcing his parties ashore Anson calmly continued embarking the treasure and what provisions he could lay his hands upon. On the third day after their arrival, November 15th, the booty had all been embarked, and the commodore set his prisoners at liberty and ordered the town to be set on fire to destroy the great quantity of merchandise which could not be found room for on board. Only the churches were spared. Six merchant vessels had been found in the bay. One, the *Solidad*, was manned as a prize, the others being taken out to sea and scuttled.

Towards midnight, having completed its work, the squadron weighed and stood out of the bay. By the sacking of Paita the Spaniards estimated their loss at a million and a half of dollars, while the wrought plate, coin, jewellery and private plunder taken on board amounted to a value of about £30,000.

Soon after sailing animosity displayed itself between those men who had landed and secured private booty and those who had remained on board and obtained nothing. Anson settled the matter in characteristic fashion by pooling the private plunder and dividing it between everybody, and by giving his own share to the common fund and ordering the officers to do the same.

Shortly afterwards the *Centurion* fell in with the *Gloucester*, who had captured two prizes. One was a small vessel with a cargo of wine, brandy, olives and about £7,000 in specie, and the second was a large sailing boat, the crew of which said they were very poor and had nothing on board but cotton. As they were found eating pigeon pie off silver plate, however, somebody's suspicions were aroused. A further search was made, and concealed amongst the cotton was found a quantity of coin to the value of £12,000.

But the richest prize of all had yet to be taken.

Far away across the Pacific in the Philippines the Spaniards collected at Manila all those commodities of India, China and the East which were most desirable in the markets of Spain and Europe. They consisted of spices, calicoes and chintzes, porcelain, filigree and other worked metal; but silk and silk goods predominated, no less than 50,000 pairs of silk stockings being exported each year to adorn the shapely lower limbs of the Spanish aristocracy. The ship that embarked this valuable collection was a large galleon commanded by a general of Spain. She was well manned and armed, and leaving Manila in July generally arrived at Acapulco, in Mexico, in the following January.

In March a similar galleon left Acapulco with money, and with the trade wind in her favour generally arrived at Manila in June. Anson had no use for silk stockings and spices. From the nature of her cargo the galleon outward-bound from Acapulco was the better prize of the two.

After leaving Paita, Anson proceeded to the island of Quibo, not far from Panama, where he hoped to take more prizes. On his way two of the captured vessels, being very slow, were burnt, and on December 5th the squadron, still consisting of five ships, arrived at its destination. Here they watered and laid in stocks of wood and food, the men being introduced for the first time to turtle, which, so far from being regarded as a luxury, they looked upon with some suspicion. Sailing again on December 9th the flagship took another small prize which was scuttled and burnt, and by the middle of February the squadron was lying off Acapulco ready to intercept the galleon due to leave in March. Boats were sent inshore at night to watch the mouth of the harbour; but a long and weary vigil at length convinced Anson that the Spaniards knew of his presence and that the sailing of the treasure-ship had been countermanded.

At length, having been four months at sea since leaving Quibo, and with only six days' water left, the squadron arrived at Chequetan, where it refitted, watered and provisioned. By this time Anson had made up his mind that further delay was useless, and decided to cross the Pacific and to wait for the galleon on the other side.

In the entire squadron at this time there were barely enough men to form the complement of a fourth-rate man-of-war. The difficult navigation and bad weather to be expected in the China Sea rendered some economy in the available man-power vitally necessary, and the commodore accordingly destroyed all his prizes after removing their valuables and determined to continue the voyage with the *Centurion* and *Gloucester* alone. After another fruitless visit to Acapulco all the Spanish prisoners were set free, and on May 6th the two ships lost sight of the mountains of Mexico and steered westward across the Pacific for the Portuguese settlement of Macao, in the Canton River. Here they would meet English ships and a civilized community, and here it was that Anson intended to refit his battered ships preparatory to lying in wait for the treasure-galleon off Cape Espiritu Santo, in the Philippines, in the following May and June 1743.

Standing well to the southward, in accordance

with the accepted rules of the period, the two ships were becalmed for seven weeks before finally meeting the favouring north-east trade wind. Soon the *Gloucester's* main-mast was discovered to be defective and dangerous, so that it had to be cut away, and once more, in spite of the fresh provisions and copious supplies of water due to the heavy rains, the terrible scurvy reappeared to play havoc with the ships' companies.

The limit of the trade wind was reached at the end of June, and for a month the ships sailed on to the westward. The crippled *Gloucester*, however, constantly lagged behind, and on July 26th the wind shifted to the west, right in their teeth, and then fell flat calm. A heavy swell and the consequent rolling occasioned the loss of the *Gloucester's* fore-topmast and fore-yard. She was taken in tow. Then arose a violent storm which forced the *Centurion* to lie to and occasioned a bad leak, so that officers and men had constantly to be at the pumps. But the *Gloucester* was in worse condition. She had been further damaged aloft and was little more than an unmanageable hulk, with seven feet of water in her hold and her sickly crew unable to keep the pumps going. Help could not be sent, for the *Centurion's* own men, what with the continual pumping and the number of sick, were wellnigh exhausted. The *Gloucester* could not be repaired at sea, and in the circumstances there was no choice but to destroy her. Two days were spent in removing the treasure and all the stores that the *Centurion* could carry, and on August 15th the wreck was abandoned and set on fire, presently to blow up when the flames reached her magazine. She had done good work.

The *Centurion*, leaking and disease-ridden, stood on alone. Of the eight ships which had left England two years before she was the only survivor.

Arriving on August 26th at the island of Tinian,

one of the Ladrone group, they found a small Spanish barque and a party of soldiers engaged in jerking beef for the garrison of Guam, an island not very far away. The barque was promptly annexed and the Spaniards made prisoners, while the *Centurion's* sick were landed to recuperate. They numbered 128, and no less than twenty-one died as soon as they were moved.

Tinian was a veritable haven of refuge. It was well wooded, with streams and smooth grassy lawns. Bread-fruit, oranges, limes, lemons and coconuts grew in abundance, while cattle, hogs and poultry roamed wild over the country-side. The commodore, himself ill with scurvy, was forced to live in a tent ashore; but by the middle of September, thanks to the change in diet, the invalids began to recover and gradually returned to duty. Ineffectual attempts were made to stop the leak in the *Centurion's* bows, and the battered ship was refitted to the best of their ability.

The only anchorage was an open bay, and as the time of the equinoctial gales drew near the ship's hempen cables were reinforced with chains and her yards and top-hamper struck. They were necessary precautions; but in spite of them the worst happened. On September 22nd a violent gale set in from the eastward. Soon there was a heavy, tumbling sea, which broke so fiercely in all directions that no boat could live. One by one the cables parted like pack-thread, and at one o'clock of a black night a furious gust of wind, accompanied by heavy rain squalls and sheets of lightning, tore the *Centurion* from her last anchor and drove her out to sea. The greater portion of the crew, including the commodore, were ashore. On board the ship there were no more than 108 men, including natives, boys and men lately recovered from scurvy. The ship was leaking badly and her only remaining anchor still hung from her bows at the end of its cable. Not a gun was lashed, nor a port barred in. Shrouds were loose, topmasts unrigged and yards struck, and not a sail could be set except the mizzen. She was unmanageable, buffeted about this way and that at the mercy of sea and wind.

In the fury of the gale and the flashing of lightning the guns and signal lights fired by the ship were neither seen nor heard by those ashore. The dawn came slowly out of the east, and the anxious watchers on the beach gazed seawards. Nothing met their eyes but league upon league of swelling ocean, the giant seas breaking and roaring like mountains rolling over mountains. The *Centurion* had vanished. Anson and 113 of his officers and men were virtually marooned.

Despondency reigned. Some instantly concluded that the ship was lost; others, believing she might weather the gale, knew how feebly she was manned and despaired of her ever regaining the island. The prospect was certainly a dismal one. The nearest friendly port was Macao, full eighteen hundred miles distant. The chance of their being rescued by a friendly ship was so slender as to be beyond all hope, and not very far away was Guam, the governor of which would presently be sending to find out what had become of his provisioning party. Inevitably, discovering the helpless condition of the castaways, he would send a force to overpower them, and once in Spanish clutches the most favourable treatment they might expect was rigorous imprisonment. At the worst, they might be put to death as pirates, for the commodore's and officers' commissions were still on board the ship.

But Anson himself, though convinced in his heart that the *Centurion* was lost, refused to admit it. She might be back in a few days, he told his men, or else she might be driven so far to leeward in the storm that she would go on to Macao to refit and return for them later.

Carpenters and blacksmiths were ashore with their tools. Wood was to be had in abundance, and calming the men's fears by his composure and steadiness he put them to work upon the little Spanish barque. It seemed an insane project; but they set about cutting her in halves and lengthening her amidships by twelve feet. This would increase her size from twelve to forty tons, and in her they would sail on to China and comparative civilization. The tents and some spare cordage left ashore would provide sails and rigging; coconuts with jerked beef and rice from a neighbouring island would serve them for food, and a small compass found in the barque and a damaged quadrant discovered in a dead man's chest would do for the navigation. They had muskets; but no more than ninety charges for them.

On October 6th, a fortnight after the *Centurion* had been driven to sea, the shore party hauled the barque ashore on rollers and proceeded to cut her in two. Working steadily, they fixed upon November 5th as the date of putting to sea; but on October 11th one of the men who had been on a hill in the middle of the island came rushing down to the landing-place shouting "The ship! The ship!"

Their joy can easily be imagined. The men shouted and laughed and leapt in ecstasy. Even the undemonstrative commodore gave way to his feelings by shedding tears of thankfulness. And by the next afternoon the *Centurion* again swung to her anchors in the road.

Those on board had performed a superhuman task. For three days the storm had continued, and expecting every moment to be dashed ashore they had set up the rigging, swayed their yards across and managed to spread a little canvas. It was five days before they finally hove up and secured the anchor; their food and water were nearly exhausted; but, achieving the impossible, they brought the ship back.

Again, on October 14th, the *Centurion* was driven out to sea by a gale, though this time the commodore and the greater number of her men were on board and she returned in five days.

Finally, on October 21st, having completed with food and water and taking on board a quantity of fruit, the ship left the island for the last time and shaped course for the China Sea. Passing to the southward of Formosa she arrived at Macao on November 13th. This port, the Portuguese settlement at the mouth of the Canton River, was frequented by European ships, many of them belonging to the British East India Company, and once more, after an absence of more than two years, the weary, weather-beaten travellers found themselves among their own countrymen.

It is unnecessary to weary the reader with a detailed account of Anson's protracted negotiations in the Canton River. The Portuguese, existing in Macao only by the sufferance of the Chinese, and fearful of giving them offence, were not very helpful, and could only advise the commodore to treat direct with the native authorities for what he required in the way of stores, provisions and means of refitting. The Chinese officials, however, used to dealing only with merchantmen, at first attempted to exact the customary dues and bribes from the *Centurion*, and without them would allow Anson no facilities for repairs and not more than one day's provisions at a time.

After much fruitless talk the commodore decided to go up to Canton to see the Viceroy in person. Permission was refused, whereupon Anson threatened to force a passage with his boats. The Chinese thought better of their refusal and the commodore proceeded to Canton in his barge, where, prevented from interviewing the Viceroy, he tried to open up negotiations through the British merchants resident there. These also were without avail, and returning to his ship in exasperation he forced the customs officials at Macao under a threat to convey a letter direct to the Viceroy, informing that potentate of his rank and status as an emissary of his Sovereign and what he required.

The Viceroy presently sent down a mandarin attended by his retinue to see the ship. The *Centurion* was the first regular man-of-war to visit the river, and Anson, judicious as ever but thoroughly determined, politely told the visitor that if he did not receive supplies, which would be well paid for, he might have to take them by force. Overawed by their reception, and the spectacle of one hundred of the crew dressed in marines' regimentals drawn up on deck under arms, the Chinese were conducted all over the ship, and lavishly entertained in the commodore's cabin. They consumed an incredible quantity of liquor without turning a hair, and departed highly pleased with all they had seen. Anson missed a gold snuff-box and some silver spoons when they had gone; but at last the native authorities were impressed with the dignity due to the British flag, for after some further delay the necessary licence was forthcoming for refitting the ship and supplying all her needs.

Methods were dilatory in the extreme, and it was not until April 19, 1743, that, refitted from truck to keelson, her stores replenished and her water-casks and provision rooms filled, the *Centurion* sailed from the Canton River. It had been noised abroad that she was bound to Batavia and thence to England, and letters for Europe were actually on board. But Anson's real destination was somewhere very different. He sailed for Cape Espiritu Santo, in the Philippines, off which it was hoped to intercept the great treasure-galleon from Acapulco.

On May 31st the *Centurion* arrived off the headland, a point invariably made by the galleon on her passage to Manila, and whence she received signals to inform her whether or not the coasts were clear of the enemy. Knowing that there were sentinels on the cape, the commodore took in his topgallant-sails and stood out to sea, where, with the land just in sight, he began to cruise on and off, keeping a good look-out.

There were some on board who did not altogether relish the idea of the coming engagement. The galleons, carrying over 500 men and heavily armed, were reputed to be very strong ships, so strong and heavily built that shot would not penetrate their sides. But Anson harangued his ship's company and allayed their fears. He would fight the enemy within pistol shot, he told them, when the shot would pass through both sides instead of rebounding. In this manner he judiciously restored the confidence of his men and awakened their enthusiasm so much that inquiring one day of his butcher why he had lately seen no mutton at his table, the man replied quite seriously that he was reserving the last two sheep for the entertainment of the Spanish captain the night his ship was taken.

During the period of waiting the men were not idle. Almost daily they were exercised at the guns in firing at a mark, while the small-arm parties were constantly practised in shooting at a target hung from the yardarm. Choosing thirty of the best marksmen Anson determined to station them aloft in action to fire down on the enemy's decks, and as there were not enough men on board to provide a full crew for all the heavy guns, he detailed two men to each weapon for loading purposes, and divided the rest into gangs who ran round the decks running out and firing such guns as were loaded. It was the habit of the Spaniards to fall flat on deck when they expected a broadside, and to rise up again after the discharge to continue the fight. By maintaining a constant rippling fire instead of volleys or broadsides this manœuvre of the enemy would be frustrated and the execution all the greater.

As the days passed the men's expectancy and impatience increased. Eager eyes ever scanned the rim of the horizon to the eastward for the welcome gleam of a sail; but a week, a fortnight, twenty days passed—and still the ocean was bare. Suspense became intolerable.

But at last, at dawn on June 20th, Mr. Midshipman Proby, at the masthead, sighted a sail low down on the horizon to the south-eastward. He hailed the quarter-deck, and instantly the men came tumbling joyfully up from below. The *Centurion* made sail towards her. By half-past seven the galleon was in sight from the deck, and firing a gun in defiance furled her topgallant-sails and came slowly on, fully determined to fight.

By noon the two ships were little more than three miles apart. Sundry manœuvres followed, and battle flags were hoisted, while the Spaniards busied themselves in throwing overboard their cattle and lumber to free their encumbered decks. Soon afterwards the action began at long range. The *Centurion* rapidly closed her adversary to within pistol shot, and keeping to leeward to prevent any attempt at escape took up her station on the Spaniard's bow, where almost all the English guns could be brought to bear, but few of the enemy's could reply. Presently some mats stowed in the galleon's nettings were set alight by the *Centurion's* wads and burnt merrily, throwing the enemy into terror and confusion. The *Centurion* also was in some danger, until, considerably to the commodore's relief, the Spaniards cut away the netting and tumbled the whole blazing mass into the sea.

The English guns, meanwhile, were plied with great vigour, while the marksmen aloft kept up a constant fire which killed or wounded practically every Spanish officer in sight. For some time the enemy fought fiercely and bravely; but sweeping their crowded decks with grape the *Centurion's* fire caused great slaughter, and at last the great flag fluttering at the galleon's masthead came slowly down in token of surrender.

The prize was the *Nuestra Señora de Cavadonga*, a ship larger than the *Centurion,* and carrying 500 men. She had 67 killed and 84 wounded in the engagement, while the *Centurion's* loss was no more than 2 killed and 17 wounded, sufficient testimony to the indifferent gunnery of the Spanish. The galleon was a very valuable capture, for she carried a quantity of dollars, wrought plate and virgin silver to the value, it is said, of £313,121.

Little remains to be told. The *Centurion*, with her numerous prisoners safe under hatches and her prize in company, arrived again at Macao on July 11th. We need not enter into a recital of Anson's various transactions there, his difficulty in obtaining what he wanted, his interview with the Viceroy at Canton, and how, true to tradition, the rascally Chinese tradesmen, selling their livestock by weight, enhanced their value by stuffing live fowls and ducks with stones and gravel and filling the carcasses of pigs with water.

The *Cavadonga* was sold for 6,000 dollars, and on December 15th the *Centurion* set sail for England. On January 3, 1744, she anchored in the Straits of Sunda for wood and water, and after staying for five days sailed for the Cape of Good Hope, arriving at Table Bay on March 11th. Here she stayed for over three weeks, putting to sea again on April 3rd.

War had been declared against France, and in a thick fog, unknown to those on board, the *Centurion* ran through a French fleet cruising in the chops of the Channel. She passed through in safety, and on June 15th, to the infinite joy of everybody on board, the battered, weather-beaten, but treasure-laden ship came to anchor at Spithead. As a fitting finale to the cruise the specie was landed at Portsmouth, to be paraded in triumph through the city of London in a procession of thirty-two wagons, the ship's company marching beside them with colours flying and bands playing.

According to a contemporary account, the treasure and plate brought home in the *Centurion* was valued at one and a quarter millions sterling, and consisted of 295 chests of silver, 18 chests of gold, and 20 barrels of gold dust.

The *Centurion's* voyage perhaps has not the originality of that of the *Golden Hind* over a century and a half before. Anson may have lacked the fiery dash of Drake and the lovable genius of Nelson; but his pluck and indomitable perseverance carried him successfully through in the face of supreme difficulty and danger where many a man would have turned back. Never for a moment did he relinquish the hope of accomplishing his purpose. Through peril and pestilence, through storm and famine, he infused new courage into his men through his own undaunted demeanour and force of character. As an example of fortitude and determination the famous voyage must ever remain without parallel in the story of the British Navy.

# CAPTAIN JAMES COOK

OUTSIDE the Mall entrance to the Admiralty buildings in London stands the statue of James Cook, the most famous circumnavigator and explorer that England has ever produced. A valuable collection of his manuscript diaries, logs and sailing directions was purchased in 1923 and is now in the Australian Commonwealth National Library. Other manuscripts and relics of the great seaman are to be seen in the British Museum, while in the Painted Hall at Greenwich is his portrait in naval uniform painted by Nathaniel Dance, R.A. A manuscript, *Directions for Sailing*, in Cook's hand-writing, and his hanger and telescope, are preserved in the museum of the Royal United Service Institution in Whitehall.

James Cook was over six feet in height, spare and rather thin, with fine features, well-set brown eyes with bushy eyebrows and a determined mouth and chin. His expression, as shown in the Green-wich picture, is austere but not unpleasing; but the strong face clearly shows the nature of the man— patient, persevering, self-reliant, self-willed and utterly fearless of danger. Grave and somewhat reserved, Cook was an indefatigable worker, a man impatient of enforced leisure and who never was tired. His fierce energy inspired others, and though, we are told, he was possessed of a hasty temper, beneath it lay a kindly and human heart. One of his chief preoccupations was ever the welfare and comfort of his crew. He commanded the respect, obedience and implicit confidence of his subordi-nates, and, himself brought up to a hard life and inured to labour, shared in his men's discomforts and privations, and was capable of enduring the severest hardship without complaint. Of good manners and simple tastes, he had no time to waste in luxurious living. He desired no better food than that served out to the seamen. His only recreation was work.

Born at Marton, Yorkshire, in 1728, Cook was the son of a farm labourer. He received some sort of an education at the village school, but when twelve years old became assistant to a shopkeeper at Staithes, a small fishing village near Whitby. But he soon tired of the life. The sea called him, and at the instance of his employer—though some accounts say he ran away—he became apprenticed for three years to a Whitby shipping firm, presently to find himself on board a vessel engaged in the coal trade up and down the east coast of England. Afterwards he served in ships plying to Norway and the Baltic.

It was a hard life, though undoubtedly the best possible school for producing a practical seaman. Cook did not neglect his opportunities. In the intervals between voyages he set himself assiduously to work to improve his general knowledge of mathematics and navigation; and that he succeeded, and was, as well, a thorough practical sailor, is evident from the fact that in 1752, at the age of twenty-four, he was mate of the *Friendship*, a great advance for a man of humble parentage. He would soon have had an independent command of his own, and but for the fact that in 1755 trouble was brewing with France and the Navy was being placed on a war footing, the services of one of its most eminent navigators, surveyors and Empire-builders might have been lost to the country.

The popular belief that Cook joined the Navy to avoid being "pressed" is contrary to fact. He realized that the Navy was short of suitable men, and knowing his own capability, saw a better prospect of advancement in the King's service than as the captain of a humble coaster. Accordingly, in 1755, when his ship was lying in the Thames, he volunteered for H.M.S. *Eagle*, joining that ship as an A.B. at Portsmouth on June 25th. Thirty-seven days later his superior qualifications had earned for him a warrant as master's mate.

It is unnecessary to deal at length with this early portion of Cook's career. He first came to notice between 1758 and 1762, when as master, or navigating officer, of the *Pembroke* and *Northumberland*, he was employed in charting the St. Lawrence and portions of the coasts of Nova Scotia and Newfoundland during the operations against the French. He also perfected his knowledge of astronomical navigation and mathematics generally, and so favourably was he reported upon that between 1763 and 1767 he was again specially employed surveying and charting the coasts of Newfoundland and Labrador. So accurate was his work that so lately as twenty years ago his charts were not entirely superseded by the more detailed surveys of modern times.

In December 1762 he had married Elizabeth Bates, of Barking.[1] The marriage is said to have been a very happy one, though Cook's home life cannot have lasted more than four years in all, and during his subsequent wanderings all over the world his wife must often have been months, and sometimes years, without news of him. The couple lived for a time at Shadwell, afterwards removing to Mile End. The house has since been identified as No. 88 Mile End Road, which now bears a tablet recording the fact.

[1] A piece of Mrs. Cook's wedding-dress is to be seen in the museum of the Royal United Service Institution in Whitehall. Mrs. Cook died in 1835, at the age of ninety-three.

In 1768 Cook's great opportunity came. At the request of the Royal Society the Admiralty had consented to send out an expedition to the Pacific to observe the transit of Venus, an event of some astronomical importance. It was at first proposed that a Mr. Dalrymple should be placed in command; but the Admiralty, mindful of a mutiny which had taken place when Dr. Halley had been given the brevet rank of captain and placed in charge of a man-of-war, steadfastly refused to countenance the appointment of a civilian. Searching for some suitable officer, they hit upon Cook, already well known as a surveyor through his excellent work in North America. And on May 25, 1768, he received a lieutenant's commission and was appointed to the *Endeavour*, a Whitby barque of 368 tons specially bought for the service.

After completing for sea at Deptford the ship finally sailed from Plymouth on August 26th, having on board ninety-four persons, including a party of scientists, and stores and provisions for eighteen months. Cook's orders were to proceed to Tahiti, which had been discovered and explored a few years before, and, after completing the astronomical work there, to continue the voyage by making discoveries in the South Pacific as far as Latitude 40° South. Then, if no land was found, he was to explore New Zealand, finally returning to England by any route that he thought fit.

The better to appreciate the importance of Cook's discoveries it is necessary briefly to mention the work of his predecessors, more particularly in the Pacific.

The discovery of a passage round the north of America into the Pacific, or the "North-West Passage," had long been a favourite British project for the purpose of discovering a shorter route to China and the Far East than the long and tedious journey round the Cape of Good Hope. Among others, the voyages of Frobisher, Davis, Hudson and Baffin in the latter part of the sixteenth and early years of the seventeenth centuries, though unsuccessful in their main object, all added to our knowledge of the geography of the ice-bound northern coast of Canada. To anticipate, the subsequent voyages of Ross, Parry, Franklin and M'Clure in the first half of the nineteenth century also had a similar object in view, and the North-West Passage, though impracticable for navigation, was actually discovered by Sir John Franklin in 1847–1848 during his final expedition, in which he and all his brave companions perished.

Drake attempted to discover the passage from the Pacific side and failed. Others also tried, and in 1777–1778, as we shall presently see, the passage was essayed by James Cook during his third and last voyage.

In 1586 Cavendish, passing through the Straits of Magellan, sailed north to California and thence to the Ladrones, capturing a rich Spanish galleon on the way. His successful exploit encouraged several emulators, but all their attempts at despoiling the Spaniards failed, and they added comparatively little to our geographical knowledge. The Falkland Islands, however, were visited and explored by Davis and Hawkins in 1592 and 1594.

During the greater part of the seventeenth century the English were too busy at home with their internal troubles and the wars against the Dutch to have much time for sea exploration. At the close of this century, however, the English buccaneers were active—men like Dampier, Morgan, Edward Cooke, Woodes Rogers, who, though all explorers after a fashion, were frankly sea rovers whose primary object was to enrich themselves at the expense of Spain.

When Anson set out on his expedition the Pacific could no longer be considered a Spanish lake, even on the authority of the Pope. The same may be said for Byron, Wallis and Cartaret, 1764–1769, who, in expeditions sent out by the Admiralty, passed through the Straits of Magellan and discovered between them the Society Islands—including Tahiti, Pitcairn, Queen Charlotte Islands, New Britain and New Ireland, and various other outlying groups in the Pacific.

But for centuries there had been a tradition that land of continental proportions existed somewhere in the southern part of the world. Various old charts show a solid belt of land, named "Terra Australis Incognita," stretching well up from the South Pole and covering the whole of the bottom portion of the globe. It was an imaginary continent, but scientific men had proved beyond any doubt that if it did not exist the world would inevitably overbalance and topple over!

The first record of Australia, as we now call it— considered to be part of a far greater southern continent than it really is—is said to have been made by the Portuguese in the sixteenth century. In 1606 Torres, a Spaniard, sailed through the strait bearing his name, while between 1618 and 1627 Dutch navigators were exploring the north, west and south coasts of Australia. In 1642 Tasman, sailing from Batavia, discovered Tasmania and a portion of New Zealand, following up his success two years later by exploring more of the Australian coast. In 1665 what we now know as Western Australia was definitely called "New Holland" at the instance of the Dutch Government.

In 1687 and again in 1699 William Dampier, the buccaneer, explored the west and north-western coasts. Subsequent voyagers did little to add to the knowledge of the continent itself, though, as we have shown, many of its outlying island groups were discovered and charted.

In the middle of the eighteenth century, therefore, at about the time Cook first set out, the coast of North and South America from Cape Horn to California, many of the Pacific islands, the Celebes, Moluccas, Java, Sumatra and China were tolerably well known. Farther south, however, a map would show only the western, and part of the northern and southern, coasts of Australia, and part of Tasmania. New Zealand would be represented by nothing more than the small angle of land skirted by Tasman. The east coast of Australia, wholly unexplored and unknown, would not be depicted at all.

Moreover, all the land shown in this quarter of the globe was considered to be part of the immense southern continent "Terra Australis Incognita." It was the mystery of this huge expanse of fabulous and unknown territory that, among other things, was finally solved by the voyages of Captain James Cook.

Having touched at Madeira and Rio de Janeiro, the *Endeavour* passed on through the Straits of Le Maire, and, on January 27, 1769, rounded Cape Horn without damage. Arriving at Tahiti on April 13th, having sighted several islands on the passage, the transit of Venus was successfully observed on June 3rd. Sailing again on July 13th Cook spent some months in visiting and exploring the other islands of the group of which Tahiti is one, and gave them the name of the Society Islands. The natives, though friendly enough, were "prodigious expert" at thieving.

On October 7th the North Island of New Zealand was sighted by a boy, Nicholas Young, the point seen being named by Cook "Young Nick's Head," and the youth being rewarded with the prize of a gallon of rum which had been offered to whoever should first sight land! The *Endeavour* spent six months on the coasts of New Zealand, the island being circumnavigated, surveyed and charted with a surprising degree of accuracy. Particular attention was paid to Cook Strait, the channel separating the North and South Islands. They had dealings with the Maoris, but found them on the whole rather unfriendly and addicted to purloining anything they fancied, including, on one occasion, Cook's sheets, which, in the wash, were trailing overboard from the stern.

Her work in New Zealand done, the *Endeavour* sailed for Australia, the coast of which, near Bass Strait, was sighted on April 19th. Ten days later they arrived at Botany Bay, near Sydney, the name being given by Cook because of the great variety of strange plants found there by the scientists. On reaching the shore in his boat for the first time tradition says that Cook ordered the midshipman, Isaac Smith, a cousin of his wife's, to jump out. The boy, afterwards an admiral, was thus reported to be the first Englishman to set foot on the soil of New South Wales, a name given by Cook because he saw some resemblance between its coast and that of the northern shore of the Bristol Channel.

Sailing on to the northward up the coast, Cook explored and examined it for upwards of two thousand miles, discovering and naming many bays, headlands and islands. It is impossible here to speak of the many thrilling adventures through which the little *Endeavour* passed at this stage of her journey. She was a small vessel of indifferent sailing qualities working on a virgin coast in waters utterly unknown and uncharted. Constantly she found herself entangled among islands and shoals, or in danger of shipwreck on the sharp coral fangs of the Great Barrier Reef. And if the ship had been lost the plight of the survivors would have been desperate, for they would have found themselves marooned on a savage, desolate coast far out of the beaten track of civilization, and with no possible hope of succour unless they could build themselves a ship and sail to Batavia, the nearest civilized port, or sail there in their boats. Once the *Endeavour* actually did run ashore, and for a time, until the leak was stopped by "fothering," or passing a sail under the bottom, was in imminent peril. For days at a time officers were stationed at the masthead conning the ship through the coral, gazing anxiously ahead for swirls in the water or the greenish tinge betokening the shallower patches. But Cook's sure judgment and sound seamanship carried her through in safety, and in August 1770 they passed the north point of Queensland through what are now known as the Endeavour Straits, south of the Torres Straits. It was thus proved beyond all doubt that New Guinea and New Holland (Australia) were separate. Before leaving the coast for the last time Cook landed and hoisted the English flag, taking possession of the entire coast he had surveyed in the name of his Sovereign.

Touching at the islands of Timor and Savu they arrived on October 10th at Batavia, where they spent some time on a badly needed refit at the hands of the Dutch workmen. "What anxieties we had escaped," says Cook, "in our ignorance that a large portion of the keel had been diminished to the thickness of the under leather of a shoe!"

Though there had been seven deaths during the voyage, none had occurred through scurvy or fever. Within a fortnight of arriving at Batavia, however, many of the ship's company were taken ill with malaria and dysentery, while seven succumbed. Sailing again on December 26th the ship touched at Prince's Island in the Straits of Sunda for water, and then shaped course for her long passage across the Indian Ocean. Dysentery was still prevalent on board. Scurvy appeared for the first time, and it was not until February 27, 1771, that the list of losses was closed by the deaths of three men, making a total of thirty since arriving at Batavia, or thirty-seven for the entire voyage.

The land near Cape Natal was sighted on March 6th, and on the 15th they came to the Cape of Good Hope. Here Cook stayed for a month refitting and recuperating his invalids. Touching at St. Helena on the way home the Lizard was sighted—again by the boy Nicholas Young—on June 10th. Two days later the gallant little *Endeavour*, passing by the white cliffs of Dover, came to anchor in the Downs.

In his first expedition Cook had given to his country Australia and New Zealand—nothing less. He was rewarded for this eminent service by promotion, at the age of forty-three, to the rank of commander, which, in modern eyes, seems a surprisingly inadequate tribute to one who had achieved so much. Cook himself, reticent and reserved as usual, is silent on the subject; but if he was never adequately recognized during his lifetime his fame has certainly passed down to posterity as one of the chief builders or pioneers of the British Empire.

For the first few months after his arrival in England in June 1771 he was hard at work collecting and putting in order for delivery to the Admiralty the vast collection of journals, notes, observations, sailing directions and charts compiled during the voyage. Meanwhile the perennial controversy about the great southern continent had broken out afresh, and Cook's recent discoveries did not in the least disprove its existence. Those who believed in "Terra Australis Incognita," and they were many, were not disposed to surrender their pet idea because Cook had not found it. He had not looked for it.

In 1675 La Roche, an Englishman, had fallen in with what is now thought to be South Georgia. In 1738 the French explorer, Bouvet, reported land in Lat. 54° South and Long. 11° 20′ East, which he called Cape Circumcision. Both these territories, as well as any other additional morsels of land seen by other voyagers driven to the south by bad weather, were invariably supposed to be part of the mainland of the southern continent.

"Terra Australis Incognita," indeed, had grown up in men's minds as a sort of Eldorado. It was thought to contain riches greater than those of the Spanish colonies in America, and to be inhabited by a race necessarily hardy because of the severe climate, but highly civilized and acquainted with the arts. "Its longitude," says one well-known writer, "is as much as that of all Europe, Asia Minor, and to the Caspian Sea and Persia, with all the islands of the Mediterranean and Ocean which are in its limits embraced, including England and Ireland. That unknown part is a quarter of the whole globe."

The Earl of Sandwich, the First Lord of the Admiralty, took a great interest in the question, and it was largely due to him that it was determined to despatch an expedition to settle the controversy. Cook was naturally selected to command it, and on November 28, 1771, after only five months ashore, he received his commission and set about making his preparations.

Two Whitby-built merchant vessels of 462 and 336 tons respectively were chosen and bought into the Navy, being named the *Drake* and *Raleigh*. Subsequently rechristened the *Resolution* and *Adventure* they were altered, armed and fitted out as sloops in Deptford dockyard. Many of Cook's old officers and men volunteered for the new expedition, and profiting by the experience of the former voyage he took every possible precaution against scurvy. Wheat was embarked instead of the customary oatmeal, sugar instead of oil, and malt, sourkraut, mustard, vinegar, salted cabbage, portable soup,[1] saloup,[2] marmalade of carrots, rob of lemons and oranges,[3] and concentrated juices of wort and beer. Some of these things were already known as anti-scorbutics, while others were tried as an experiment and failed in their effect. Nevertheless, surprising as it may seem, this was the first occasion in the history of navigation in which careful preparations were made for combating the dreadful disease which regularly carried off a considerable proportion of the crews embarked for long voyages.

Cook's orders are too long and too complicated to be quoted in full. Briefly, he was to call at Madeira for a supply of wine and then to proceed to the Cape of Good Hope to recuperate his men and revictual. He was then to sail south to search for Bouvet's "Cape Circumcision," supposed to lie some 1,200 miles to the southward of the Cape of Good Hope. If found, he was to survey it and to ascertain whether or not it was an island or portion of a continent. If it proved to be a continent he was to explore it so far as possible, cultivating friendly relations and trade with the inhabitants, if any. He was then to proceed either east or west, keeping as far south as possible, to continue his discoveries until such time as the health of the crews necessitated a return to a civilized port, whence he was to make the best of his way back to England.

[1] A cake of the portable soup which was on board the *Endeavour* is in the museum of the Royal United Service Institution in Whitehall. It looks like a slab of whitish-coloured glue.

[2] "Saloup." A decoction made from the root of a meadow plant, or from sassafras, used as a beverage before the introduction of tea and coffee.

[3] "Rob of lemons and oranges." A sort of jelly made from the fresh fruit.

If Cape Circumcision proved to be an island, or if he did not find it, he was to stand on to the southward so long as he thought there was a chance of falling in with the continent. If the latter was not found he was to steer east and to circumnavigate the world, keeping as far to the south as he could and exploring any islands or land that he fell in with. Having done this he was to return to the Cape of Good Hope and thence to England. He was given full permission to proceed to the northward at any time to any known place to refit and revictual his ships and recuperate his men, returning to the southward when circumstances allowed it. If the *Resolution* was lost the voyage was to be continued in the *Adventure*.

On July 13, 1772, the two ships, after considerable delay due to alterations, finally left Plymouth. Touching at Madeira for fresh food, wine and water, they arrived on October 30th at the Cape of Good Hope, where they were afforded every assistance by the Dutch authorities.

Leaving the Cape again on November 22nd they sailed on to the southward to search for Cape Circumcision, the weather soon becoming bitterly cold and stormy and the men being served out with the fearnought jackets and trousers provided by the Admiralty. For a week they were blown eastward by a heavy gale in which no canvas could be carried and much water found its way on board, and on December 10th ice was first sighted. For another six weeks they sailed among icebergs and pack-ice, with fog, rain, sleet and snow. Much of the livestock purchased at the Cape perished in the cold and wet, so that salt provisions had to be served out and scurvy made its appearance among the ships' companies. It was kept under by liberal doses of the various preventatives.

Christmas Day, we are told, was celebrated by

the seamen "with savage noise and drunkenness," and though, soon afterwards, the vessels reached a position ninety-five miles south true of the reported position of Cape Circumcision,[1] there were no signs of the great continent of which it was supposed to form a part.

By New Year's Day, 1773, the ships were in Lat. 60° South, and seventeen days later crossed the Antarctic Circle. Still there were no signs of land, and soon they found themselves hemmed in by ice, some of which being taken on board and melted proved excellent for drinking purposes, which allayed Cook's anxiety in regard to fresh water. But the weather was bad and the ice to the southward impassable. No further advance could be made without endangering the ships, and Cook was forced to retreat northward before resuming an easterly course. On February 8th the *Adventure* was lost sight of in a severe gale and thick weather. The *Resolution* fired guns and burnt flares to attract her attention; but the ships did not meet again until May 18th, in New Zealand.

Sailing on alone, the *Resolution* steered first northerly, then south-easterly, and then east along the parallel of 60° South. Still no land was sighted, and on March 16th the course was altered for New Zealand. The weather, says one of the civilian passengers, was very severe, the ship constantly rolling gunwales under in the heavy sea, masts and sails being damaged or blown away, and rigging so encrusted with ice that it cut the men's hands. The sailors, however, do not seem to have regarded it as unusual. On March 26th, after a run of 3,600

1 "Cape Circumcision," it may here be said, is now supposed to have been Bouvet Island, rediscovered in 1898 by the German Deep Sea discovery ship *Valdivia*. Its position in Lat. 54° 26′ South, Long. 3° 24′ East, is considerably to the westward of the position given to Cook.

leagues and having been 117 days at sea without a sight of land, the *Resolution* arrived at Dusky Bay, New Zealand. So efficient had been Cook's precautions that there was only one man sick of the scurvy.

After refreshing his men with game, fresh fish and spruce beer, Cook continued his survey of the coast, arriving at Queen Charlotte's Sound on May 18th, where he found the *Adventure*. She had been there for six weeks, and some of her crew were down with scurvy.

On June 7th the two ships sailed in company for Tahiti, and by the end of July twenty of the *Adventure's* men were suffering from scurvy and one had died. It would seem that sufficient precautions had not been taken to combat the disease, for the *Resolution* herself had only one man afflicted with it. After sighting various islands they arrived at Tahiti on August 16th, and in coming to an anchor in a light wind and a strong tide the *Resolution* struck a reef, though luckily without serious damage.

Remaining at beautiful Tahiti for about a fortnight, Cook recuperated his men and met many natives whom he had seen during his previous voyage. Then, sailing again on September 1st, the ships spent some time in cruising among the other islands of the group. At Huahine the *Adventure* ran ashore but got off without great damage, and here again Cook met many old friends and was supplied with everything he wanted in the way of pigs, fowls and fruit. The only unpleasant incident that occurred was to one of the botanists, who, roaming in the interior by himself, unwittingly transgressed some native law and was bereft of everything save his nether garments.

On November 3rd the *Resolution* again arrived in New Zealand. The *Adventure*, however, lost company during the passage and was seen no more during the voyage. At Queen Charlotte's Sound Cook refitted his ship and overhauled his stores, when about 4,000 lb. of biscuit was found to be rotten and utterly useless as food and another 3,000 lb. nearly as bad. It was as well that they were able to lay in an abundant supply of wild celery, scurvy grass and vegetables from the seeds planted during their previous visit. Before sailing some of the officers discovered a party of Maoris eating human flesh. They did not indulge in the practice from shortness of food, but seemed to be in the habit of regaling themselves upon the bodies of enemies slain in battle.

Leaving orders behind in a bottle in case the *Adventure* came in, Cook sailed again on November 25th for his second voyage southward into the icy, windswept wastes of the inhospitable Antarctic.

When clear of the land the *Resolution* steered to the south-eastward. On December 12th the first ice was sighted. There was constant danger of the ship being wrecked during fog on the numerous bergs and heavy floes; but working south whenever he could, Cook reached, on January 30, 1774, a position in Lat. 71° 10' South, Long. 106° 54' West, a record that was not beaten until 1823.

The rigging, encrusted in ice, became so thick when covered with frozen sleet that it could hardly be grasped by the largest hand. Icicles hung from the men's noses, and their bodies were sometimes cased in frozen snow as if in armour. There was little or no scurvy on board; but men suffered from fever brought on by the cold and wet.

To the south, east and west the sea was covered in an immense sheet of impenetrable ice, mostly flat, but rising here and there in hummocks, sometimes into great hills like mountain ranges. Along the edge of the great barrier there was a mile's width of broken ice, grinding, rising and falling with the movement of the sea. Further progress to the south was out of the question, and satisfied in his mind that there was no land within the Antarctic Circle except so far south as to be practically inaccessible, Cook turned to the northward.

There was still plenty of unexplored space in the great Pacific. It was his intention to fix the position of Juan Fernandez, to visit Easter Island, and then to return to Tahiti, where he hoped to find the *Adventure*. That ship, after parting company with Cook near New Zealand three months before, had been blown off the land by a severe gale which wrought considerable damage to sails and rigging. Compelled to seek shelter for temporary repairs and water, she did not reach Queen Charlotte's Sound until November 30th, six days after Cook had sailed. The bottle containing the orders was found; but the *Adventure* was delayed by having to refit and rebake a large quantity of her biscuit. On December 17th a boat's crew sent ashore for vegetables quarrelled with the natives and were killed to a man, some of them being eaten. Portions of the bodies were found and recognized. It was not until December 23rd that the *Adventure* sailed. She stood to the south-east and thence for Cape Horn, and after passing it, crossed the South Atlantic and searched again for Cape Circumcision, but without success. Accordingly she sailed for Table Bay to refit, and departing thence on April 16th arrived at Spithead on July 14, 1774.

To revert to the *Resolution*. From February 6 to 12, 1774, there was heavy weather, which wrought great havoc with the sails and running rigging, and not long afterwards Cook himself was severely ill with what he lightly calls "a bilious colic." For a long time, it must be remembered, they had been living upon salt provisions—beef so fibrous, tough and impregnated with salt as to be loathsome; biscuit little better than mouldy dust. A dog on board was killed and made into soup, and, says Cook, "I received nourishment and strength from food which would have made most people in Europe sick." Whether or not it was the effect of this fresh meat cannot be said, but on March 4th, to the great joy of everybody on board, the captain was well again.

Juan Fernandez was searched for in its reported position, but without success, and on March 12th the *Resolution* reached Easter Island, remarkable for its large stone statues carved by native hands in the dim ages, some of which are to be seen in the British Museum. They obtained a limited amount of fruit and vegetables from the natives; but the water was bad, and after a stay of four days the ship sailed on to the Marquesas Islands. Here they traded with the natives; but except for fruit and very small pigs, forty or fifty of which were necessary for one meal for the crew, little fresh food was obtainable. Sailing on again, the ship visited two more islands, and on April 22nd, to the great joy of all on board, she arrived again at Tahiti, where she remained three weeks.

Until October they cruised among the Society and Friendly Islands, making several new discoveries, and, passing on, a month was spent surveying the group now known as the New Hebrides. On September 4th Cook discovered and named New Caledonia. Norfolk Island was discovered on October 10th, and on the 18th the *Resolution* arrived again in Queen Charlotte's Sound, New Zealand.

Sailing again to the eastward on November 10th the ship crossed the Pacific between Lat. 54° and 55° South, seeing nothing until December 17th, when she raised the land at the western entrance of the Straits of Magellan. Proceeding southward down the bleak and desolate coast of Tierra del Fuego they reached Christmas Sound, where they met the miserable, half-starved, evil-smelling natives, and obtained wood, water, wild celery and sufficient geese to provide all hands with a feast on Christmas Day.

Cape Horn was passed on December 29th, and on New Year's Day, 1775, they visited Staten Island, proceeding again on January 3rd to search for the southern continent. It was not seen; but South Georgia was discovered, named and formally taken possession of, though Cook was not of the opinion that the island, its peaks covered with snow even in the height of the Antarctic summer, would ever benefit any one. He was mistaken, for South Georgia is now the scene of an extensive and profitable whale fishery.

On January 30th the Sandwich group was discovered and named, and on February 23rd, after another attempt to find Cape Circumcision on the other side of the South Atlantic, course was altered to the north for the Cape of Good Hope. The ship anchored in Table Bay on March 22nd, and after refitting and provisioning turned her bows for home. After touching at St. Helena, Ascension and Fernando de Noronha, the *Resolution* finally arrived at Spithead on the morning of Sunday, July 30, 1775. She had lost no more than four men during the entire voyage, three by accident and one only by disease, a most remarkable contrast to the terrible mortality incurred by Anson's unhappy squadron.

Cook's second expedition must always remain one of the most remarkable feats of navigation ever performed. In an absence of three years and sixteen days he had put a complete girdle round the globe on or near the Antarctic Circle. He had crossed the southern ocean in all directions, had skirted the edge of the Antarctic ice until he could force his way no farther south. The question of any inhabitable continent in the extreme south was settled for ever. It did not exist.

Forty-eight years of age, Cook had spent thirty-four years at sea. He had achieved more than any living person; had probably added more to geographical knowledge than any man since Columbus. But, as before, his reward was meagre. He was graciously received by the King and was promoted to post-captain, a step he might well have obtained several years before. He was appointed by the Admiralty to be one of the Captains of Greenwich Hospital, a sinecure which, if he wished it, provided him for life with a house and an income of £200 a year and allowances. The Royal Society recognized his worth by electing him a Fellow, and in 1776 by conferring upon him the Copley Gold Medal, awarded annually for the best experimental research of the year, for his paper on the prevention of scurvy read before them.

In every way Cook was a great man, a valuable servant of the State, highly respected in his own country and abroad. But he received no distinction in keeping with his services, not even a simple knighthood.

As already stated, the discovery of a north-west passage with a view to shortening the route to the Far East had long been a matter of interest to British navigators. In the middle of the eighteenth century the subject was revived, and an Act of Parliament had been passed offering £20,000 to any ship which should discover it. Many failures to find it from the Atlantic turned men's thoughts to the Pacific, and Lord Sandwich, the First Lord of the Admiralty, consented to send an expedition with a view to finding the passage from that ocean.

It is said that in February 1776 Cook was dining with Lord Sandwich when the conversation turned upon the proposed expedition and who was best fitted to command it, possibly with a view to inviting Cook to volunteer. The snug retreat at Greenwich Hospital, which, apparently, he had not yet taken up, was by no means to the liking of a man full of a restless energy, and fired with his old enthusiasm for exploration Cook instantly offered his services, which were accepted.

The *Resolution* was again chosen for the voyage, her consort being the *Discovery*, a Whitby-built vessel of about 300 tons. Cook received his commission in February, and the next month his old ship was hauled out of dock to complete for sea, many of those who had served in the previous voyages again coming forward as volunteers. An extra supply of warm clothing was taken on board for the men, together with articles of "trade" for bartering with the natives. A bull, two cows and their calves, together with some sheep, were also embarked as presents from King George to the natives of Tahiti.

Cook's orders were simple. He was to proceed to the Cape of Good Hope, and then to look for some islands discovered by a French navigator well south of Mauritius. Thence he was to proceed to New Zealand, and afterwards to Tahiti. Leaving there about February he was to sail across the Pacific to the coast of Drake's "New Albion," in North America, and, sailing northward, was to explore any inlets or rivers that seemed likely to lead to communication with the Atlantic. For the winter he was to retire to a Russian port in Kamtchatka, or other suitable place, and the following spring was to resume his search for the North-West Passage.

Sailing from Plymouth on July 12th the *Resolution* touched at Teneriffe, and arrived at the Cape on October 18th. The next month she was joined by the *Discovery*, which had been delayed in England,

and on November 30th, having refitted, watered, stored and embarked so many animals that the *Resolution* resembled a Noah's Ark, the two ships sailed to the eastward.

The weather soon became cold and stormy, so that spars were carried away and some of the animals perished; but on December 12th they sighted the islands discovered by the Frenchmen Marion du Fresne and Crozet some years before. Cook called them Prince Edward's and Marion's Islands, and gave the name of Crozet Islands to another group farther east. Desolate Kerguelen was reached on Christmas Eve, and here they spent six days watering and surveying. During the run eastward they had considerable fog and bad weather; but on January 26, 1777, put into Adventure Bay, Tasmania, to obtain a new spar in place of a broken topgallant-mast. It was still thought that Tasmania—or Van Diemen's Land—was part of Australia, and no attempt was made to disprove it.

Queen Charlotte's Sound, New Zealand, was next visited for a fortnight, and until the end of the year the two ships cruised among the islands in the southern Pacific, making many new discoveries, the natives, though thievish, being generally friendly. They visited their beloved Tahiti, and by the end of August, considerably to his satisfaction, Cook got rid of the last of his live-stock, horses, cows, sheep, a turkey cock and hen, a gander and three geese, a drake and four ducks, not omitting a peacock and peahen, which he had brought out for stocking the islands. How this menagerie was found room for in the confined space on the deck of a small ship, and how they were kept alive on the passage, it is impossible to imagine.

On December 23rd the two ships crossed the Equator sailing northward, and on the 25th discovered a low island which they named Christmas

Island, whence they obtained a quantity of fish and turtle. The Sandwich Islands—named after the First Lord of the Admiralty—were next found, and here they had no difficulty in getting water, together with pigs and other provisions. On March 7, 1778, they sighted the shore of North America, near Vancouver Island, and passing on up the coast, surveying and exploring, they were soon off the Alaskan shore. The various journals mention the predatory instincts of the wretched natives, the extreme cold, the hunger, the bad food, and how they killed walruses and ate the rank flesh, which, "disgustful as it was," was still better than the abominable salt beef out of the casks. One and all, except Cook, bitterly lamented their departure from fair Tahiti, with its abundance of fresh food, its pretty girls and its fine climate.

The summer was spent in searching for the North-West Passage, and by August 18th, having passed through the Behring Straits, the two ships were well within the Arctic Circle and had reached their most northern latitude, 70° 44′. No farther advance was possible, for from east to west, as far as they could see, the sea was covered by an unbroken sheet of ice standing six feet above the water.

Turning back, Cook cruised for some time on the Siberian and Alaskan coasts and among the islands. Here he met Russian traders who showed him their charts, and to one of them Cook entrusted a letter and chart to be forwarded via Siberia and St. Petersburg to the Admiralty. After their long journey overland they were duly delivered in London the following year.

During the voyage in the northern Pacific no less than 1,200 leagues of coast were examined and the sea crossed in many directions. The main object of the expedition failed, as it was prevented by the ice; but no previous navigator had carried out such extensive and accurate surveys in this remote corner of the world.

On October 26th the two ships sailed southward, and a month later discovered Maui, another island of the Sandwich group. Here Cook procured a quantity of sugar-cane and ordered it to be utilized for brewing a sort of beer, both palatable and wholesome, intending it for use instead of spirits with a view to conserving the latter for use in colder climates. But the men would have none of it. As Cook says, "every innovation whatever, tho' ever so much to their advantage, is sure to meet with the highest disapprobation from seamen." The eighteenth century sailor, not unlike his twentieth century brother, was suspiciously conservative in his likes and dislikes.

On the last day of November they came to the larger and more important island of Hawaii, which Cook spent some time in exploring and surveying, and on January 17, 1779, anchored in Karakakooa Bay.

The place was crowded with natives, many of them coming off in canoes laden with provisions, and the sea being alive with hundreds of others who swam round the ships like shoals of fish. The vessels soon became so crowded that the men could scarcely find room to work; but the visitors, though very friendly, were adepts at thieving— stealing, among other things, the rudder off a boat, the lids of the coppers in the *Resolution's* galley, and cutting the *Discovery's* standing rigging for the sake of the iron. Ashore Cook was treated with honour as a great chief, being given the title of "Orono" after uncouth native ceremonies in which figured idols and a much decomposed pig. He also exchanged visits with King Terreeoboo, the king presenting Cook with valuable feather cloaks and quantities of provisions, and Cook, in turn, investing the king with a linen shirt and sword. As time went on, however, inquiries began to be made as to when the ships were going to leave, hints being given that provisions were running short.

The *Resolution* and *Discovery* left on February 4th to seek a better anchorage, the king presenting quantities of vegetables and a herd of pigs before they sailed. Soon afterwards they ran into a succession of heavy gales, in the course of which sails were split and the *Resolution's* fore-mast so badly sprung that it was necessary to unstep it for immediate repair. This could not be done at sea, and in the circumstances there was no alternative but to return to Karakakooa Bay, which was reached on February 11th.

Their reception, however, was very different to that on their first arrival. Not a canoe came off. The natives seemed shy and diffident, and by no means satisfied when it was explained to them why the ships had come back. And looking at it from their point of view one can well understand it. They had got rid of most of their superfluous provisions during the first visit, and when the vessels returned they saw themselves confronted with demands for further supplies, which, without going short themselves, they could not easily provide.

However, the mast was got ashore for repairs and everything went well until the afternoon of the 13th, when trouble was caused by natives interfering with a watering party. They began, also, to arm themselves with stones and became noisy and truculent. Then a pair of carpenter's tongs were stolen from the *Discovery*, the thief being captured, flogged and put in irons until they were returned. Other thefts took place, and some canoes with stolen property on board were chased by two ship's boats, the crews of which were stoned and roughly handled by the natives on reaching the shore.

The next morning the *Discovery's* six-oared cutter was missing from her moorings. It was more than Cook could stand. He determined to teach the natives a lesson, and providing himself with a shot-gun, he landed with a party of armed marines to take some of the chiefs as hostages until the boat was returned. Ship's boats were also sent to prevent any canoes from leaving the bay.

With his marines Cook proceeded to the village, where he saw the king; but, naturally enough, could not persuade him to come on board. The use of force could only have ended in bloodshed, for a large and threatening crowd was present. Very soon news came that an important chief had been killed by one of the boats on the other side of the bay. Matters now became serious, for the natives instantly began donning their war-mats, while Cook himself was threatened by an excited man with a stone in one hand and an iron spike in the other. He was told to be quiet, but only became more furious, and in exasperation Cook fired a charge of small shot into him, the mats, however, saving him from injury. Stones began to fly and the marines were attacked, and Cook, firing his second barrel loaded with ball, killed a native. Instantly the place was in an uproar and the stone-throwing increased, whereupon the marines fired a volley. Before they could reload they were charged by the natives, four out of the seven being killed and all the remainder, including the officer, being wounded.

Retreating to the water's edge followed by a mob of natives, Cook unwisely turned his back to them to order the boat's crews to cease firing and pull inshore. The moment he did so he was clubbed from behind, and staggering forward, fell on his hand and knee and dropped his musket. Before he could recover his foothold he was stabbed in the back of the neck, and as he fell into the water a crowd of natives leaped on him and tried to keep him under.

A boat was not more than five or six yards distant, but in the confused mêlée and the excitement nobody seems to have been able to do anything to save their leader, for Cook, bleeding and half-drowned, but still struggling fiercely, was clubbed again. His dead body was then hauled ashore by the natives, who snatched the daggers from each other's hands and plunged them again and again into the corpse.

Portions of the body, which had been burnt and dismembered, were subsequently recovered from the natives, and, at sunset on February 21st, with the booming of minute guns and the colours at half-mast, were reverently committed to the deep.

It is unnecessary here to describe the rest of the voyage to Kamtchatka and their ineffectual attempts to discover the North-West Passage, before, in October 1779, they started homewards by way of Japan, Macao, the Straits of Sunda and the Cape of Good Hope. The *Resolution* and *Discovery* finally arrived in England on October 4, 1780, having been absent four years, two months and twenty-two days.

Thus, in a petty quarrel terminating in a fight, in the midst of a brilliant career, perished James Cook, one of the greatest navigators of any age.

No other seaman has ever so enlarged our knowledge of the world. In eleven years he explored New Zealand, proving it to consist of two islands, and surveyed the east coast of Australia for 2,000 miles and showed it had no connection with New Guinea. He discovered the Society Islands and the Sandwich Islands—explored New Caledonia and the New Hebrides, not to mention numerous other islands scattered throughout the Pacific. He crossed the Antarctic Ocean from end to end and proved conclusively that no habitable continent existed to the southward. Far south in the Atlantic he found South Georgia and the Sandwich group, and in the northern Pacific explored over 3,500 miles of coast, and penetrated to the Arctic Sea in search of the North-West Passage.

A chart of the world with the courses of Cook's voyages marked upon it is more eloquent than words. North, south, east and west, his tracks run, crossing and re-crossing in all directions, sometimes so interlaced as to be scarcely comprehensible. From Cape Horn they pass right round the world and back again, with here and there a V-shaped indentation showing a dash towards the South Pole. From England they pass to the Cape of Good Hope, and thence across the Indian Ocean to the Straits of Sunda and New Zealand. In the Pacific they are especially thick, from Easter Island to New Caledonia —from Polynesia away up through the Behring Straits and into the Arctic Ocean.

Cook's record is wonderful. Compared with his achievements the voyages of other British navigators fade into insignificance. Of our famous seamen he **was the** greatest Empire-builder of them all.

# SIR JOHN FRANKLIN IN
# THE ARCTIC

IN Waterloo Place, London, close to the Athe-
næum Club, stands the bronze statue of Sir John
Franklin, one of the most renowned Arctic explorers
that this, or any other, country has produced.
Erected in 1866, it is inscribed to "Franklin. The
great navigator, and his brave companions who
sacrificed their lives in completing the discovery of
the North-West Passage, A.D. 1847–48."

Certain relics of this great explorer and of the
members of his last and most famous voyage have
been recovered from time to time by expeditions sent
out to discover his fate. They included portions of
watches, compasses, telescopes and guns obtained
from the Esquimaux who had found them, also
silver spoons and forks bearing the crests and initials
of the officers, together with a round silver plate
engraved with Sir John's name and the star of an
order of which he was a member.

The most important discovery of all, however,
was made in 1859 by an expedition under the
command of Captain McClintock, when Lieutenant
Hobson found beside a cairn of stones a tin canister
containing a written record of the lost expedition.
First deposited in 1847 and added to in 1848, the
written paper stated that Franklin's ships, the *Erebus*
and *Terror*, had been beset in the ice in September
1846, and that Sir John himself had died the following June. No trace of the ships themselves was ever
found; but various skeletons and other relics, including a large boat mounted on a sledge, were
discovered on the western coast of King Wliliam

Island on the route taken by Franklin's unfortunate followers when, having abandoned their ships, they tried to save their lives by retreating to the mainland.

The rust-stained record, written on an Admiralty printed form, is preserved in the Royal Naval Museum at Greenwich, where are also lodged many of the relics. Others may be seen in the museum of the Royal United Service Institution in Whitehall.

Born at Spilsby, Lincolnshire, on April 16, 1786, John Franklin was the youngest son of a large family of four boys and six girls. It was intended that he should become a clergyman; but a visit to the seaside as a boy first fired his ambition to go to sea. To cure his craving in this direction his father withdrew him from school at the age of thirteen and sent him for a voyage to Lisbon and back in a merchant ship. The experience, however, so far from discouraging him, had the very opposite effect, for though he saw that life in the mercantile marine would not be to his taste, he became determined upon joining the Royal Navy.

Realizing it was useless to thwart his wishes, his father obtained for him an appointment as a first-class volunteer on board the *Polyphemus*, a two-decker of sixty-four guns. He joined in October 1800, and the following April was present at the Battle of Copenhagen. The end of the same month saw him appointed a midshipman to the *Investigator*, an old vessel bought into the Navy some years before. She was being fitted out for a voyage of discovery to New Holland, as Australia was then called, and was commanded by a relative of the Franklin family, Matthew Flinders, who had already made his mark as a navigator and explorer. Manned by eighty-three officers and men, the ship sailed from England on July 18, 1801.

In this voyage Franklin early distinguished

himself by his seamanlike capacity and aptitude as a surveyor. Arriving in King George's Sound, in Western Australia, in December, the *Investigator*, after refitting, sailed along the southern shore of Australia, surveying the coast as she went. In May 1802 she arrived in Sydney Cove, Port Jackson, then a tiny settlement, and here the crazy old ship was overhauled and refitted and an observatory set up on shore.

Leaving again in July, she proceeded up the east coast of Australia, rounded its north-eastern extremity and penetrated into the Gulf of Carpentaria, which was minutely examined. By this time, however, the vessel was unseaworthy and rotten. She had been in bad condition on leaving England and during the voyage out; but now it was estimated that she could not last for longer than six months, while the first really bad gale would probably send her to the bottom with all her men. Completing his survey, Flinders therefore had no alternative but to make the best of his way back to Port Jackson. He proceeded thither round the west coast of Australia and arrived in June 1803, very short of provisions, and with many of the crew suffering from scurvy and dysentery.

On being examined the *Investigator* was found to be past all repair, so Flinders and some of his officers and men were transferred to the *Porpoise* for passage home to England. She sailed from Sydney in August in company with the East Indiaman *Bridgewater* and the *Cato*, with the intention of proceeding to Batavia by way of the Torres Straits. Six days after leaving, however, both the *Porpoise* and *Cato* struck on an outlying reef off the badly charted coast. The *Bridgewater*, to the everlasting disgrace of her captain, abandoned them to their fate and sailed on alone.

When daylight came it was discovered that the

two ships had grounded upon a reef of coral practically awash at high water, and about 900 feet in length by 150 feet wide. The *Cato* had already been battered to pieces by the heavy surf; but the *Porpoise*, in a better position, remained intact, and landing on the little island the shipwrecked men set about salving stores and provisions, together with what sheep and pigs had escaped death by drowning. By August 23rd everything that could be saved had been landed from the wreck, including the *Investigator's* charts and records. On taking an inventory it was found they had sufficient food and water to last the ninety-four survivors for three months on bare rations.

But even so the situation was desperate enough. The nearest land, the uninhabited coast of Australia, was 180 miles away, while Sydney, the only place whence help could be obtained, was about 750 miles distant. It was the stormy season of the year and navigation in the reef-strewn waters was fraught with danger; but on August 26th, undeterred, Flinders himself with twelve men embarked in a cutter belonging to the *Porpoise* to seek assistance.

The survivors on the reef, meanwhile, set to work to build a couple of decked boats, lest the attempt to reach Sydney should come to nothing. They intended to sail for the mainland at the end of October if they were not rescued beforehand; but on October 7th, when they had nearly made up their minds for the worst, three sail hove in sight off the island.

The ships were the *Rolla*, bound for Canton, and the two schooners *Cumberland* and *Frances*. Flinders, who had accomplished his hazardous boat journey in safety, was on board the *Rolla*, and in four days, having embarked the survivors and what stores were worth saving, the *Frances* returned to Sydney; the *Cumberland*, with Flinders, two of his officers and ten men, sailed for England by way of the Torres Straits and Mauritius, while the other survivors, including Franklin, embarked in the *Rolla* for passage to England via Canton.

Flinders, touching at Mauritius for water, was made a prisoner by the French and detained for six and a half years, in spite of the fact that he had a passport from Napoleon. Franklin and his companions arrived safely at Canton, to find there a squadron of sixteen East Indiamen and a number of smaller ships, all laden with the valuable products of the East, on the point of sailing for England. The squadron was under the command of Commodore Nathaniel Dance, of the East India Company's Service, and the officers and men of the *Investigator* were distributed among the different vessels, Franklin himself being sent to the *Earl Camden*, which flew the commodore's broad pennant.

War was in progress with France, and the East India Company's vessels of those days were craft of over 1,000 tons built on man-of-war lines. Their hulls were painted in imitation of line-of-battle ships and frigates the better to deceive the enemy's cruisers and privateers, while they carried from thirty to thirty-six light guns apiece for purposes of defence. Their crews, though well disciplined, were not very numerous and included a proportion of Lascars and Chinese, so from the point of view of guns and men the East Indiamen were no real match for men-of-war with their heavy armaments and large ship's companies.

On February 14th, when the convoy was entering the Straits of Malacca, some strange vessels were seen ahead. They were soon identified as a French squadron under Admiral Linois, comprising the *Marengo*, a line-of-battle ship of seventy-four guns; the *Belle Poule*, of forty-eight guns; two other ships of thirty-six and twenty-four guns respectively, and an eighteen-gun brig. In fighting power this formidable collection was more than a match for the East Indiamen and their consorts.

But Dance was not the man to submit without a fight, while Linois, who had previous information of the English squadron's sailing and its strength, noticed that there were three more vessels than he had been led to expect. He promptly jumped to the conclusion that they were men-of-war.

His supposition was further supported by Dance's bold behaviour, for instead of crowding on all sail and endeavouring to escape, he formed his ships into line of battle and prepared for action. The evening was drawing in, and the French admiral, very perplexed, decided to postpone his attack until daylight.

During the night Dance might have escaped without much difficulty; but, instead of that, he hove-to during darkness and stood on under easy sail at dawn. Linois then manœuvred to cut off some of the ships in the rear of the English line, whereupon Dance, with his ships in battle array, promptly faced about and hoisted signals: "Tack in succession. Bear down in line ahead. Engage the enemy."

The action that ensued was inconclusive, for after a few ineffective broadsides the French, still of the opinion that they were engaged with a superior force, hauled their wind and made all sail to escape. Hardly able to believe in his good fortune, Dance, with sublime impudence, ordered his ships to chase, and for two hours he and his crews enjoyed the astonishing spectacle of sixteen English merchantmen in hot pursuit of a French squadron of war.

The danger past, and fearing that a lengthy chase would carry him too far out of his way, Dance continued his voyage and eventually reached England in safety. His losses amounted to one man killed and another wounded, and for his exploit, one of the most magnificent pieces of bluff on record, the commodore was rewarded with a knighthood, together with £5,000 from the Bombay Insurance Company and a pension of £500 a year for life from the East India Company.

Soon after reaching England in August 1804, Franklin was appointed midshipman of the *Bellerophon*, in which vessel he was present at the Battle of Trafalgar. His ship incurred a loss of 300 men; but Franklin, who, as signal midshipman, was on deck throughout the engagement, escaped without a scratch.

In 1807 he joined the frigate *Bedford*, being promoted to lieutenant early the next year. For two years the ship was kept in South American waters, but in 1810 was recalled to England to take part in the unfortunate Walcheren Expedition, and spent the next two years in the dreary task of blockading Flushing and the Texel. This monotonous sort of work did not suit the adventurous disposition of Franklin, and in 1812, having already served for five years in the *Bedford*, he petitioned the Admiralty to be allowed to exchange into a frigate. His request was not granted.

The year 1812, however, saw the outbreak of war with America, and in 1813 the *Bedford* was employed convoying a fleet of merchantmen to the West Indies. Then followed another nine months' blockade duty off the Dutch coast, while in 1814 the ship was again sent to the West Indies with a convoy and thence to North America to take part in the operations against New Orleans.

It is unnecessary here to describe the arduous little campaign, in which Franklin was slightly wounded during a boat attack upon some gunboats. May 1815 saw his return to England in his ship, and soon afterwards, having enjoyed a short spell of leave, he was appointed to the *Forth* as first lieutenant. He had been for no less than seven and a half years in the *Bedford*.

His service in the *Forth* calls for no special remark. In 1818, however, soon after his thirty-second birthday, having fought in two great naval battles and various minor engagements, besides having taken part in a voyage of exploration to little-known Australia, John Franklin started his career as an Arctic explorer.

It was in 1773 that Captain Phipps, with the *Racehorse* and *Carcass*, the latter bearing the young Horatio Nelson, had sailed from Sheerness with orders to proceed to the North Pole or as near to it as circumstances would permit. The two ships, in an absence of three months, actually attained a latitude of 80° 48′ N.

By 1818 England was again at peace after her wars against France and America, and after a lapse of forty-five years the subject of Arctic exploration again took possession of the minds of the Government, the Admiralty and various learned societies. So far back as 1745 an Act had been passed offering a reward of £20,000 to the owners of any vessel which should first discover a north-west passage from Hudson's Straits along the north coast of America to the Pacific, while in 1776 quarter this sum was offered to any one who should approach the North Pole by sea within one degree.

This last provision was modified by another Act in 1818 establishing a sliding scale of awards—£1,000 to the vessel which first succeeded in reaching 83° north; £2,000 for 85° north; £3,000 for 87° north; £4,000 for the 88th parallel, and £5,000 for the discovery of the Pole.

Apparently unaware of the great difficulties of Arctic navigation, the authorities seem to have thought it quite possible that the Pole would be reached. Indeed, the tone of easy familiarity with which the Admiralty of the period talked of it in their sailing orders to various expeditions is somewhat astounding. "Should you reach the Pole, your future course must mainly depend . . ." they airily say. "If . . . the weather should prove favourable, you are to remain in the vicinity of the Pole for a few days, in order to the more accurately making the observations which it is to be expected your interesting and unexampled situation may furnish you with."

But however lightly the Admiralty talked they certainly spared no efforts in fitting out expeditions. Four vessels were prepared, two of which, the *Isabella* and *Alexander*, under the command of Captain Ross, were to proceed to the northward via Baffin's Bay, while two more, the *Dorothea* and *Trent*, were to go by way of Spitzbergen. These last-named were brigs of 370 and 250 tons respectively, hired for the service and specially fitted and strengthened, the *Dorothea* being under the command of Captain Buchan, who was also in charge of the expedition, while John Franklin was chosen to command the *Trent*.

Sailing from the Thames on April 25, 1818, they were instructed to pass between Spitzbergen and Greenland and to endeavour to reach the Pole. Thence, if possible, they were to shape course direct for Behring Strait.

Spitzbergen was duly sighted on May 26th, and passing up its western coast with considerable difficulty from ice and bad weather the vessels came to a harbour on the north-western coast of the island. Leaving again on June 7th, they stood along the margin of the pack-ice seeking for an opening. But no passage could be found, and soon afterwards the ships were driven by the wind into the pack, where they were beset in the ice.

It was a situation of no little danger, and on one occasion the little *Trent*, though seemingly locked fast, was suddenly raised four feet into the air by a gigantic mass of ice under her keel. The *Dorothea*, too, was in similar peril, and both were subjected to terrible pressure by the ever-moving bergs and floes. For a time the crews made attempts to drag their ships through the ice whenever the smallest water-lanes opened in front of them, and by dint of warping, working the ice-saws and using their sails wherever possible they actually succeeded in making a few miles' progress. But at the end of it they found the whole pack was being carried southward by the current faster than they were progressing north, and on July 19th Buchan was forced to the conclusion that any further attempt was useless. All that could be done was to regain open water as soon as possible, and then to proceed westward along the ice in the hope of finding a clear channel.

It took nine days' incessant labour before the ships were free of the pack, and hardly were they clear when there came a furious southerly gale with a heavy, tumbling sea. They were on a lee-shore of ice, and to escape almost certain destruction were forced to the desperate expedient of taking shelter in the ice itself, and set about protecting the hulls of their ships to the best of their ability with fenders of hemp cable, walrus hides and iron plates.

As they approached, no opening could be seen in the wall of ice, against which the mountainous seas were breaking furiously to set the immense masses in violent agitation. "At one moment," says one who was present,[1] "it (the sea) bursts upon these icy fragments, and buries them many feet beneath the wave, and the next, as the buoyancy of the depressed body struggles for the ascendancy, the water rushes in foaming cataracts over its edges, while every individual mass, rocking and labouring

[1] Lieutenant Frederick Beechey, Franklin's first lieutenant. A well-known explorer, he died a rear-admiral in 1856.

in its bed, grinds against and contends with its opponent until one is either split with the shock or upheaved upon the surface of the other. Nor is this collision confined to any particular spot; it is going on as far as the sight can reach. . . ."

Into this awful, heaving turmoil, with the men watching the masts and every one holding on for their lives, the two ships dashed under reduced canvas. Cutting her way through the thin ice, the *Trent* came into violent contact with the main mass. The little ship shook and staggered under the impact and seemed to recoil, while men were flung sprawling, the masts bent like fishing-rods and the sound of cracking timbers from below told of under-water damage. The next great wave, curling up under her stern, broke and drove her bodily about her own length into the pack, where she gave one heavy roll and was then thrown broadside on to the wind by the succeeding wave.

Encompassed on all sides by great masses of ice, rolling and pitching violently, literally tossed from piece to piece, little could be done but await the issue, though Franklin, by crowding on more sail, forced his ship farther into the pack where the motion was a little less violent. In a few hours the gale blew itself out as suddenly as it had arisen.

The vessels succeeded in extricating themselves the next morning and made their way to a bay on the northern shore of Spitzbergen. Both were badly damaged after their severe gruelling, the *Dorothea's* port side being so battered that it was little short of a miracle that she had remained afloat.

Further contact with the ice was obviously out of the question so far as the *Dorothea* was concerned. In accordance with his orders from the Admiralty, Buchan was fully authorized to continue the voyage in the still seaworthy *Trent* and to send his own ship home. The state of the *Dorothea*, however, made it inadvisable for her to undertake the voyage alone, and accordingly, on August 30th, after taking magnetic observations and doing a certain amount of survey work, both vessels sailed for England. They arrived at Deptford on October 22nd, having been absent nearly six months.

Early the next year, 1819, two more expeditions were organized by the Admiralty. The first, consisting of the *Hecla* and *Griper*, commanded by Lieutenant Parry, was to proceed up Baffin's Bay and thence to endeavour to reach the Pacific through any channel leading to the westward. The second expedition, commanded by Franklin, was an entirely new departure, for it was to proceed overland from the north-west shore of Hudson Bay, thence across a great tract of practically virgin country to a point on the shore of the Arctic Ocean in the vicinity of the Coppermine River. From here the explorers were to travel eastwards along the coast, and, if possible, to effect a junction with Parry and his ships.

The overland journey was a hazardous undertaking, for only two men, Hearne and Mackenzie, had previously crossed the country from south to north. Nobody knew what difficulties and dangers the new expedition might have to contend with, or how great were the risks of perishing through the intense cold or starvation.

Franklin, who seems fully to have realized the risks and uncertainty of his mission, chose as his companions Doctor Richardson,[1] a naval surgeon and a keen and well-trained scientist; George Back[2] and Robert Hood, midshipmen who had served with him in the *Trent*, and two seamen. There were also four boatmen from the Orkneys.

---

[1] Afterwards Sir John Richardson, well known as an Arctic explorer.
[2] Afterwards Sir George Back, who made a reputation as an independent Arctic explorer.

Leaving England in one of the Hudson Bay Company's ships on May 23, 1819, the little party arrived at York Factory, on the western shore of Hudson Bay, on August 30th. Here they remained for a week collecting stores and equipping a boat, and finally started on their journey on September 9th. The details of the route were left more or less to Franklin; but, using portable boats or canoes, his idea was to follow the line of rivers and lakes ending with the Great Slave Lake and Coppermine River.

Progress was slow and very difficult, for the boat was heavily laden, while there were numerous rapids to contend with. They managed to drag their unwieldy craft over the smaller rapids after lightening her; but when it came to negotiating the steeper waterfalls they were compelled to unload and to carry her bodily over the dry land to the next stretch of water. Twenty-one miles was the actual length of these "portages," though as seven trips had to be made on each occasion to transport all the stores, the distance actually traversed on foot and heavily laden was nearly 150 miles. However, after a weary journey of between 800 and 900 miles, the party reached Fort Cumberland, a station on the Saskatchewan River, on October 23rd.

Here, to his great disgust, Franklin found that he was unable to obtain the guides, hunters, interpreters and other necessary people that he had been told would be readily available. This unfortunate state of affairs was largely brought about by the jealousy between the Hudson Bay Company and their rivals the North-West Company, who in those days divided between them the jurisdiction over the wild region through which Franklin was passing. The matter was serious, for it necessitated a lengthy journey to obtain the assistance without which the expedition could not proceed.

Leaving Richardson and Hood at Fort Cumberland to bring on the stores and provisions in the boats as soon as the river was navigable, Franklin, with Back and one seaman, started on foot for Fort Chipewyan, on the shore of Lake Athabasca. They had a couple of dog sledges and fifteen days' food, and travelling in a temperature so low that it froze the mercury in the thermometer and "the tea in our teapots before we could drink it," finally reached their destination on March 26th.

Here they spent the rest of the long, dreary winter; but again their efforts to obtain the necessary outside assistance met with ill success due to the friction between the two companies. Richardson and Hood rejoined Franklin at Fort Chipewyan as soon as the state of the rivers permitted, and on July 18th the expedition left for Fort Providence, on the northern shore of the Great Slave Lake, with a very scanty supply of ammunition and little more than a day's provisions.

Hunting and fishing to support themselves on the way, the party arrived at Fort Providence on July 29th, leaving again on August 2nd. By this time they had recruited outside help, and the expedition now comprised twenty-eight people, including Canadian guides and hunters and interpreters, together with three women and three children. They were also joined on the way by a party of Indian hunters, and on August 20th, after very slow progress, arrived at Winter Lake. Here they spent the first few days building log huts wherein to spend the winter, and the spot is still shown on maps as Fort Enterprise, the name given to it by Franklin.

The winter, with its snow and bitter cold, came on earlier than was expected, and at Fort Enterprise the party remained until June 14, 1821, nearly ten months, suffering from great scarcity of provisions through the reindeer having unexpectedly shifted their ground. The stock of food fell so low, indeed, that it became necessary to obtain food from Fort Chipewyan, a service for which Back volunteered. Leaving in November, he returned in March with a party bringing food, having travelled more than 1,100 miles on snowshoes, sometimes without food for two and three days at a time, in a temperature sometimes so low as 50°, and protected at night by only one blanket and a deer-skin.

On June 14th the expedition was at last able to leave Fort Enterprise for the sea, the party consisting of twenty in all. They had with them two large canoes and several sledges, while, before leaving, Franklin arranged with the Indian chief to deposit a supply of food at Fort Enterprise lest another winter should have to be spent there.

Progress was very slow. Often they had to traverse tracts of barren ground and rugged hills carrying the canoes on their backs, so it was not until July 1st that they finally launched their little craft on the Coppermine River. For another fortnight they travelled down it, obtaining their first sight of the sea from a hill on July 14th. Seven days later they were at the mouth of the river and afloat on the Arctic Ocean.

Sometimes sailing, sometimes paddling, they proceeded to the eastward along the sterile and inhospitable coast bounded by rugged cliffs and fringed with heavy masses of ice rising and falling with the motion of the sea, and against which the frail canoes were in constant danger of being destroyed. The voyage must rank as one of the most memorable pieces of exploration ever carried out, for following all the indentations of the coast, accurately charting it as he went, and naming all the principal capes, bays and islands, Franklin travelled a distance of no less than 555 miles. On August 18th he arrived at what was christened Cape Turnagain, in 69° 19' N.,

111° 5′ W., on the eastern side of Bathurst Inlet. Hence, with only three days' pemmican left, with increasing severity in the weather and the absence of Esquimaux, from whom they hoped to obtain food, they were forced to turn back.

Owing to the shortness of food Franklin decided that the homeward journey to Fort Enterprise must be made by the quickest possible route, and determined to return by way of Hood's River, which seemed to offer a short cut. They reached it on August 25th and proceeded up it; but on the third of the following month the stream curled to the westward away from the direction in which they wished to travel. Leaving it, they struck off across country to the south-westward, having first broken up the large canoes and rebuilt them into smaller craft which they could conveniently carry with them. The story of their subsequent sufferings is one of the most poignant on record.

Even on starting up Hood's River food was so scarce that only a few mouthfuls of pemmican could be issued to each person, and at breakfast on September 4th they consumed all that remained of their supply of meat. From now on they would practically have to depend upon what natural food the inhospitable country would provide.

Reindeer were seen the day after leaving the river; but they were so wild that the hunters could not get near enough for a shot. Then followed a heavy storm of wind and rain which confined the travellers to their tents for three days. It was bitterly cold, and on re-starting the march, tents, clothes and belongings were frozen stiff, while the moss, the only available fuel, was covered in ice and snow, so that there were no means of making a fire. Suffering the awful pangs of extreme hunger they struggled on— sometimes through snow a foot deep, sometimes across swamps and marshes, sometimes over streams and hill-sides strewn with boulders and slippery stones. The men carrying the canoes were often hurled headlong through slipping or by the violence of the wind, and one of the canoes was so badly damaged as to be unserviceable. Making a fire of the bark and timber thus obtained they cooked what remained of the portable soup and arrowroot, and the resulting meal, though scanty enough for men who had been three days without food, seemed to satisfy their hunger for a time and to build up their strength. A few partridges were killed on the evening of the first day after leaving camp, and half a bird was issued to each man for his supper, being boiled with a small quantity of "tripe de roche" over a fire of frozen willows collected from under the snow.

"Tripe de roche," it should be explained, was simply an unpalatable, unwholesome lichen which grew on the rocks in places. It was described as "edible," though, very bitter, it proved nauseous to all and noxious to many, producing severe internal disorders.

On this miserable food and what remained of the partridges they lived for the next three days; but by September 10th starvation again stared them in the face. Then, providentially, a herd of musk-oxen were seen ahead, one of which was shot. The men were so ravenous that the raw intestines of the animal were devoured on the spot and pronounced excellent. Supper that evening was the first full meal for seventy-two hours.

The flesh of the musk-ox lasted for three days, after which they were again reduced to their detestable diet of "tripe de roche." The going, too, was becoming increasingly difficult, for they found themselves confronted by a great lake and were compelled to negotiate its rocky shores. Two more deer were killed and saved them from starvation for a time; but by September 21st they were subsisting again on the lichen, eked out by bits of deer skin and bones, the remains of an animal killed and partly eaten by the wolves during the preceding spring. Five days later they were lucky enough to kill five small deer; but by this time the Canadian "voyageurs" were becoming demoralized. Two of them, who had been carrying the remaining canoe some way in rear of the main party, left it behind, alleging that it had been damaged by a fall and was entirely useless. The Canadians, indeed, having given up all hope of ever getting through alive, were quite out of hand. Nothing could make them exert themselves.

September 26th found the expedition on the banks of the Coppermine River, which it was necessary to cross. They were now within forty miles of Fort Enterprise as the crow flies, and with a canoe might have negotiated the rapid stream without difficulty. For some time no materials could be found for building another; but in searching the neighbourhood for materials they came across the carcass of a deer in a cleft of rock into which it had fallen many months before. The flesh was putrid; but they lit a fire, and cooked and ate it on the spot.

A raft was eventually constructed of willows, and on September 29th they endeavoured to use it for crossing the river. It would not support more than one man, however, and could not be paddled or poled across owing to the rapidity of the stream and the depth of water. It was then that Dr. Richardson volunteered to swim across with a line, an attempt which all but cost him his life.

The cold was bitter and a heavy snowfall set in. For three more days, while waiting for a lull in the weather before attempting another crossing, the party subsisted on scraps of leather and "tripe de roche." Finally they built themselves a canoe of painted canvas stretched over a wooden framework, and in this crazy craft, one by one, they were drawn across the swollen stream in safety.

Things began to look more hopeful, and even the spirits of the Canadian "voyageurs" revived. Franklin realized, however, that in their enfeebled state the entire party could never hold out against starvation for the time it would take them to reach Fort Enterprise. Back, with three Canadians, was accordingly sent on ahead to the Fort to return with all possible speed with some of the food that should have been deposited there by the Indians. Franklin himself, with Dr. Richardson, Hood, one of the seamen, eight "voyageurs" and an Indian named Michel, struggled on in rear, their progress painfully retarded by deep snow.

They lived on scraps of roasted leather and "tripe de roche." Two of the Canadians collapsed and could hardly walk on, while Hood was very feeble. At last, leaving Hood with Dr. Richardson and one of the seamen—Hepburn—in a tent, Franklin went on with the others. They had not travelled more than four and a half miles before they were obliged to camp, one of the Canadians and Michel being utterly spent and declaring they could go no farther. Franklin finally consented to their going back to rejoin Richardson, and himself went on with the remainder; but during the day two more men collapsed and were allowed to return, leaving him with four companions. Their food during the dreadful march consisted of the lichen and fried leather with "tea" made of gathered herbs, as nauseous as it was unsustaining. At last, on October 11th, five days after leaving Richardson, Franklin and his men reached Fort Enterprise, only to find it empty of food. The Indians had failed in their trust.

They found a note from Back saying that he had arrived and had gone on in search of the Indians, and that, if he could not find them, he intended going on to Fort Providence and to send on food from there. Franklin, meanwhile, his heart full of terrible anxiety for the safety of Richardson and his party, had to feed his own men. In an outhouse they came across some rotting deer-skins left from the year before, and with these, the inevitable "tripe de roche" and decomposing bones from an ash-heap, produced "a very palatable mess." Their weakness was so great that they could not move more than a few yards at a time. Their eyeballs were dilated, their mouths raw and bleeding as a result of their miserable food, their joints and limbs hideously swollen. They were, in point of fact, in the grip of that dread disease—scurvy.

Nine days passed in utter misery, and at last, with two men, Franklin started off in search of the Indians. Only one day out, however, he was forced to return by the breaking of one of his snow-shoes, one of the Canadians going on in search of help.

Another week crawled by, the wretched men at Fort Enterprise getting weaker and weaker, and some of them already so feeble that they could not leave their beds in search of food. On October 27th Franklin wrote in his journal: "I have this day been twenty-one years in H.M. service, and exposed to many hardships in my professional career, but was never placed in such a melancholy and affecting situation as at present. However, with sincere praises to Almighty God for His past goodness and protection, I will humbly confide in His gracious mercy and hope for deliverance from this severe trial."

On the 29th, quite unexpectedly, Richardson and Hepburn staggered into the fort. They were the only survivors of those who had stayed behind or had subsequently turned back, and their tale was a ghastly one. Two of the men who had returned from Franklin had been missed, and though the exact nature of their death was never verified, there were strong grounds for believing that the Indian, Michel, had done them to death and devoured their bodies. Moreover, on October 20th Hood, who had been temporarily left behind in camp while Richardson and Hepburn searched for food and fuel, had been foully shot through the head by the Indian. It is impossible here to enter into all the details of the tragedy; but Richardson decided to push on for Fort Enterprise at all cost, and on the 23rd, by which time both he and Hepburn were convinced that Michel intended to kill them also, the doctor avenged Hood's death by shooting the murderer through the head with his pistol.

By November 3rd two of the Canadians at the Fort had died of starvation and the party was now reduced to Franklin, Richardson, Hepburn and the interpreter. The days rolled on, each one worse than the last. Hope was practically given up, and by the 6th they were all on the verge of absolute exhaustion and starvation. The end could not long be delayed.

On the very next day, however, relief came. "Praise be unto the Lord!" wrote Franklin in his diary. "We were this day rejoiced by the appearance of Indians with supplies at noon."

It was to the gallantry of Back that they owed their lives—Back, who after enduring incredible hardships and supporting life upon an old pair of leather trousers, a gun cover, a pair of old shoes, and what little "tripe de roche" he could find, had at last fallen in with the Indians on November 4th.

Little remains to be told of this expedition. On the 16th the survivors left Fort Enterprise, to arrive at Fort Providence on the 11th of the following month. Hence, after a few days' rest, they made their way to Moose Deer Island, where they spent the rest of the winter. Progress was resumed in May 1822 and York Factory, on the shore of Hudson Bay, was reached in July. Sailing for England, they reached home in October, having been absent three and a half years and having journeyed, by land and water in the northern continent of America, a distance of 5,500 miles.

Franklin had been promoted to commander in his absence, and on November 20, 1822, was advanced to captain, being also elected a member of the Royal Society. Of his companions Richardson was appointed surgeon of the Chatham division of the Royal Marines, while Back, having been promoted to lieutenant, was sent to the West Indies.

During the summer after his return Franklin became engaged to Miss Eleanor Anne Porden, whom he had known for some time. They were married on August 19, 1823.

By the end of 1823 Franklin was submitting schemes for further expeditions to the Arctic, and his ideas were accepted by the Admiralty. The *Blossom*, under the command of Captain Beechey, Franklin's old first lieutenant in the *Trent*, was to proceed by way of the Pacific and to enter the Arctic Ocean through the Behring Straits, and thence to sail eastward along the coast of North America towards the mouth of the Mackenzie River. Franklin, at the same time, was to conduct another overland expedition through northern Canada and down the Mackenzie River. On reaching its mouth the party was to divide, Franklin himself proceeding west along the coast with a view to meeting the *Blossom*, while another party went east as far as the Coppermine River to connect up the new survey with the work already done in 1821.

Mrs. Franklin, who was in failing health, gave birth to a daughter in June 1824, and on February 16, 1825, Franklin and his officers, having been preceded by the men and stores, sailed from England for New York. Dr. Richardson and Back were again members of the expedition, and arrangements had been made with the Hudson Bay Company for the conveyance of the men, stores and provisions to a depôt on the Great Bear Lake. They took with them three boats specially built for the project, craft capable of holding seven or eight men apiece, but light enough to be carried overland to avoid falls and rapids, and sufficiently large and seaworthy for work in the open sea.

Arriving at New York on March 22nd, Franklin and his officers made their way to Penetanguishene, a remote naval station on Lake Huron, and it was here, on April 22nd, that he learnt of the death of his wife exactly two months before.

Proceeding by the chain of lakes stretching north-westward, and thence by the Saskatchewan, Franklin overtook the boats and the remainder of the party, and on July 15th arrived at Fort Chipewyan, on Lake Athabasca. From here, travelling down the Slave River, they went to Fort Resolution, on the Great Slave Lake, August 2nd finding them in their boats on the Mackenzie, having made arrangements with the Indians for the supply of food during the forthcoming winter.

Fort William was reached after six days' travelling, whence Back was sent to the Great Bear Lake to construct the huts for winter quarters afterwards known as Fort Franklin. Richardson also proceeded to explore the northern shore of the lake, while Franklin, in the few weeks in which travelling was still possible, started down the Mackenzie in one of the boats with the idea of reaching its mouth and gaining some knowledge of the condition of the ice in the Arctic Ocean. He reached his destination on August 14th without undue incident, hoisting the silk Union flag made by his dying wife.

By September 5th all the members of the expedition had returned to winter quarters at Fort Franklin, and here, in the log huts erected by Back and his men, they spent the next nine months until further travel was possible. The temperature sometimes fell as low as 49° below zero, but the huts were well warmed and comfortable, and the supplies of food—reindeer, moose, and trout collected by the Indians—plentiful.

On June 24, 1826, the summer expedition started, and on the third of the following month, near the mouth of the Mackenzie, Richardson parted from his leader for the journey to the eastward. In about two months he accomplished the stupendous task of tracing nearly 900 miles of rugged, undiscovered coast which lay between the Mackenzie and Coppermine Rivers.

Franklin himself went on to the mouth of the Mackenzie, which he reached on July 7th, and here the boats were attacked by a party of Esquimaux 300 strong, desirous for loot. The scuffle lasted several hours, and for a time things looked decidedly serious. Indeed, had it not been for Franklin's tact and forbearance in refusing to open fire when beset by a crowd of natives armed with knives, bows and arrows and spears, his entire party, hopelessly outnumbered, would probably have been massacred.

July 14th saw the boats at sea; but for five days further progress was prevented by masses of ice. Finding a way through, they eventually pushed on, though the advance was depressingly slow. For days at a time they were held up by gales, ice and thick fogs, the boats themselves being damaged by rough contact with the floes. By the 27th, however, they reached the imaginary line of demarcation between Great Britain and Russia, the latter country, at that time, still being mistress of Alaska. Here, underneath a pile of driftwood, they deposited a tin box containing a record and hoisted the Union flag.

Going on to the westward, sometimes paddling, sometimes sailing, they were further delayed by fog and ice; but on August 18th, having mapped the coast for 374 miles since leaving the Mackenzie, were reluctantly compelled to turn back. The autumn was advancing. Another six weeks would see the setting in of winter, when further voyaging would be impossible and the reindeer, upon which they depended for food, would have deserted the coast. The abandonment of the project for completing the exploration of the coast westward to the Behring Straits by effecting a junction with Beechey in the *Blossom* was a bitter disappointment, though in the circumstances there was no alternative.

Franklin was not to know until after his arrival in England how narrowly he had escaped complete success. Beechey had arrived with his ship at Icy Cape and from here had sent a boat to the eastward. On August 25th this boat reached a point only 160 miles to the westward of where Franklin had decided to turn back a week earlier.

September 21st saw all the exploring parties back at Fort Franklin, where they spent the winter of 1826. Early the next year the expedition left for home, and proceeding by way of Forts Simpson and Chipewyan and thence through Montreal and New York, Franklin arrived in England on September 26, 1827, having been away for two years and seven months.

Though not perhaps so spectacular as the first overland journey, this second expedition achieved important results, for it brought about the discovery and charting of over 1,200 miles of absolutely unknown coast, while the geological, magnetic and meteorological observations were of great value to science. Franklin was presented with the gold medal of the Paris Geographical Society soon after his return; but it is a little surprising that it was not until the spring of 1829 that his services were officially recognized in his own country by the bestowal of a knighthood. In the same year the degree of D.C.L. was conferred upon him by the University of Oxford.

Eighteen years were to elapse before Franklin again set out for the Arctic on his last and most famous expedition.

In September 1828 he married Miss Jane Griffin, a close friend of his first wife, and after two more years of unemployment was appointed on August 23, 1830, to the command of the twenty-six gun frigate *Rainbow*, then fitting out at Portsmouth. In this ship he sailed for the Mediterranean towards the end of the year, to spend the greater portion of the year 1831 at Corfu.

In the spring of 1832, however, there came a chance of more active employment. Greece, though nominally free, was still labouring under a heavy yoke of oppression. The Turks had been expelled; but the country seethed with anarchy and rebellion, and a host of soldiers, sailors, government officials and private adventurers lived idly at the public expense while the miserable agricultural population died of famine. The *Rainbow* was sent to Patras to assist the French and Russian vessels to keep order and to protect life and property, and until December 1833, when the ship returned to England, Franklin was employed on one of those semi-diplomatic, semi-political tasks of maintaining tranquillity in a foreign country which sometimes fall to the lot of the naval officer. It is unnecessary here to enter into details; but he carried out his difficult duties with great tact and firmness, being created for his services a Knight Commander of the Guelphic Order of Hanover by William IV, and having the cross of the newly instituted Grecian Order of the Redeemer conferred upon him by King Otho.

In spite of asking the First Lord of the Admiralty for immediate employment on his return to England, Franklin was to remain for over two years without an appointment, inactivity which many naval officers had to put up with in those days of peace, when, the Navy having been reduced to save expense, there were few ships and numerous applicants to command them.

By the spring of 1836, wearied of the humdrum monotony of doing nothing, he was again petitioning the Admiralty and forwarding a record of his service for the past thirty-six years. In March the Colonial Secretary offered him the governorship of Antigua, an appointment which he refused for the reason that he considered the salary of £1,200 a year insufficient, while, as lieutenant-governor, he would not be in direct communication with the Colonial Office, but more or less under the jurisdiction of the governor of the Leeward Islands. The refusal stood him in good stead, for less than three weeks later he was offered, and accepted, the governorship of Van Diemen's Land, or Tasmania, whither he and his wife and daughter sailed towards the end of 1836.

We need not dwell upon the seven years spent by Franklin in an appointment in which he had much that was unpleasant to contend with; but by June 1844 he was once more at home in England.

During his absence much had been done in the way of discovery in the frozen north. The gap of 160 miles left between Franklin's turning-point in 1826 and the spot reached by the *Blossom's* boat had been charted by two officers of the Hudson Bay Company, while the same pair had surveyed the coast between Cape Turnagain and the Great Fish River. Parry, in his expedition of 1827, when he reached a latitude of 85° 45′, thus establishing a record which remained unbroken for nearly half a century, had pushed westward in the region of the 74th parallel of latitude. But for the finding of a passage of less than 300 miles linking Parry's discoveries with those farther south, the finding of the North-West Passage along the northern seaboard of North America was complete.

Towards the end of 1844 the Admiralty was proposing another expedition to finish the work, Franklin and other well-known Arctic explorers being asked for their advice concerning it. Anxious for congenial employment, Sir John wished to command the new venture, and his application was backed up by the Royal Society. On February 5, 1845, he visited Lord Haddington, the First Lord of the Admiralty, by appointment, who told him that the Government had approved of the expedition. To the First Lord's observation that the undertaking was a risky one for a man aged sixty, Franklin replied that he was only fifty-nine and perfectly fit; and after a lengthy conversation Lord Haddington promised to consider the matter. Two days later Sir John received a letter from the Admiralty appointing him to the command he so earnestly desired.

The two ships selected for the new expedition were the *Erebus* and *Terror*, ex-bomb-vessels with specially strengthened hulls which had taken part in previous Arctic and Antarctic expeditions. The *Erebus*, 372 tons, was built at Pembroke in 1826, and the *Terror*, 362 tons, at Topsham thirteen years earlier. These two "bombs" each carried two guns and 8 carronades. For the first time in the history of Polar exploration steam was used as an auxiliary to sail, both ships being fitted with screw propellers and engines of fifty horse-power, power which seems puny compared with that of even the smallest steamers of the present day.

The *Erebus* was to be commanded by Franklin himself, with Captain Fitzjames as his second-in-command, while Captain Crozier was appointed to the *Terror*, whose captain he had been during her Antarctic voyage of a few years before. Each ship had a complement of sixty-seven officers and men. They carried stores and provisions sufficient to last for three years and were provided with everything in the way of equipment that human ingenuity and forethought could devise.

All the officers of the expedition seemed confident of being able to find their way through to the Pacific, and it was Franklin's intention to take Parry's recently discovered route through Lancaster Sound and Barrow Strait, and then to turn south-westward after passing North Somerset and to endeavour to reach the Behring Strait by as direct a passage as he could find. At that time, it must be remembered, the space between Banks Land and the coast of America was entirely unknown, and navigators were as yet ignorant as to whether it was occupied by detached islands affording passage between them or by a solid tract of land. Franklin, as we shall see, had to modify his plans.

The two ships sailed from the Thames on May 24, 1845, and after an uneventful passage reached the coast of Greenland at the beginning of July. From Whalefish Island, in Disco Bay, where they remained for ten or twelve days embarking stores and provisions from a transport brought with them, Franklin wrote the last letter that his wife was ever to receive from him. The expedition left Disco on July 14th, and twelve days later was sighted and spoken with by a whaler in Melville Bay, on the Greenland coast, in 74° 48' North, 66° 13' West. The ships were, at the time, made fast to an iceberg with their crews well and in good spirits, and the news was duly published in a London paper on October 27th.

This brief glimpse was the last sight of the ships vouchsafed to any one unconnected with the expedition, apart from the wandering tribes of Esquimaux.

As early as the winter of 1846–1847 there were gloomy forebodings in England that all was not well with the Franklin expedition, and in 1847 arrangements were made with the Hudson Bay Company for large supplies to be sent overland to the Arctic coast, lest the explorers should have been forced to abandon their ships and make for the mainland.

By the winter of 1847–1848, when there were still no tidings, there was general uneasiness throughout the country, and the year 1848 saw the despatch of the first of a long series of search expeditions. Between 1848 and 1859, indeed, there were no less than thirty-eight such expeditions, mostly British and by sea, some sent out under Government auspices and some by private enterprise. A number of journeys were also carried out overland.

In 1850 the first clues to the movements of the *Erebus* and *Terror* were found by Captain Ommanney of H.M.S. *Assistance*, in his discovery at Beechey Island, an islet on the coast of North Devon near the mouth of Wellington Channel, of traces of Franklin's winter quarters of 1845–1846. There were three graves of men who had died there, together with a hut and a great pile of preserved meat tins supposed to have been supplied by a rascally contractor and condemned because the contents were uneatable. There was no written record.

In the vicinity, also, were seen traces of sledge journeys carried out by the missing explorers, and to experts unmistakable signs showed how little they understood the necessity of making their equipment light and portable, and how greatly the sledges were overloaded through inexperience.

Four years later, in 1854, Dr. Rae, despatched

on an overland journey by the Hudson Bay Company, came across a party of Esquimaux, from whom he obtained information that some seasons before, probably in 1848, a party of about forty white men had been seen travelling over the ice near King William Land with a boat and sledges. They all looked thin and were obviously starving. At a later date the bodies of about thirty white men had been found by the natives on the mainland near Point Ogle at the entrance to Back's or the Great Fish River, and others on Montreal Island, not far away. Some of the bodies had been buried, some were in a tent or tents, and several lay scattered about. One of the corpses on the island was evidently that of an officer, since he had a telescope strapped over his shoulders and a double-barrelled gun beneath him.

On evidence obtained from the same source, Dr. Rae says in his report dated September 1, 1854: "From the mutilated state of many of the bodies, and contents of the kettles, it is evident that our wretched countrymen had been driven to the last dread alternative as a means of sustaining life." The same conclusion was also arrived at in 1864 by Captain Hall, the American explorer, as a result of prolonged conversations with the Innuit Esquimaux, whose language he knew well. All Esquimaux tales, however, must be regarded with suspicion, and it is possible that they knew more about the deaths of the survivors than they cared to admit.

From the natives Dr. Rae obtained many relics of the expedition, including parts of broken up watches, compasses and instruments; crested silver spoons and forks, a silver plate with Sir John Franklin's name, and his star of the Royal Guelphic Order.

The substantial truth of the fate of Franklin's expedition having been thus confirmed by Dr. Rae, the British Government, involved in the Crimean War, did not consider itself justified in sending out further search expeditions in a cause considered as hopeless. It therefore devolved upon Lady Franklin and her friends to probe the mystery of her husband's last voyage and death.

In 1857 she purchased the steam yacht *Fox* and sent her north under the command of Captain Leopold McClintock, already well known as an Arctic explorer. Leaving the *Fox* at Port Kennedy, at the eastern end of the Bellot Strait dividing North Somerset from Boothia, McClintock devoted the spring of 1859 to extensive sledge journeys, which not only completed the Franklin search, but also the geographical survey of many portions of Arctic America left unfinished by former expeditions.

In March 1859, while sledging along the western shore of Boothia, McClintock came across a party of Esquimaux and noticed a naval button on one of their dresses. It came, they said, from some white men who had died of famine near Back's or the Great Fish River, as did also the iron of which their knives were made. None of them had actually seen the white men; but in the possession of the tribe were many relics of Franklin and his men, most of which McClintock bought. They consisted of six silver spoons and forks bearing crests, a silver medal, portions of a gold chain, some buttons, and knives, bows and arrows made of materials from a boat.

The next month McClintock obtained other relics from Esquimaux in the same neighbourhood, and after much inquiry was told that several seasons before two ships had been seen by the natives off King William Land. One of them, crushed in the ice, had disappeared in deep water; but the other, badly battered, had been forced ashore. From her the natives had obtained most of their wood and iron, while on board they had discovered the body of a very large man with long teeth. The crews of these ships, they added, had gone away to "the large river" taking boats with them, and in the following winter their bones had been found there.

Further relics, consisting of pieces of silver plate[1] bearing the crests of Franklin and other officers of the *Erebus* and *Terror*, together with bows and arrows made of English wood and buttons, were obtained from Esquimaux on the eastern shore of King William Land. On Montreal Island, also, which McClintock visited, he found hidden away by the natives a piece of a meat tin, an iron hook, and scraps of iron and copper.

On May 25th, however, McClintock happened upon a human skeleton lying face downwards in the snow. With the remains were a brush and comb, a leather pocket-book containing nine or ten letters —mostly indecipherable—and fragments of clothing. From what could be read of the letters and a parchment certificate the skeleton was thought to be that of Henry Peglar, one of the petty-officers of the *Terror*.

The most important discoveries of all, however, were made by Lieutenant Hobson, who, at Point Victory, on the north-west coast of King William Land, found by a cairn a written record of the long-lost expedition. Contained in a tin cylinder and so badly stained with rust that in a few years it would have been unreadable, it consisted of a printed form of the sort supplied to discovery ships for the purpose of being thrown overboard at sea to ascertain

[1] The quantity of plate recovered is probably accounted for by the fact that the officers' silver spoons and forks were served out to the men prior to the abandonment of the ships. No iron spoons of the kind commonly used by the seamen were found among the natives.

the set and drift of the currents, blanks being left for the date and position and a request being printed in six languages that the finder would forward it to the Secretary of the Admiralty.

This record gave the first authentic news of Franklin, for upon it was written:

"28 of May, 1847.    H.M. Ships 'Erebus' and 'Terror' wintered in the Ice in Lat. 70° 5' N., Long. 98° 23' W.

"Having wintered in 1846-7[1] at Beechey Island in Lat. 74° 43' 28" N., Long., 91° 39' 15" W.

"After having ascended Wellington Channel to Lat. 77° and returned by the West side of Cornwallis Island.

"Sir John Franklin commanding the Expedition. All well.

"Party consisting of 2 Officers and 6 men left the Ships on Monday, 24th May, 1847.

"Gm. Gore, Lieut.
"Chas. F. Des Voeux, Mate."

The news contained in that portion of the record was good, for it showed that important discoveries had been made and that Sir John Franklin was alive. Round the margin of the paper, written by another hand, was an additional message:

"(April 25)th, 1848—H.M. Ships 'Terror' and 'Erebus' were deserted on the 22nd April, 5 leagues N.N.W. of this (spot hav)ing been beset since 12th September 1846. The Officers and Crews consisting of 105 souls under the command (of Cap)tain F. R. M. Crozier landed here—in Lat. 69° 37' 42" N., Long. 98° 41' W.

[1] This is an error for 1845-6.

*Sir John Franklin died on the 11th June 1847, and the total loss by deaths in the Expedition has been to this date 9 officers and 15 men.*

"*James Fitzjames,*
"*Captain, H.M.S. 'Erebus.'*

*F. R. M. Crozier,*
  *Captain & Senior Offr.*

*and start on to-morrow, 26th, for Back's Fish River."*

The words under Crozier's signature were added in his own hand, the rest being written by Fitzjames together with the further information:

"*(This) paper was found by Lt. Irving under the cairn supposed to have been built by Sir James Ross in 1831, 4 miles to the Northward, where it had been deposited by the late Commander Gore in June 1847. Sir James Ross' pillar has not however been found, and the paper has been transferred to this position, which is that in which Sir J. Ross' pillar was erected.*"[1]

A great variety of articles lay scattered about the cairn where the record was found, among them being four heavy sets of boats' cooking stoves, pickaxes, shovels, iron hoops, old canvas, a large single block, part of a copper lightning conductor, many long pieces of hollow brass curtain-rod, some instruments, and a small sextant. There was also a great pile of clothing four feet high.

In another spot was discovered a duplicate record deposited in 1847 by Gore and without Fitzjames' amendments, while in Erebus Bay was found a twenty-eight-foot boat mounted on a heavy sledge.

---

[1] Portions in brackets are supplied by conjecture, as the record is obliterated by time and rust.

Her bows were pointed to the north-east, and she had been carefully equipped and lightened for the ascent of the Great Fish River, and inside were two human skeletons, beside one of which were five watches and two double-barrelled guns, one barrel in each being loaded and cocked. In the boat there were also five or six small books, mostly devotional, and an amazing collection of stores and clothing, including toilet articles, silver spoons and forks, twine, nails, saws, files, sailmakers' palms, powder, bullets, shot, cartridges, knives, needle and thread cases, bayonet scabbards cut down into knife sheaths, two rolls of sheet lead, and other articles too numerous to mention. Perhaps the most pathetic relic of all was the fragment of a pair of embroidered slippers bound with red silk ribbon, and probably worked by some wife or sweetheart in England.

The only provisions found were a small quantity of tea and forty pounds of chocolate. But here, as at the cairn where the record was found, the quantity of articles of one sort and another were astonishing in their variety. For the most part they would have been considered by experienced sledge travellers as comparatively useless superfluities, mere dead weight likely to exhaust the already waning strength of the sledge crews.

On the coast of King William Land, between Point Victory and Cape Felix, other traces were found of the lost expedition. The relics already described, however, provide sufficient evidence to reconstruct the course of the *Erebus* and *Terror*, their abandonment when provisions became scarce, and the subsequent terrible journey of their starving, scurvy-stricken crews.

It is known from the record that the ships duly entered Lancaster Sound and proceeded to the westward. On reaching the entrance to Barrow Strait it seems probable that further progress west was stopped by impenetrable ice, whereupon, as described by Gore, they proceeded north through the Wellington Channel.

Up this they must have sailed or steamed until what is now known as Grinnell Land was sighted ahead, and then, turning to the westward, tried to find a passage north of the Parry Islands. Again baffled by thick ice extending for hundreds of miles, they were forced to turn south, to find that the land to the west of Wellington Channel was an island, now called Cornwallis Island. Eventually they arrived once more in the Barrow Strait about one hundred miles west of where they had left it, and by this time it was probably too late in the year for further exploration. Accordingly they went east to find a suitable site for winter quarters, eventually selecting Beechey Island.

When voyaging again became feasible in July or August 1846 the ships left Beechey Island and proceeded through Barrow Sound. They soon came to a new channel leading to the southward, now known as Peel Sound, and passing down it, entered what is now called the Franklin Strait, finally to emerge into the icy region between Boothia and Victoria Land.

Their progress had been very slow, for they had covered only between 200 and 300 miles since entering Peel Sound, and on September 12th, some twelve miles to the north of King William Land, the ships were beset in the ice. From this date until April 22, 1848—a period of 587 days—the wretched crews were held fast in an icy prison, whence the survivors, their food nearly exhausted, broke out only to die miserably.

No records are available as to how the winter of 1846-1847 was spent; but Franklin evidently hoped that with the arrival of summer the ice would disperse and permit him to resume his journey south.

But it was not to be. The ships, securely held in a gigantic stream of heaped-up pinnacles and floes drifting slowly south, were never to emerge. In eighteen months the southerly drift was no more than about nineteen miles.

Had Franklin only known it there was comparatively clear water to the eastward of King William Land, whence he might have reached the American coast and thence proceeded westward to his destination through the Simpson and Dease Straits. But in the charts of those days King William Land was shown as connected with Boothia, thus barring any passage to the westward round the south of it. His only chance was to enter the ice-stream or pack and with it to drift slowly to the south-west in the hope that it would eventually break up and free him.

In May 1847 two sledge parties left the ship, one probably led by Fitzjames and the other by Graham Gore, first lieutenant of the *Erebus*. The last-named advanced southward along the west coast of King William Land and deposited the record afterwards found by Hobson and now in the museum at Greenwich. Then, though there is no corroborative evidence to prove it, he probably went south to discover the Simpson Straits, the last undiscovered link between the Atlantic and Pacific Oceans. In any case the honour of discovering the North-West Passage is rightly ascribed to the Franklin expedition.

When the sledge parties returned to the ships early in June they found that Sir John Franklin was dying. Nothing is known of the manner of his death; but he was sixty-two years of age, and since a boy of fifteen had led a life of activity and exposure. He must have been depressed at the seeming ill-success of the expedition and worn out with anxiety for the safety of his men, while the rigours of two successive winters in the Arctic at his advanced age must undoubtedly have told upon his constitution.

Before his death he may have heard of Graham Gore's possible discovery, which completed the finding of the North-West Passage; on June 11, 1847, the gallant old explorer died, probably to be buried in the ice-floes of his Arctic prison, a scene reproduced in the bas-relief beneath his statue in Waterloo Place.

The command of the expedition now devolved upon Captain Crozier, and for the next few months he must have watched with intense anxiety and suspense the gradual advance of the Arctic summer in the hope that the ice would break up and free the ships. Ice-saws and gunpowder were probably used in attempts to break up the ice; but every expedient was futile. The ships were immovable.

The winter of 1847–1848, the third since they had left home, was spent in the pack. The ships were provisioned only for three years and food was becoming scarce, and by the spring of 1848, cold, hunger and scurvy had all had their effect. The losses by death on the abandonment of the ships amounted to nine officers and fifteen men, as we know from the record, but many others must have been weakened through disease and famine. Provisions and stores would be exhausted in August, so even if the ships did get free of the ice during the summer it would be too late to save their crews. The choice lay between a lingering death by starvation and an attempt to reach the mainland in the hope of finding salvation there, and on April 22, 1848, sledges having been prepared and packed, the survivors, to the number of 105 officers and men, abandoned their ships and made for King William Land in the hope of reaching the Great Fish River.

They took with them the two whale-boats mounted on runners and the heterogeneous mass of articles already referred to. That so much was taken speaks of inexperience in Arctic travel, and can only be accounted for because they required things for barter with the Esquimaux. The men dragging the sledges and heavy boats, however, were woefully overladen, and the articles found by McClintock at Point Victory, fifteen miles from where the ships lay in the ice, were abandoned when the sledge crews found the task too much for them and realized that their lives were in jeopardy.

Near Point Victory, too, Lieutenant Irving of the *Terror* found the record left by Gore nearly a year before. It was removed from its tin canister, and Crozier and Fitzjames, after thawing their ink, penned their last message to the outside world. The canister was not resealed, probably through lack of solder.

Having freed themselves of all possible encumbrances the crews started off again. The distance from Point Victory to Cape Herschel as the crow flies is only about sixty miles, though, as the relics found by McClintock show, they followed the irregular coast-line and thus trebled the distance. Suffering agonies of scurvy and hunger, many of the men must have already been very feeble, for in Erebus Bay the party divided, the stronger members going on with one boat and the remainder electing to return to the ships for a reason that will never be known.

That the party did so divide seems proved by the boat found by McClintock with her bows to the north-east, and it is probable that the skeletons left in her were those of two men who, unable to keep pace with their companions, were left behind with what food could be spared until the others could return from the ships with a fresh supply.

How many of the returning party, if any, succeeded in reaching the ships is also a mystery. The natives, it will be remembered, told McClintock that they had found one corpse on board the vessel which drifted ashore.[1] The fate of the others can never be known—they may either have reached their vessels to die of slow starvation and to be buried by their companions, or else have dropped and died in their tracks as they trudged wearily

[1] On April 20, 1851, while on a passage from Bristol to Quebec, the brig *Renovation*, near the edge of the Newfoundland Banks, fell in with icebergs. One of them was very large and had field-ice attached to it, and on it were two three-masted vessels close together with upper masts and yards struck and no sails bent, as if snugged down for the winter. There were no signs of life on board.

They were in sight for three-quarters of an hour at a distance of about five miles and were seen by more than one person, one ship lying over on her beam-ends and the other, upright, on a higher portion of the berg. Their size approximated to that of the *Erebus* and *Terror*, while the absence of spars and boats indicated that their abandonment had been unhurried and deliberate. It was blowing fresh at the time and the *Renovation*, whose master was ill, did not stop to examine the wrecks. They were also sighted a few days later afloat, but in a sinking condition, by a German barque, which did not examine them closely.

The news became public only in 1852, when it was thought that the wrecks might be those of Franklin's ships. The Admiralty held an inquiry into the matter, though the result was necessarily inconclusive.

Three whalers were overwhelmed in the ice in Baffin's Bay in 1849, and none in 1848, 1850 and 1851; but no crew finding their vessel suddenly nipped in the ice would stop to dismantle her aloft. The three whalers lost, moreover, were reported to have been crushed.

The Esquimaux statements to McClintock in 1859 in regard to the vessels seen off King William Land must be regarded with caution, particularly in regard to the year in which they were seen. The natives had an unenviable reputation for lying, and had a habit of stating as true what they imagined was most favourable to inquirers. Moreover, in spite of the position in which, from the record, it is known that the *Erebus* and *Terror* were abandoned, it is not impossible that the ships seen by the *Renovation* were Franklin's. The *Resolute*, abandoned in 1854 in Barrow Strait, was picked up by an American whaler in Davis Strait, having drifted 1,000 miles in a year.

back along the bleak coast. The absence of skeletons would readily be accounted for by the presence of bears, wolves and foxes ashore, while more often than not the men were moving over the sea-ice fringing the coast, which would eventually disperse and melt.

Many of the party advancing towards Cape Herschel must have died in a similar manner, for in the piteous words of an old Esquimau woman who saw them and subsequently told the tale, the white men "fell and died as they walked along the ice." The only human remains discovered in this neighbourhood, however, was the skeleton seen and examined by McClintock.

That about thirty survivors, of which Crozier is believed to have been one, succeeded in gaining the entrance to Back's or the Great Fish River is proved by the remains and relics found by the Esquimaux near Point Ogle and on Montreal Island. Of the last sufferings of these gallant survivors, and their lingering deaths through disease and starvation, we happily know nothing.

Every man of the expedition which left England in the *Erebus* and *Terror* on May 24, 1845, perished. It is pleasing to think, however, that their supreme sacrifice was not made in vain, for the grand object of their voyage, the discovery of the North-West Passage, was achieved.

The monuments to Franklin and his followers in Waterloo Place and Westminster Abbey, as well as at Spilsby in Lincolnshire and Hobart in far-away Tasmania, together with the relics now lodged at Greenwich and in the Royal United Service Institution, are fitting memorials to those 129 heroic souls who died in the frozen Arctic as gloriously as if they had laid down their lives for their country on the field of battle.

# CAPTAIN SCOTT IN THE ANTARCTIC

ON January 3, 1902, a little ship crossed the Antarctic Circle on her voyage to the southward, and before long was forcing her way through the ice-pack.

As far as the eye could reach the surface of the sea presented an expanse of dead, snowy white, broken here and there by the dark shadows indicating pools and narrow channels of clear water. There was an intense stillness, relieved by the regular chugging of the ship's engines and the measured "ssh" of the floes as they ground ceaselessly together with the gentle movement of the swell. Now and then came the sharp, smashing crunch as the armoured bows met and divided a floe, and the grating sound as the fragments passed alongside.

The pack teemed with life. Bluish-gray southern fulmars and brown-and-white Antarctic petrels circled constantly round, while there were giant petrels and fierce skua gulls intent upon robbing the smaller birds of their hard-earned food. Also many snow petrels, delicate birds with white plumage and black feet and beaks, and numerous penguins in their picturesque plumage of black and white. The penguins, perhaps, were the most interesting birds of all. Alternately running and diving from floe to floe, they came bustling inquisitively towards the ship to see the strange monster that had invaded their icy domain, standing in open-eyed astonishment to gaze at her as she drove past, and squawking to their friends to come and do likewise. They were companionable birds, and before long, by imitating their call, the seamen learnt how to attract them from a distance.

There were many seals asleep on the floes, and both they and the penguins knew no fear. In the water they were preyed upon by killer whales and fierce sea-leopards; but on the ice had never known an enemy and so could imagine none.

Some seals were killed for food to eke out the supply of fresh meat on board and to accustom officers and men to a diet they would presently have to rely upon. From the first their flesh was found palatable, and before long seal liver and kidneys were regarded as a luxury. But every particle of blubber had to be removed before the meat was cooked, otherwise the meal was more than a human stomach could bear.

After five days' pushing through the pack the little ship passed through the ice-field and emerged into an open sea beyond, the Ross Sea. Late the same evening, January 8th, while the sun still hung low over the southern horizon, the travellers had their first view of the Antarctic continent, for far away to the south-westward the dim bluish outlines of the great peaks of Victoria Land could be seen silhouetted against the pale opalescence of the cloudless sky. Those mountains were full a hundred miles distant; but the goal was in sight. The *Discovery's* long voyage out from England by way of the Cape of Good Hope and New Zealand was nearly finished. The chief work of her officers and men, that of exploring the great Antarctic continent, had still to be done.

From the beginning of the sixteenth up till the close of the nineteenth century various navigators had explored the southern seas. Captain Cook in 1773–1774 was the first actually to cross the Antarctic Circle, which he did three times in different localities. He found fog and many icebergs, and though eventually stopped by thick pack-ice, successfully exploded the theory of the existence of the great southern continent shown on all maps as "Terra Australis Incognita." Voyages made by Bellingshausen, Weddel, Biscoe, Balleny, Dumont D'Urville, Wilkes and many others during the nineteenth century added to our knowledge and traced out many points of land about and within the Antarctic Circle. It was Captain James Ross, however, in 1841, with the *Erebus* and *Terror*, who pushed through the pack and found within the Antarctic Circle to the southward of New Zealand the deep indentation of moderately clear water now known as the Ross Sea. Sailing on, he discovered and named the great chain of mountains nearly 500 miles long which form the coast of Victoria Land, christened Mounts Erebus and Terror—the former an active volcano —and discovered McMurdo Sound. He completed his work by sailing 400 miles to the eastward along the huge wall of solid ice which he named the "Great Barrier," and at the end of this journey reached a point nearly four degrees to the southward of any previous navigator.

Ross, indeed, did all that was possible in the way of exploration by sea. The next step was for his discoveries to be followed up on land, and the Ross Sea was the starting-point of all the subsequent sledging expeditions culminating in the discovery of the South Pole. But nearly sixty years was to elapse before any further real progress was made, for until the *Discovery* expedition of 1901–1904 the map of the Antarctic remained practically unchanged.

In 1893 Sir Clements Markham, the president of the Royal Geographical Society, had decided upon an expedition to the Antarctic, though it was not until 1899 that the project, finally carried out under the joint auspices of the Royal and Royal Geographical Societies, at last became practical.

In Waterloo Place, London, close beside the United Service Club, and also in the dockyard at Portsmouth, are statues of Robert Falcon Scott, captain in the Royal Navy and one of the most celebrated Antarctic explorers that Britain has produced. Both statues are the work of Lady Scott,[1] herself a well-known sculptor, and that in London shows her husband grasping a ski-stick and clothed as for a sledge journey. Perhaps the most pathetic memorial of all, however, is the sledge diary kept by Scott during his last journey to the Pole and back in 1911–1912. The note-books were subsequently found by the relief expedition with the bodies of Scott and his companions, and are now in the British Museum. In their pages are recorded the daily doings and progress of the Polar party, written in pencil in Scott's clear handwriting, until, on that fateful March 29, 1912, when all hope had gone, there comes that last sad entry: "For God's sake look after our people."

Born at Devonport on June 6, 1868, Scott entered the Royal Navy in 1882. By 1897, after serving in various ships and having qualified for torpedo duties in the *Vernon*, he was appointed to the battle-ship *Majestic*, flagship of the Channel Fleet, retaining this appointment until his promotion to commander on June 30, 1900.

Sir Clements had first met Scott as a midshipman in 1887 and had taken a great liking to him, and saw him again as a lieutenant some years later. In June 1899, however, by which time Scott was in the *Majestic*, he happened to be spending a few days' leave in London. Walking down Buckingham

---

[1] Captain Scott's widow, whom he married in 1908, received the rank and precedence of the wife of a K.C.B. subsequent to her husband's death. In 1922 she married the Right Honourable Edward Hilton Young, P.C., D.S.O., D.S.C., M.P. (now Sir Edward).

Palace Road he saw Sir Clements on the opposite pavement, and crossing over, made himself known. He finally accompanied Sir Clements to his house, and here, for the first time, heard that an Antarctic expedition was actually in the wind. Within forty-eight hours he wrote applying for the command. Sir Clements consulted various officers with whom Scott had served. The replies were so favourable that on his promotion to commander in June 1900 he was appointed in command.

Meanwhile the keel of the *Discovery* had been laid at Dundee in March, her launch taking place a year later, after which she was brought to the Thames for the final fitting out. Built on the general lines of the vessels used in the Arctic expedition of 1876, she was the first ship built in this country especially for scientific exploration and was constructed of wood, which has the strength and resilience necessary for work in the ice. Barque-rigged, with engines and a two-bladed lifting screw, she was provided with an overhanging bow specially designed for charging ice-floes and strengthened on the waterline by solid thicknesses of wood protected on the outside by steel plates. The ship carried provisions and stores for two years and was designed to accommodate forty-three officers, scientists and men.

Of the five officers, Royds, the executive officer and meteorologist, Barne, the second lieutenant and also in charge of the deep-sea trawling and sounding apparatus, and Skelton, the engineer officer, who also had charge of the dark-room and helped with observations and bird-skinning in his spare moments, were all officers of the Royal Navy. Armitage, the navigator, also in charge of the magnetic observations, and Shackleton (afterwards Sir Ernest) both belonged to the Royal Naval Reserve.

There were two doctors, Koettlitz, also botanist, and Wilson, the vertebrate zoologist, who soon

became Scott's firm friend and was afterwards to
perish with his leader during that terrible journey
back from the South Pole in 1912. The other scientists
were Hodgson, invertebrate zoologist, Ferrar, geologist, and Bernacchi, physicist.

As regards the men, the Admiralty provided
twenty-two petty officers, able seamen and stokers
together with two marines. Extra men were engaged
from the merchant service as seamen or dog atten-
dants, so nearly all the ship's company belonged to the
Royal Navy.

That officers, scientists and men lived in cramped
surroundings in the greatest harmony for three long
years speaks volumes for the care with which they
were chosen.

Scott was instructed to explore the Antarctic
continent by land in the neighbourhood of Ross's
discoveries, spending the winter on the coast of
Victoria Land. Surveys and scientific researches of all
kinds were to be carried out, while attention was
called to the discovery of new coast-lines, the depth
and nature of the ice, and the formation of the
mountain ranges and their underlying rocks. Any
mention of the South Pole as an objective was
purposely omitted.

By July 31, 1901, the arduous work of preparation
was complete and the ship sailed from London
Docks. At Cowes on August 5th she was visited by
King Edward and Queen Alexandra, Scott being
invested with the M.V.O. Soon afterwards the coast
of England was fading into the dim distance and
the little ship had started her long voyage.

On November 30th the *Discovery* arrived at
Lyttelton, New Zealand, and was put into dry-dock.
After a thorough refit, and having embarked a
quantity of stores, sledge-dogs and forty-five sheep,
she left on December 21st, coaling at Port Chalmers
and sailing to the southward on Christmas Eve, 1901.

On January 2, 1902, she was in sight of Victoria Land. Pushing on, she came to an anchor on January 9th in Robertson Bay, close to Cape Adare, where there was a hut which had been used by Borchgrevink's expedition of 1898–1900. In the hut, still in fairly good condition, was placed a tin cylinder containing a report of the voyage up to date. A year later this was found by the relief ship *Morning*, whose captain thus knew of the *Discovery's* safe arrival.

For the next twelve days the ship steamed southward along the coast, identifying the various peaks and mountains of Victoria seen by Ross sixty years before. Once she was nearly wrecked among icebergs, sometimes she struggled against heavy ice, and had gales in which the spray froze as it fell. By the morning of January 21st, however, the *Discovery* was in the middle of McMurdo Sound, within a few miles of the place where the expedition eventually spent the winter.

The next day another post and tin cylinder were put up near Cape Crozier, at the eastern extreme of Ross Island, and this, though very difficult to see even at a short distance, was eventually found by the *Morning* and brought that ship into McMurdo Sound. It was here that Scott and two companions climbed to the top of one of the nearest volcanic cones and had their first view of the Great Barrier, a gigantic expanse of ice stretching north and south and far away over the horizon to the eastward to a distance of over 400 miles.[1] On the 23rd the ship started to steam to the eastward to investigate the Barrier, which had an average height of 150 feet but at one place towered 280 feet above the sea.

Six days later the *Discovery* was to the eastward of Ross's extreme position. The same evening the

[1] The Great Barrier is not frozen sea, but ice which has overflowed from the glaciers inland. Its outer edge is afloat and its southern portion aground.

character of the Barrier changed, its height diminishing and the surface behind it rising in snow-clad, rolling ridges which showed it to be land. A dense fog prevented further investigation; but on the evening of the 30th the weather cleared and afforded them a glimpse of a few black patches which presently resolved themselves into rock. They were looking at land which had never before been seen by mortal eyes, land now shown on our maps as King Edward VII Land.

On February 1st, by which time they could see many miles of new coast rising in a chain of sharp peaks, the *Discovery* started to retrace her course along the Barrier. At one place where it was no more than twenty feet high the ship was made fast to the ice, and while a sledge party landed to explore Scott ascended in the captive balloon. By the 8th, however, the ship was once more in McMurdo Sound, where a suitable site for winter quarters was selected at the southern end of a long spur of land[1] running down from the slopes of Mount Erebus. Here they proceeded to erect the large hut brought out in sections, together with two smaller huts for the magnetic instruments. Kennels for the dogs were also built ashore, and a quantity of provisions, oil and stores and fifteen tons of coal safely landed. The ship was still to be used for living purposes, though before sledging parties could be sent off to explore it was necessary that there should be some sort of depôt ashore in case she was blown off to sea in a gale.

There was plenty of work to be done before the Antarctic winter set in, though in the intervals there was time for football and ski exercise, in which they all required practice. On the 19th the first sledging party set off, and returning three days later were so full of their experiences that they could

[1] Hut Point.

hardly answer questions. Very unwisely they had continued to march through a snowstorm, and on stopping to camp were so exhausted that frost-bites were numerous. The tent and cooking apparatus were unfamiliar and difficult to manage. "It is strange now," Scott wrote three years later, "to look back on these first essays at sledging, and to see how terribly hampered we were by want of experience."

As the month of March drew to an end the hours of daylight rapidly grew shorter. On April 23rd the sun vanished for four months, and with their ship fast locked in the ice the explorers settled down to a spell of darkness in a spot nearly 500 miles south of a point where any human being had wintered before.

Often there were gales and fierce blizzards in which the temperature sometimes fell to –40°, which meant 72° of frost. These nearly occasioned the loss of the *Discovery's* boats, which, to give more room on board, had been hoisted out on to the ice, where they were buried by successive blizzards. Periodical digging had to be resorted to, but it was not until the following December, after much sawing and blasting with explosives, that they were finally freed in rather a mangled condition.

The sun made its reappearance on August 22nd and the final preparations were set afoot for the spring sledge journeys. Before going any further, however, it seems desirable to give some idea of the sledging equipment.

The tents were small bell-shaped affairs of green Willesden canvas spread on bamboos seven feet long joined at the top, thus giving a floor space about six feet in diameter. The sledges were of various lengths, those of eleven and nine feet being the most useful. One of those used in Scott's subsequent expedition of 1910–1913 is to be seen in the museum of the Royal United Service Institution at Whitehall. The sleeping-bags, some single, some to hold three men, were made on board of reindeer-skin with the hair inside, and had a flap which, on being buttoned over, completely covered the occupants.

The sledging food, the most important consideration of all, was worked out on a scientific basis. Pemmican—dried beef pounded and mixed with lard—and biscuit were the main items; but oatmeal, Plasmon, pea flour, cheese, chocolate, cocoa, sugar and "red ration"—the latter a mixture of pea flour and bacon generally used for thickening the nightly soup or "hoosh"—were also served out in various proportions. Tea, onion powder, pepper and salt were issued weekly. Three men formed the complement of a tent, and matters were so arranged that each took it in turn to cook for a week.

The cooker consisted of a central cylindrical boiler of aluminium surrounded by another annular container fitting round it, the whole heated by a Primus lamp burning paraffin. The ingredients of the "hoosh"—pemmican, oatmeal and pea flour —were first placed in the central portion and snow in the outer receptacle. When the "hoosh" was ready it was served out in the pannikins and eaten, and the snow in the outer boiler, now melted, transferred to the central cooker for the final brew of cocoa.

The other equipment carried on the sledges included spades, ice-axes, spare clothing, medical repair and tool-bags, an alpine rope, instruments, and a camera, with skis and ski-boots for the entire party. Sledge travellers took little extra clothing beyond warm footgear for the night and spare socks and mittens, living and sleeping in one costume until their return. Each wore a thick suit of under-clothing, one or two flannel shirts, a jersey or sweater, lined pyjama jacket and pilot-cloth trousers. Some, but not all, used mufflers. The outer garments of all were blouse, trousers and leggings of wind-proof gabardine, while the headgear varied according to the taste of the wearer. Gloves, slung round the neck, were of thick fur or felt worn with mittens underneath, while the boots, worn over two pairs of socks and padded with dry grass, were generally Norwegian "finnesko" reaching above the ankle and made of reindeer hide with the fur outside. "Crampons" fitted with steel spikes were used when negotiating ice.

The sledges could be pulled either by the men themselves or by dogs, and there were two methods of using the latter. They could either be brought back safe and sound, in which case their food for the whole journey had to be carried on the sledges, or else they could be used for as long as possible and then slaughtered one by one to serve as food for the others. Scott, as can be understood, was very averse to using them in the second way, though as things turned out he was compelled to do so.

The first sledging expedition after the long winter started off on September 2nd, and for two months there were a number of other journeys to test the equipment, reconnoitre the ground, and lay the necessary depôts for more extended operations. Members of one party returned suffering from scurvy, which led to a medical examination of the entire ship's company and disclosed the fact that several other men had slight symptoms. The disease was successfully checked by serving out seal meat instead of tinned meat, and by a thorough airing, cleaning and disinfection of the ship herself.

The two most important expeditions carried out during the season 1902–1903 were those led by Scott and Armitage. The last-named started out to the westward on November 29th, and, after much difficulty and many adventures, climbed the Ferrar Glacier and reached a spot on the Antarctic plateau 8,900 feet above the sea. We cannot describe his progress; but he and his party returned to the ship on January 19, 1903, with much invaluable information, having discovered a practicable route into the interior of Victoria Land.

November 2nd saw Scott's departure to the southward with Wilson, Shackleton, five sledges and nineteen dogs, a supporting party of one officer and eleven men accompanying them, half until the 13th, the remainder until the 15th, to increase the distance they could travel by carrying additional food for dogs and men. Depôt "A," containing provisions, had already been laid out on the Barrier about sixty miles south of the ship, and on the 13th the travellers were up to the 79th parallel, farther south than any man had ever been before. The dogs were pulling well, so that they were making a good twelve miles a day.

They were travelling, it must be remembered, over the frozen surface of the Great Barrier, ice many fathoms deep.[1] Sometimes the going was good, sometimes deplorably bad, and very soon the dogs began to weaken. Before long the travellers were compelled to divide their load into two, taking half on at a time, which meant that every foot of ground had to be traversed thrice, so though the ground covered daily was fifteen miles, the distance made good was no more than five. They soon sighted high land far away to the westward stretching in a northerly and southerly direction, a chain of mountains that had never before been seen by mortal eyes. But the dogs were rapidly declining, their weakness probably being caused by their food

---

[1] One crevasse in Latitude 79° S. was seen to be more than 200 feet in depth with no bottom visible.

—Norwegian stock-fish—used on the advice of Arctic travellers. It had evidently deteriorated during the passage through the tropics, and so induced a form of scurvy.

Starting to edge in towards the land the travellers struggled on for their daily five miles, crossing the 80th parallel on the 25th. The driving of the dogs was sickening work, the poor animals rapidly becoming worn out. By December 3rd they were close enough to the shore to make out some of its details, and on the same day Scott notes that the pemmican bag had been slung near a tin of paraffin so that their food both smelt and tasted of oil. They were too hungry to care.

As they progressed the march became harder and harder on account of the bad going, and soon the dogs were utterly useless and the men were doing all the work. The paraffin, moreover, was dwindling rapidly, and to eke it out they had to curtail the cooking of the evening meal and to content themselves with frozen seal meat and biscuits for lunch. The daily distance diminished from four miles to three, and then to two, and on December 6th one of the dogs, utterly ravenous, made away with over a week's ration of the precious seal meat intended for the men. The temperature was normally above zero, though sometimes it fell to 30° below zero.

Scott, whose diary is full of homely little details, describes how their faces were burnt black by the sun and the smoke of the cooker, while their nostrils were bare of skin, their lips cracked and bleeding and their fingers gashed and torn. They each carried a toothbrush which they used fairly frequently with snow, while there was one cake of soap among them with which, not very often, they washed their hands and faces with snow.

The first dog died on December 9th, being used as food for the others. Five days later they were near enough to the land to obtain accurate bearings, so made another depôt, "B," where they deposited three weeks' provisions and some dog food. Then they struggled on, and by the 18th the men themselves had passed from the merely hungry to the ravenous, and could divert neither their thoughts nor conversation from food. They felt sick from hunger during the marches, and woke up at night with an awful feeling of emptiness. To add to their misery they were all suffering more or less from snow-blindness.

Another dog died on the 20th, while the rest were in a pitiable condition, mere bundles of skin and bone. On the 21st, however, to make matters worse, Wilson discovered symptoms of scurvy in Shackleton. He was not told at the time; but they took the precaution of issuing an increased allowance of seal meat. Things were looking very bad indeed, but, said Scott, "Things must look blacker yet before we turn."

The men's rations were now reduced to about a pound and a half of food a day, barely sufficient to keep them alive in the terrible conditions of cold and bodily exertion. For breakfast—tea and fried pemmican mixed with biscuit; for lunch—frozen seal meat, half a biscuit and some lumps of sugar; for supper—about three-quarters of a pannikin of "hoosh" followed by tepid cocoa with the powder improperly dissolved. Their fuel supply was too precious to bring it properly to the boil, and lest any one portion of food should be slightly larger than another, they evolved a system of drawing lots to avoid unfairness.

Scott and his companions were weakening fast, and they soon found that by using skis they could drag the laden sledges no more than a mile an hour, and then only with terrible exertion. But it had to be done, for any day the dogs might give out altogether.

They trudged on, the snow clogging their weary progress and every step an agony.

Christmas Day came with a sky gloriously clear and not a cloud to mar its surface. It was dead calm, and away to the westward stretched a long line of coast gleaming in the sun. To celebrate the occasion they breakfasted more luxuriously and finished with a spoonful of jam, and for once had a hot lunch of cocoa and Plasmon, a whole biscuit and more jam. The going was better; but the three men had to pull the sledges while the dogs walked idly in the traces. That evening they laid themselves out to enjoy a Christmas feast, pouring a double quantity of everything into the cooker, and making a "hoosh" in which a spoon would stand upright. Then, as a surprise, Shackleton produced a plum-pudding the size of a cricket-ball from the toe of a spare sock, which they heated in the cocoa as it boiled. "We shall sleep well to-night," says Scott; "for us this has been the reddest of red-letter days."

They had long since come to the conclusion that, in order to lighten the load, they had stinted themselves too much in the way of food. Apart from the physical distress of mere hunger, they were slowly sapping their strength through virtual starvation; but still they were determined to go forward.

On December 22nd Wilson's snow-blindness, brought on by sketching the coast in the glare, was so bad that he had to trudge blindfold alongside the sledge. On the 29th they were kept to their tent by a raging blizzard. The next day they struggled on until lunch, when Wilson and Scott, leaving the sledge, set forth on skis. But the weather was thick and they were forced to return after travelling a mile.

They had shot their bolt. It was their last camp, and from here, in 82° 17′ South, on the last day of the year, they set their faces homewards. Depôt "B" was about 110 miles distant, and they had no more than fourteen days' provisions left.

After finishing the march on New Year's Day another dog died, while by January 3rd only seven of the animals remained alive. There was a southerly wind, and they were able to improvise sails for the sledges; but by the 7th the dogs that remained were merely walking weakly alongside and the men were doing all the work. The next day the surface was very bad, and after three hours' laborious work they covered only one and a quarter miles. They were still fifty miles from Depôt "B" with less than a week's provisions left.

By the 9th only four dogs remained, and on the 10th the party were marching in a blizzard so strong that the sledges with their sails were over-running them. Good progress was made, though on the next day the surface was again abominable. January 12th and 13th were days of fog and cloud in which all landmarks were obliterated. They were somewhere near Depôt "B", and the contents of the food-bag were so diminished that they could have consumed them at a sitting and still have felt hungry. In the thick weather finding the depôt was like looking for a needle in the proverbial truss of straw; but luck was on their side. The sky cleared momentarily, and Scott tumbled out of the tent with the theodolite to take an observation. He obtained the best result he could, and casually lowering the telescope swept it round the horizon. Suddenly a black dot seemed to flash by. Swinging the telescope back he saw a speck in the white expanse of snow with two smaller specks on either side of it. It was the depôt, and in five minutes everything was packed up and they were on the march. In two hours, with thankfulness in their hearts, they had arrived at last in a place of comparative plenty.

They stripped the runners of the two large sledges

of their German-silver covering, and found a distinct improvement, and with about 130 miles to travel to the next depôt, things looked a little more hopeful. However, they were all feeling the effects of hunger and privation, and their faces were haggard and worn, their hair and beards long and matted, and their clothing in rags. On January 14th a medical examination showed that Shackleton's scurvy was worse, while both the others showed traces of it. The same afternoon Shackleton's condition gave rise to great anxiety, and it became obvious that his breakdown could not long be delayed. There was nothing for it but to make as rapid a journey as possible back to the ship, while the invalid, whom hitherto nothing on earth could persuade not to do his fair share of the work, was peremptorily ordered to take things easy. Every effort had to be made to keep him on his legs, for if once he collapsed Wilson and Scott could only carry him on a sledge by doing relay work.

On January 15th the two last surviving dogs were killed; but as they marched northward with their two sledges over bad surface they were out of sight of land and had great difficulty in steering a straight course in the overcast weather. Shackleton, moreover, was fast becoming worse. Sometimes, when the wind was favourable, they used the sail to help them, while the invalid was generally sent on ahead on skis directly breakfast and lunch were over, leaving the other two to drag the sledge after him. By the evening of January 25th Depôt "A" was twenty or thirty miles distant, and on the 28th they reached it.

Here they found letters from the ship with good news and any amount of food, including sardines, marmalade, and soup squares. Supper that night was a gluttonous orgy, the effects of which were unfortunate. "For the first half-hour everything was pure joy," says Scott, "but soon our clothes seemed to be getting extraordinarily tight, and the only conclusion we could come to was that the concentrated food was continuing to swell . . . discomfort speedily gave place to acute suffering."

Shackleton was worse than ever, and by February 2nd he was very near a total collapse, while scurvy was rapidly gaining on the others. But the familiar landmarks round winter quarters were creeping up over the horizon, and on February 3rd the returning travellers were sighted by watchers from the hills near the ship, and Skelton and Bernacchi hurried out to meet them. They had great tidings, for the relief ship *Morning* had arrived, bringing a whole year's news from the outer world.

And so, on the evening of February 3rd, the wanderers came back to their friends. They had covered a distance of 973 statute miles, equal to a journey from Portsmouth to the north coast of Scotland as the crow flies and thence nearly back to Oxford. For ninety-three days they had plodded and toiled over a limitless snow plain bare even of birds and animals, living the while in a tent just large enough to hold them, and existing in conditions of privation and hunger and bodily exertion that are wellnigh indescribable. Such an expedition would be regarded as something extraordinary if carried out in the depths of winter in England; but the bitterest cold in this country is nearly tropical compared with that of the windswept wastes of the Antarctic.

Immediately after the *Discovery's* departure from England Sir Clements Markham, being aware that the disaster to the Franklin expedition was largely due to the absence of a relief ship, at once set about raising the necessary funds to procure such a vessel.

The ship purchased was the *Morning*, which

sailed from England in July 1902 under the command of Captain William Colbeck, R.N.R., and proceeded to New Zealand, finally leaving Lyttelton for the Antarctic on December 6th. Scott, before leaving home, had intimated where he would leave records to guide the relief ship, and those at Cape Adare and Cape Crozier were duly found and brought her into McMurdo Sound.

On the evening of December 23rd she was sighted from the hills near the *Discovery's* winter quarters, and the next day a large party set off to greet the new-comers and to obtain welcome news of the outside world. It was a long trudge of ten miles across ice and snow; but soon daily communication was established between the ships, and the *Discovery's* officers and men were enjoying letters from home, newspapers, and all manner of little luxuries which had long been absent from their daily bill of fare.

Prior to his departure for the South Scott had given orders that the *Discovery* was to be ready for sea by the end of January, by which time he expected the ice would have broken up and they would be free to sail. The possibility that she might remain frozen in throughout the season had not occurred to him, for the previous year, at the same time, the bay had been comparatively free from ice. But it was now realized that the conditions were utterly different to those which had obtained in 1902. There were still six miles of solid ice between the *Discovery* and freedom, and at last Scott was forced to see the undesirability of detaining the *Morning* much longer, lest she also should be beset by the ice of the rapidly approaching winter. At the same time he realized that the chances of getting his own ship away were becoming more and more nebulous, so the men were set to work to transfer the necessary stores and provisions from the relief ship.

It had been decided to reduce the *Discovery's* crew by eight men, who were sent to the *Morning*. Shackleton also was in a very bad state of health, and much against his will was sent to the *Morning* for passage home, his place being taken by Mulock, a sub-lieutenant R.N. The latter, a qualified surveyor, was a most valuable acquisition for collating the hydrographical information already obtained and for making the necessary charts.

On March 3rd the *Morning* finally sailed, nearly the whole of the *Discovery's* crew assembling at the ice edge to wave their farewells, while wondering how long it would be before they also would take the northern track. But soon it became evident that the ship was a fixture for that season, and on March 14th Scott notes in his diary: "We have admitted the certainty of a second winter, and to-day orders have been given to prepare the ship for it."

There was a lot to be done—boilers emptied, engines pulled to pieces, small steam pipes disconnected, sails unbent, ropes unrove and stowed away, the winter awning prepared, snow brought in upon the decks and so forth. They also set about replenishing their meat supply and establishing a larder ashore in the ice cave, which they soon stocked with the frozen carcasses of seals, skua gulls, and sheep received from the *Morning*. The year before the skua gulls were not regarded as fit for human food, but on one of the sledging expeditions someone had caught one and put it into the pot with quite satisfactory results.

The preparations were completed by April 7th, and a fortnight later the sun vanished for the last time and the explorers settled down to another dark winter. The months that followed need not be described, for, as before, officers, scientists and men were fully employed on their various tasks, and also in preparing for the sledging journeys to be undertaken during the following spring. The sledge equipment, however, was badly worn and in very poor condition—skins of inferior quality having to be used for sleeping-bags, while tents, blackened with use, were threadbare and patched, the cookers very much the worse for wear, and wind-clothes almost worn out. They had even to fall back upon sheets and tablecloths to make the small bags for carrying provisions and so on.

The sun reappeared on August 21st, and early the next month the first sledging expedition set out. Leaving the ship on September 9th, Scott left for the westward with five companions to find a new route to the Ferrar Glacier and to lay a depôt. This was successfully accomplished in spite of the thermometer registering 82° of frost at night, and they returned to the ship after an absence of eleven days. In the meanwhile another sledge party had endured temperatures of –70°, or 102° of frost, one of the men being severely frost-bitten. It was quite an hour before they could get any signs of life into a frozen foot, and then it was only done by the officers taking it in turns to nurse it against their bare chests. It was found impossible to keep it in contact with the skin for more than ten minutes, at the end of which time it had to be handed over to someone else.

Scott with twelve men again started out on October 12th for a long journey to the westward to explore the Ferrar Glacier and the ice cap on the plateau beyond. They were forced to return, however, as the icy surface split the German silver on the sledge runners, and finally they set out again on October 26th. But very soon they were once more having trouble with the sledges, and Skelton and the stokers of the party were constantly at work stripping off the torn metal and renewing it as best they could.

By November 3rd they had reached a height of 7,000 feet. On the next day, half-way up a bare icy slope, the full force of the gale burst upon them. Faces became frozen; but struggling on, they looked for a camping ground, eventually finding a patch of frozen snow. Here they pitched the tent, and, exhausted and frost-bitten, crept inside and got into their sleeping-bags.

For a week the gale raged incessantly, and the outside world was enveloped in a mist of blinding snow. Scott describes it as the most miserable week he had ever spent. Twenty-two out of the twenty-four hours they spent in their sleeping-bags, but twice a day rolled them up and prepared a hot meal. Sleep was practically out of the question, and he mentions how they took it in turns to read their one and only book, Darwin's *Cruise of the Beagle*, until their frozen fingers refused to turn the pages. It was not until the 11th that they were able to continue, and then the weather conditions were terrible and they found themselves among chasms and crevasses in the ice. By the evening of the 13th, however, they had reached the summit of the glacier 8,900 feet up, and with nearly five weeks' provisions in hand started off to westward across the great snow plain. The going was very difficult and the weather vile; but up till the 17th they made tolerably good progress. The severe conditions, however, were beginning to tell upon their strength, and soon they were forced to do relay work. On November 22nd Scott ordered some of the party to return in charge of Skelton, and he himself, with two seamen, Evans and Lashly, went on with a single sledge.

They were now out of sight of landmarks; but in spite of the surface of broken and disturbed snow waves and terrible conditions of cold, made rapid progress. By November 30th they had travelled

200 miles from the edge of the ice cap. They were cut to pieces by the wind, with deep cracks in their cheeks, lips, nostrils and fingers. Says Scott: "We can see only a few miles of ruffled snow, bounded by a vague wavy horizon; but we know that beyond that horizon are hundreds and even thousands of miles which offer no change to the eye. . . . Nothing but the terrible limitless expanse of snow! It has been so for countless ages and will be so for countless more. . . . Could anything be more terrible than this silent wind-swept immensity?"

They had reached the end of their tether, and on December 1st the little party turned homewards, struggling on day after day over the rough snow ridges in thick weather. By December 9th hauling was sheer agony and they could advance no more than a mile an hour. They were in a tight place, for only seven days' food remained and their whereabouts was a matter of uncertainty.

On December 15th they found themselves on a hard glazed surface with ice hummocks and disturbances ahead. They tried to avoid them by turning, but without success, and were soon among crevasses and pinnacles of ice. Then the surface became smoother and steeper and the sledge began to overtake them. Evans and Lashly were put behind to hold it back, but the latter slipped, the sledge took charge and started to career down a steep slope, dragging the three men after it. They were soon travelling on their backs with the speed of an express train, now and then leaving the ground and bumping heavily. For 300 yards this headlong progress continued, until they were finally brought to rest by softer snow. No bones were broken; but badly bruised and shaken they staggered to their feet, and on looking round, Scott, to his amazement, saw they were well on towards the entrance of the Ferrar Glacier. Half an hour before they had been utterly lost. Now, well-remembered landmarks were in sight, and not many miles ahead was a great hummock of rock where a depôt of provisions had been established. It was almost too good to be true.

Hurrying on, they made for the depôt; but that same afternoon were again in mortal danger. They were all three joined up to the harness ahead of the sledge. It started to skid, and Lashly was told to pull wide to steady it. Hardly had he moved out to do so when Scott and Evans trod upon nothing and disappeared headlong. By a miracle Lashly checked himself and sprang back with his whole weight on the trace. The sledge tore past him and providentially bridged the crevasse down which his companions had fallen. Scott and Evans, brought up with a jerk, found themselves dangling at the end of their traces with walls of blue ice on either side of them and a fathomless chasm below.

Taking off his goggles, Scott saw Evans just above him. He was unharmed, and twelve feet overhead was the sledge, one side badly cracked by their abrupt descent. Wearing steel spiked crampons, Scott groped round with his feet and found a thin shaft of ice wedged between the walls of the crevasse, upon which he and Evans presently succeeded in obtaining a foothold. It was the only support of its kind in sight, and its position was providential. The cold was intense and there was no time to lose if they were to save themselves.

Lashly, still on the brink of the crevasse, could not let go of the sledge in case it slipped. His presence of mind, however, undoubtedly saved the lives of the others, for with one hand he withdrew the skis from the sledge and slid them beneath the broken runner. Scott and Evans, meanwhile, were becoming badly frost-bitten about the face and fingers; but there was nothing for it but to swarm up the thin rope. It seemed an impossible task in thick clothing and heavy footgear; but after an agonizing effort Scott at last succeeded and flung himself panting on the snow. For a full five minutes he lay there helpless, his bare hands frost-bitten to the wrists. Putting them into his chest the circulation gradually returned, and then with difficulty Evans was hauled up. They had escaped death by a miracle; but Evans' only remark on reaching the surface was, "Well, I'm blowed!"

We need not dwell longer upon the journey, for the food depôts were reached without further incident, and on Christmas Eve the gallant little party returned to the *Discovery*. They had been away for fifty-nine days, for nine of which they had been confined to the tent. They had travelled 725 miles at a daily average of fourteen and a half miles in the worst imaginable conditions, probably the greatest Polar journey on record without dogs.

It is unnecessary here to describe the sledge journeys undertaken by other members of the expedition; but Barne and Mulock, in an absence of sixty-eight days, reached Barne Inlet, making an accurate survey of the coast as they went. Perhaps their most important discovery of all, however, was that Depôt "A," established thirteen and a half months before, had shifted 608 yards northward, which gave a very good indication of the movement of the Great Barrier ice sheet.

Meanwhile all the available men from the *Discovery* had been set to work at sawing the ice some ten and a half miles to the northward where the ship lay, with the idea of assisting in her liberation. They camped out in a tent near the scene of their labours and worked with great eighteen-foot saws, operated by ropes from a tripod. From the first, however, it was a hopeless business, and on Scott's return, work was relinquished.

January 5, 1904, found Scott and Wilson camped within half a mile of the ice edge. They were really enjoying a holiday, and having finished breakfast, Scott was looking dreamily out through the open door of the tent when a ship suddenly entered his field of view. A few moments later another vessel hove in sight. They stared at them in amazement, hardly able to believe their eyes.

What had happened was this. The *Morning* had been got ready for her second relief voyage and arrangements had been made for embarking all the officers and men of the *Discovery* if that vessel could not be freed. Then, for various reasons which need not be mentioned, the Government undertook the responsibility of the relief expedition, and purchasing one of the finest whalers, the *Terra Nova*, equipped her and sent her out post haste to New Zealand to assist the *Morning*.

On establishing communication Scott learned that it was the general opinion in England that the *Discovery* was stuck fast in the ice for all time. His spirits were considerably damped, as were also those of his men, by the receipt of orders from the Admiralty that if his ship could not be freed in time to accompany the relief ships to the northward she was to be abandoned.

Necessary as this order was, it placed Scott and his companions in a very cruel dilemma. The ties which bound them to the *Discovery* were no ordinary ones, and involved a depth of sentiment not in the least surprising when one remembers what the ship had meant to them. Thoughts of abandoning her had never entered their heads, and they were quite prepared to spend their third winter in the Antarctic if need be. Now they were confronted with the fact that if twenty miles of ice did not break up within six weeks they must bid a long farewell to their beloved vessel and return to England more or less as castaways with the feeling of failure hanging over them.

The prospect was a dismal one, and day after day the signal station erected for the purpose reported no change in the ice conditions, and soon preparations were in train for sending the scientific collections, instruments and records from the *Discovery* to the relief ships. On January 18th, however, some large pieces of ice broke away, and five days later the relief ships were four or five miles nearer in. On the 28th the whole ice sheet began to rise and fall very slowly under the influence of a long swell, while the *Discovery* was gently moving in her icy bed. By the 30th the *Terra Nova* and *Morning* were not much more than eight miles distant. In the last five days, six miles of ice had broken away, and it was just touch and go whether or not the *Discovery* could be freed in time. Meanwhile all the collections, instruments and library had been transported to the relief ships, while personal belongings were packed ready to follow. Then came several days of alternate hope and anxiety, Scott meanwhile firing explosive charges to help in the dispersion of the ice.

It was finally on February 14th, when they were at dinner on board the *Discovery*, that the officer of the watch called down the hatch, "The ships are coming, sir!" The meal was entirely forgotten, and rushing on deck they found the ice breaking up right across the strait with a rapidity that they had thought impossible. By 10.30 p.m. scarcely half a mile of it remained between the *Discovery* and the relief ships. By midnight the three vessels were lying almost side by side.

The *Discovery* was prepared for sea, and on the 16th the little ship at last swung to her anchor with the blue water lapping her sides. But even yet their adventures had not ended, for on the 17th there came a furious gale with a heavy sea and the ship was driven ashore near Hut Point. Hour after hour she lay there crashing and grinding on her rocky bed, until, at seven o'clock that evening, the wind lulled, and soon afterwards she began to move astern. By dint of working the engines and running the men from side to side she eventually slid free, little worse for her pounding.

On April 1, 1904, the *Discovery*, *Terra Nova* and *Morning* arrived at Lyttelton, New Zealand, where they were accorded a wonderful reception. The *Discovery* sailed again on June 8th across the southern Pacific, and after passing through the Straits of Magellan, and visiting the Falkland Islands and the Azores for coal, arrived at Spithead on September 10th.

The expedition in its many discoveries and scientific results, which included the discovery of King Edward VII Land, the accurate charting of the mountain ranges of Victoria Land, the investigation of the ice of the Great Barrier and the Antarctic plateau, and the discovery of the position of the South Magnetic Pole, more than fulfilled the object for which it was sent out. Scott richly deserved the honours showered upon him, which included promotion to the rank of captain and the bestowal of the C.V.O. by King Edward. But perhaps most precious of all was the octagonal silver Polar Medal which, with its plain white ribbon and bar inscribed "Antarctic, 1901–04," was awarded to every officer and man who had taken part in the gallant exploit. Seldom has an honourable badge of merit been more thoroughly earned.

Between the end of 1905 and the middle of 1910, Scott held various appointments afloat and at the Admiralty. He was married on September 2, 1908, to Miss Kathleen Bruce, his son, Peter Markham Scott, being born in September 1909. In the same month he published his plans for the British Antarctic

Expedition to be carried out the following year. Though it was his chief object to reach the South Pole and to secure the honour of that achievement for the British nation, he also had in his mind an extended scientific programme to continue the work of the former expedition.

The necessary funds were raised partly by a grant from the British Government and partly by public subscription, many firms sending gifts in money or in kind. Grants were also forthcoming from the South African, Australian and New Zealand Governments. The *Terra Nova*, a Scottish whaler twenty years of age, which had served as a relief ship in the former expedition, was purchased for the new venture, being handed over to Lieutenant Evans, who had previously served in the *Morning*, for fitting out and equipment. Scott himself was busy with the scientific programme and the question of finance. The ship was to sail under the White Ensign and burgee of the Royal Yacht Squadron, of which Scott had been elected a member.

It is unnecessary here to deal with the work of preparation, but on June 1, 1910, the *Terra Nova* sailed from London, finally leaving Cardiff a fortnight later. October 28th saw her at Lyttelton, New Zealand, whence she sailed for the Antarctic on the 29th of the following month. She was manned by fifty-nine officers, scientists and seamen, and left New Zealand a very full ship. Besides 400 tons of coal, she carried three years' provisions, two huts in sections, forty sledges, many fur sleeping-bags, bales of warm clothing, and the thousand and one items of equipment necessary to a Polar expedition. In stalls under the forecastle were nineteen Siberian ponies, and on the upper-deck thirty-four sledge dogs, three motor sledges, 2,500 gallons of petrol, paraffin, and a deck cargo of coal in bags.

Two days after sailing, the ship ran into a heavy

gale, in which, deeply laden, she was soon plunging heavily and taking in green water over the lee rail. Wind and sea rapidly increased so that it became impossible to keep the ponies on their feet, while the packing-cases and coal-bags broke loose and charged about the deck like battering rams. The ship had to be hove-to, but the weather quickly got worse, the waves being logged as thirty-five feet high and constantly sweeping the deck from end to end and cascading waist deep over the poop. She rolled sluggishly and very deeply, many tons of water finding their way below.

Early on December 2nd there came word from the engine-room that the floor-plates were under water and the pump suctions choked. The water gradually rose higher and higher until it was in contact with the boilers, and fires had to be drawn. With no means of coping with the inflow it seemed only a matter of time before the ship filled and sank. All that could be done was for a party of officers and scientists to bale out the ship with buckets, which they did, working in watches, with the ship all the while being swept fore and aft by mountainous seas and rolling and pitching like a mad thing. Even so, with death almost staring them in the face they did not lose heart, but singing all the songs they knew, passed the three iron buckets ceaselessly from hand to hand for a whole day and night.

In the meanwhile a hole was cut in the engine-room bulkhead, and headed by Lieutenant Evans a party scrambled through and found there was just room to wriggle their way to the pump shaft over the coal in the hold. Tearing down some planks, Evans got inside and went to the bottom of the ship, and there, sitting on the keel, with the filthy water up to his neck and at times completely submerging him, passed up twenty buckets full of the nauseous mixture of coal-dust and oil with which the suction pipes were choked. It was a piece of work which undoubtedly saved the ship, for presently the pumps were again in working order and the water could be discharged. On December 3rd the weather moderated and the *Terra Nova*, sadly battered, and with the loss of two ponies, one dog and a portion of her deck cargo, was able to continue her voyage.

Passing many icebergs, the pack-ice was reached on December 9th and the ship pushed on through it for 200 miles under sail and steam. She was then retarded to such an extent that the engines were stopped to save coal. They spent the time taking observations and soundings, and on December 30th, having traversed 380 miles of ice, passed out into the open waters of the Ross Sea. On January 3, 1911, the ship reached the Great Barrier, five miles east of Cape Crozier, where Scott had thought to make his winter quarters. But no good site could be found, and standing to the westward the ship entered McMurdo Sound and was made fast alongside the ice. An ideal spot for winter quarters was presently found close by a little headland on Ross Island, afterwards known as Cape Evans. The *Terra Nova*, having landed the shore parties, was due to return to New Zealand, and presently the men were busy disembarking the huts and the necessary provisions, stores, sledges, ponies and dogs.

The work was soon in full swing, Lieutenant Pennell taking over command of the ship, Lieutenant Campbell supervising the transport arrangements, and Lieutenant Evans being put in charge of the base. Scott himself acted as general supervisor. One of the motor sledges unfortunately went through the ice and was lost; but by January 12th practically everything had been landed and the huts were ready for habitation. Stables for ponies had also been built outside, and ice caves dug wherein to stow the mutton and a quantity of seals and penguins.

On January 24th Scott, with eleven companions, eight ponies and two dog teams, set off to lay a depôt to assist the southern journey to the Pole due to take place later on in the year. It was important that this should be done before the Antarctic winter set in, and nearly a ton of provisions was transported on sledges to a point 144 miles from the hut, known as "One Ton Depôt."

A part of the plan was that Lieutenant Campbell should explore King Edward VII Land with a party of three other officers, three men and two ponies, and on January 26th the *Terra Nova* had left McMurdo Sound and proceeded east along the Barrier. No suitable landing-place could be found in King Edward VII Land, and on their return journey they found, on February 5th, Amundsen's *Fram* moored to the ice edge, her men busily unloading stores and building a hut in readiness for a dash to the Pole after the winter. Campbell and his party accordingly returned to Cape Evans, left their ponies, and then went on in the *Terra Nova* and were eventually landed in Robertson Bay, near Cape Adare.

Scott returned on February 22nd, and his feelings on hearing of Amundsen's arrival on the Great Barrier about 400 miles to the eastward may more easily be imagined than described. It is true that when the *Terra Nova* had arrived at Melbourne the previous October he had received a telegram from Madeira saying, "Beg leave to inform you proceeding Antarctic.—AMUNDSEN"; but the knowledge that the Norwegian had definitely arrived came as something of a shock. At first Scott and his men were naturally furious, regarding Amundsen as something of an interloper on what they regarded as their preserve. But on sober reflection it was realized that the only thing to do was to go forward with their own preparations as if nothing out of the ordinary had occurred. There was no doubt, however, that the Norwegian's plan was a severe menace to Scott being first at the Pole.

Amundsen had sixty miles less to travel. He had 120 well-trained dogs, used to sledge work, and his men, all expert ski-runners, were hardened to a cold climate.

By March 4th all the parties which had been laying depôts were safely housed in the *Discovery's* old hut at Hut Point with two dog teams and two ponies, all that remained out of the eight they had taken with them. For six weeks they remained there, communication being impossible with Cape Evans across the sea-ice, until on April 13th they joined the main party and settled down for the winter.

A winter sledging journey carried out by Dr. Wilson with Bowers and Cherry-Garrard started off on June 27th for Cape Crozier to observe the incubation of the Emperor penguins at their rookery there. It is unfortunate that limitations of space prevent our describing a journey which is probably the worst ever undertaken. They were absent for thirty-five days, enduring at times temperatures of $-77°$, or $109°$ of frost. The going was abominable, and even on the bitterest days they perspired, the perspiration freezing and accumulating inside their clothes until they could shake down ice and snow inside their trousers whenever they changed their footgear. Sleeping-bags and clothes became armour-plated with ice, garments being so encrusted that they felt as if they were walking in suits of sheet lead. Frost-bites were numerous, and at one time the fluid inside the large white blisters on Cherry-Garrard's fingers became frozen so that it was difficult not to howl with agony.

For days on end proper sleep was unobtainable

on account of the cold. Paraffin for cooking and food ran short, and daily, almost hourly, they were in danger of their lives amidst crevasses and ice cliffs.

On arriving at their destination they built themselves a tiny hut of boulders banked up with snow, leaving the tent pitched outside. Presently there came a blizzard which tore the canvas roof of their hut into shreds and blew away the tent. For forty-eight hours they lay in their sleeping-bags in the roofless hut, gradually being snowed-up, while all the time the wind whistled and howled with demoniacal fury and the air was full of scurrying snow. For two days they had no food, and at the back of their minds was always the dreadful knowledge that without their tent for the return journey they were practically doomed to death by starvation.

By the mercy of God the tent was eventually found half a mile away when the weather cleared, and finally, famished and exhausted, the party fought their way back to winter quarters.

It was a miracle that they survived, and two years later, in 1913, three penguins' eggs, for which those brave souls had risked their lives and had strained themselves to the limit of human endurance, were handed over to the official of a London museum.

The sun returned on August 22nd, and for the next two months there were various subsidiary sledge journeys while the final preparations were made for the southern journey to the Pole.

The plan was as follows: Lieutenant Evans with three men and two motor sledges, towing six other sledges laden with three tons of stores, were to leave winter quarters in advance of Scott and proceed to "Corner Camp," thence to "One Ton Depôt," and thence due south as far as Latitude $80\frac{1}{2}°$ S., the object being to carry forward stores and provisions and to relieve Scott's ponies as much as possible. The pony party, consisting of Scott,

Wilson, Oates, Bowers, Cherry-Garrard, Atkinson, Wright, and Petty Officers Evans, Crean, and Keohane, was to advance after the motors and independently of them, while the dog teams, starting later, were to join Scott at "One Ton Depôt."

The main object was to get twelve men with the necessary food to the foot of the Beardmore Glacier. Thence, with three units of four men it was hoped to extend the Polar party to the required distance.

The motor party, setting out on October 24th, had constant difficulty with the sledges, and very soon one of them had to be abandoned. By November 2nd, however, they arrived at "Corner Camp," where they deposited some of the food for dogs and ponies. Soon afterwards they were forced to abandon the second motor, continuing on foot with six weeks' food supply for four men on a single sledge. The motors, though they had not been altogether successful, had advanced the stores fifty-one miles, thereby husbanding the strength of Scott's ponies as far as "Corner Camp."

In spite of their heavy load, Lieutenant Evans' party made good going, dragging their sledge fifteen and a half to seventeen miles a day. On November 9th they reached "One Ton Depôt," where they embarked extra provisions and stores and continued on their way. Six days later, after some very bad going, they reached Latitude 80½°, where they remained until November 21st, when Scott arrived with the pony party and the dog teams. The combined parties now numbered fifteen officers and men, all in excellent health and spirits.

But already, far over the southern horizon, though they knew it not, Amundsen with his dog sledges was within about 330 miles of the South Pole and rapidly approaching it. Scott had still over 600 miles to travel.

The march southward continued at the rate of

fifteen miles a day, Lieutenant Evans and his party going on in advance on foot and building snow cairns at intervals. Scott and the pony party came next, the rear being brought up by the speedier dog teams.

The days passed without undue incident, the sun being visible throughout the entire twenty-four hours, so that there was no difference between night and day. Day and Hooper turned back from Lat. 81° 15′, and on December 4th, after a spell of bad weather and difficult surface conditions, the others arrived within twelve miles of the entrance to the Beardmore Glacier. The land visible extended from S.S.W. through S. to N.W., range after range of glistening mountain peaks and great ridges of snow-covered rock. The least interesting portion of the journey across the monotonous surface of the Barrier was nearly finished.

On December 5th, by which time five out of the ten ponies had been slaughtered, there came a severe blizzard which held up the march for four days. The delay, within a day's march of the glacier, was not only exasperating, but, by diminishing the valuable food supply without any corresponding advance, was one of the contributory causes to the subsequent disaster to Scott and his brave companions.

On December 9th the march recommenced through a morass of thick snow in which the men sometimes wallowed up to their thighs, and on the evening of that day the last ponies were killed and cut up for food for men and dogs.

According to plan, three teams, each of four men, now started up the glacier, Meares with his Russian dog driver and the dog teams accompanying them until the evening of the 10th and then turning back for the 450-mile march home to Cape Evans.

The advance up the Beardmore Glacier was considerably retarded by soft snow, and until the

13th they could march no more than four miles a day with the heaviest exertion. By the 16th, however, they had reached a height of 3,000 feet, and in spite of delays through crevasses and pressure-ridges of ice, made tolerably good progress. From this time on the daily marches increased from thirteen to twenty-three miles, and by the 21st they were 6,800 feet up on the plateau above the glacier in 85° 7′ S., all fit and eager to go forward. Here they established another depôt of stores and provisions, and the third supporting party, Atkinson, Wright, Cherry-Garrard and Keohane, turned back for their 584-mile march home. Scott and his two remaining sledge teams,[1] each of four men, pushed on, maintaining an average speed of fifteen miles a day.

They steered to the south-west to avoid pressure-ridges and ice falls, but on December 23rd came across many yawning crevasses as wide as a London street. They were nearly all bridged across by narrow pathways of frozen snow, and taking them at a rush, they managed to get across with no more serious results than occasionally falling in up to their armpits. But here, high up on the Antarctic plateau, they were already beginning to experience the bitter wind that Shackleton had met during his journey in 1909 by the same route to 88° 23′ S. Noses and ears were constantly being frost-bitten, while their breath turned their unkempt beards into cakes of ice. By Christmas Eve they had reached 85° 35′ S., and Christmas Day found two tiny tents pitched on the glittering waste of snow that lay between the summit of the Beardmore Glacier and the South Pole.

They marched seventeen and a half miles that

---

[1] The members of the teams were Scott, Wilson, Oates, and Petty Officer Evans; Lieutenant Evans, Bowers, Crean, Lashly.

day in excellent spirits, though Lashly celebrated his 44th birthday by tumbling headlong into a crevasse, where he hung spinning round in his harness with a clean drop of eighty feet beneath him. He was hauled up with great difficulty, and facetiously wished a happy Christmas, to which his reply was more forcible than polite. However, the Christmas dinner—pemmican with pieces of pony meat in it, a chocolate and biscuit "hoosh," plum-pudding, cocoa, ginger and caramels, after which they felt so replete that they could hardly summon the energy to change their footgear or to get into their sleeping-bags—more than made up for it.

New Year's Day, 1912, found the explorers in 87° 7' S., and on January 3rd Scott told Lieutenant Evans that he was confident of reaching the Pole if Bowers could join his party. This change was made, and on the 4th, in 87° 34', Lieutenant Evans, Crean and Lashly turned their faces to the north for the long march of between 750 and 800 miles to Cape Evans. The last the returning party saw of Scott and his four companions was a series of tiny black dots far away on the southern horizon as they trudged towards the goal of their desire, 146 miles distant. Little did the returning party think that they were the last men who would ever see their five gallant comrades alive.

The return of Lieutenant Evans and his men is an epic in itself, though unfortunately it cannot be dealt with here at any great length. They had many hairbreadth escapes among ice cliffs and crevasses; and on January 30th Evans discovered he was suffering from scurvy. It gradually got worse, until the stricken man could not step out and could only push himself forward on skis. Then came the inevitable collapse and Evans fainted right away. Regaining consciousness, he ordered Crean and Lashly to leave him behind in his sleeping-bag with what food they could spare. But the gallant souls refused to do so, and putting him on the sledge in his sleeping-bag, trudged doggedly on. For ten days they covered ten miles a day with their suffering burden jolting behind them.

Then came a blizzard in which they were forced to camp. Crean and Lashly, having marched nearly 1,500 miles, were exhausted and spent, while Evans was at death's door.

The two men consulted together as to what was to be done. Crean, if anything, had had the easier time, having been with the pony party on the outward march, and so with no more food than three biscuits and two sticks of chocolate he set out on February 18th to cover the thirty-five miles to Hut Point, leaving Lashly behind to nurse his officer.

Utterly exhausted, Crean accomplished his journey after a wonderful march of eighteen hours, and Dr. Atkinson and the Russian dog-driver Dimitri, with a dog team, set off to rescue Evans and Lashly. They reached them on the 20th, and two days later arrived at Hut Point with the invalid, who was subsequently embarked in the *Terra Nova* and made a complete recovery.

Lashly and Crean between them, at the risk of their own lives, had saved Lieutenant Evans from almost certain death, and for their gallant conduct were both decorated with the Albert Medal by His Majesty the King.

By noon on January 16th the Polar party were in 89° 42′ S. with another twenty miles still to travel. That afternoon, however, they saw a black spot ahead, and marching on, found it was a black flag, while not far off were the remains of a camp with sledge and ski tracks and the clear marks of dogs' paws, many dogs. These signs meant that Amundsen had forestalled them, that the prize upon which Scott and his men had set their hearts had been wrenched from their grasp. The shock was almost unbearable, and their hearts full of disappointment and bitterness, the gallant five struggled on.

January 17th saw them at the Pole, which they fixed accurately by means of a theodolite. They also took a photograph[1] of themselves with Queen Alexandra's silk flag fluttering in the breeze and their sledge flags displayed. Not very far away they found Amundsen's tent with the Norwegian flag flying. There was a considerable amount of gear left inside, also a record of five Norwegians having been there on December 16th and a letter from Amundsen to King Haakon with a request that Scott would forward it.

On the 18th, having been out for two and a half months, Scott and his four companions left the Pole behind them, and turned their faces northward for the weary 900 statute miles of sledge dragging which lay between them and safety.

They made rapid progress for the first few days, finding their cairns one by one. But very soon things were in a bad way. Petty Officer Evans, besides a septic knuckle due to a previous injury, had badly frost-bitten fingers, and presently his nails were coming off. Oates' feet were in a bad condition from frost-bite, while on the 30th Wilson strained a tendon in his leg, and for a time could do nothing but hobble alongside the sledge.

February 4th found the party among crevasses, both Scott and Evans falling into them, and three days later they commenced the descent of the Beardmore Glacier. Struggling on, they made fairly good progress, though Evans' condition soon gave rise to serious anxiety. It was thought he had injured his brain by a severe fall, for he had become dull and listless, very unlike his usual energetic

---

[1] The roll of films was subsequently found in the tent with the bodies of Scott, Wilson and Bowers, and was successfully developed.

self. And soon the party were being delayed on his account, so that the food supply was diminishing too rapidly in relation to the distance travelled. Things were beginning to look serious. It was, indeed, the beginning of the end.

During the march on February 17th, at the foot of the Beardmore Glacier, Evans, who had left the sledge to adjust his footgear, dropped some distance behind. Again, on camping for lunch he was a long way off, and the others, becoming alarmed, hastened back towards him. Scott was the first man to arrive, and found the poor fellow on his knees with his hands uncovered and frost-bitten and a look of madness in his eyes. He was asked what was the matter, and replied slowly that he did not know, but thought he must have fainted. They managed to get him to his feet; but after a few steps he collapsed, and a sledge had to be fetched to take him up to the camp. He was practically unconscious when he reached the tent, and died quietly the same night at about 10 o'clock. The strongest man of the party, a tried sledger and a veteran in Antarctic experience, was dead. With heavy hearts and dismal forebodings the four survivors struggled on.

On the 18th they reached the old camp where the last of the ponies had been slaughtered on the outward journey, and laid in a supply of pony meat. Everything now depended upon good marching, but very soon the surface became terrible, and in their weakened condition the daily progress became less and less. Their best march on the Barrier was twelve miles; but in the later stages the distance dropped to four, and the food depôts were some sixty-five miles apart. Temperatures, moreover, were abnormally low. Already they must have realized that their chances of reaching Hut Point were infinitesimal, though as late as March 4th Scott pathetically observes in his diary, "We are in a very tight place indeed, but none of us are despondent yet, or at least we preserve every semblance of good cheer."

Things were as bad as they could possibly be, and by March 6th Oates' feet were so bad that he was no longer able to pull. He suffered terrible agony, and as the days passed gradually became worse and worse.

"Things steadily downhill," says Scott on March 10th—"Oates' feet worse. He has rare pluck, and must know that he can never get through. He asked Wilson if he had a chance this morning, and of course Bill had to say he didn't know. In point of fact he has none. Apart from him, if he went under now, I doubt whether we could get through. . . ."

Provisions were very short, and they were delayed by blizzards, and on March 11th, six miles a day was about the limit of their endurance. Seven days' food was left, and they were fifty-five miles from "One Ton Depôt," thus leaving them thirteen miles short in their distance. Even if things got no worse, Oates was very near the end.

"What we or he will do, God only knows," says Scott. "We discussed the matter after breakfast; he is a brave, fine fellow, and understands the situation; but he practically asked for advice. Nothing could be said but to urge him to march as long as he could. . . . I practically ordered Wilson to hand over the means of ending our troubles to us. Wilson had no choice between doing so and our ransacking the medicine case."

March 15th came, and when the tent was pitched for lunch Oates said he could no longer go on, and proposed that he should be left behind in his sleeping-bag. This the others would not do, and induced him to struggle on for a few miles during the afternoon. By the evening he was worse, and knew that the end had come. He had suffered intensely for weeks without complaint, and never for a moment had given up hope. He went to sleep that night hoping not to wake up. The morning came with a blizzard, and getting up, Oates said to the others, "I am just going outside, and may be some time." He left the tent and was never seen again.

"We knew that poor Oates was walking to his death," says Scott, "but though we tried to dissuade him, we knew it was the act of a brave man and an English gentleman. We all hope to meet the end in a similar spirit, and assuredly the end is not far."

By midday on March 18th they were within twenty-one miles of "One Ton Depôt," but the wind and drift were ahead, and they had to stop marching. "My right foot has gone, nearly all the toes," says Scott, and there was not much to choose between his condition and that of the others. By lunch-time on the 19th they were fifteen and a half miles from the depôt, and ought to reach it in three days; but they had only two days' food left and barely a day's fuel. The condition of their feet was worse, and the temperature was down to -40°. "Amputation is the least I can hope for now," Scott observes.

By the night of the 19th they were within eleven miles of the depôt; but from the 20th onwards had to keep to their tent on account of a raging blizzard. On the 21st, as a forlorn hope, Wilson and Bowers proposed going to the depôt for fuel.

"22 and 23," writes Scott. "Blizzard as bad as ever—Wilson and Bowers unable to start—to-morrow last chance—no fuel and only one or two of food left—must be near the end. Have decided it shall be natural, but we shall march for the depôt with or without our effects, and die in our tracks."

Then a long gap in the diary; "Thursday, March

29th," comes the next entry. "Since the 21st we have had a continuous gale from W.S.W. and S.W. We had fuel to make two cups of tea apiece, and bare food for two days on the 20th. Every day we have been ready to start for our depôt, eleven miles away, but outside the door of the tent it remains a scene of whirling drift. I do not think we can hope for any better things now. We shall stick it out to the end, but we are getting weaker, of course, and the end cannot be far.

"It seems a pity, but I do not think I can write any more.

"R. Scott."

The last entry in the diary was, "For God's sake look after our people."

The *Terra Nova* had arrived at Cape Evans from New Zealand on February 4, 1912, and landed stores as well as mules and additional dogs.

It had been intended that Dr. Atkinson, now left in command at winter quarters, should take the dog teams out as far as "One Ton Depôt" prior to the return of the Polar party. It was not a relief expedition, for Scott should have had ample provisions to reach Hut Point; but was to accelerate his return in order to permit him to catch the *Terra Nova* before she sailed. Scott had not quite made up his mind whether or not he would remain south for another year; but in any case was anxious to send news back by the ship.

On February 13th Atkinson and the Russian dog-driver had left Cape Evans for Hut Point, intending to leave on their journey on the 20th. On the 19th, however, Crean arrived with the news of Lieutenant Evans' collapse at "Corner Camp," and, as already described, Atkinson set out to rescue him on the 20th after a day's delay due to a severe blizzard. Atkinson was the only doctor available on the spot, and as Evans was very seriously ill and could not be left, he deputed Cherry-Garrard with Dimitri to proceed to "One Ton Depôt" with the dog teams with all possible speed and to leave there a fortnight's surplus food for the Polar party.

After a terrible journey Cherry-Garrard and his companion reached "One Ton Depôt" on March 4th. The weather was very bad, and on his arrival he had to decide whether he would remain there as long as his food lasted, or whether he should proceed farther south and run the risk of missing Scott and of incapacitating the dogs, which he had explicitly been told were not to be hazarded in view of their employment in the subsequent spring. Very wisely he decided to remain where he was, staying until March 10th, when he and Dimitri turned their faces homewards. They arrived at Hut Point on the 16th after a very bad journey, in the course of which the Russian practically collapsed and the ravenous dogs were very difficult to manage.

As yet there was no undue anxiety about the Polar party. March 10th was considered the earliest possible date for their return; but as day after day passed with no signs of them, Atkinson began to fear the worst, and on March 27th, by which time the *Terra Nova* had sailed with Lieutenant Evans on board, he started southward with Keohane, in terrible conditions of weather and temperature. On the 30th they reached "Corner Camp," left some provisions, and went a little way beyond. But the winter was fast approaching. Already it was too late for sledging, and they were soon forced to turn home, arriving again at Hut Point on April 1st. It was now morally certain that the southern party had perished. Indeed, on March 29th, eleven miles south of "One Ton Depôt," Scott had made the last entry in his diary.

Further search expeditions would have been sheer folly and unnecessary risk of life, and on May 1st the remaining six officers and seven men, with

Atkinson in command, settled down for the winter at Cape Evans.

We must diverge from the main story to give a very brief account of Lieutenant Victor Campbell and his party, who, after meeting Amundsen, had been landed at Cape Adare. Here, living in a hut, they did much valuable research work, and in January 1912 were re-embarked and landed farther south in Terra Nova Bay, to sledge round Mount Melbourne. The ship was to pick them up again on February 18th; but was never able to come within thirty miles on account of the ice. In consequence, Campbell, with Dr. Levick, Priestly—the geologist —and three men were left to face the Antarctic winter with four weeks' sledging rations and 270 lb. of biscuit.

Realizing they were marooned, they replenished their scanty food supply with penguins and a few seals. Also they dug themselves an "igloo," or snow-house, in a slope of hard snow, lining it with seaweed and constructing a tunnel-like entrance. The floor-space measured thirteen feet by nine, and for six and a half months the party remained there. Their experiences beggar description.

Their hair and beards grew to such an extent and their faces were so blackened by the smoke of the blubber stove that they were only recognizable by their voices. Food became scarce, so that the biscuits had to be reduced from eight to two a day, then to one, and finally to none at all. Their two meals—breakfast and supper—consisted of small allowances of pemmican, cocoa, fried blubber and seal "hoosh," and the tea used on Sundays was reboiled on Mondays and served out as tobacco on Tuesdays, being smoked mixed with wood shavings. Seaweed was used as a vegetable; a small piece of chocolate and twelve lumps of sugar were issued weekly. Twenty-five raisins were served out on the last day of each month.

For days at a time they were confined to their igloo, and did Swedish drill to keep themselves fit; but in spite of their dismal hardships and abominable food the party remained cheerful. On September 30th, with one man so ill that he had to be carried on the sledge, they set out for Cape Evans, arriving on November 7th. The wonderful achievement of Campbell and his men in the face of danger, hardship and privation is one of the most stirring tales of Polar exploration on record.

It was on October 30th, the earliest possible moment, that a large party set out from Hut Point to find out what had become of the Polar party. It was thought that they must have perished in the crevasses of the Beardmore Glacier; but on November 12th, eleven miles due south of "One Ton Depôt," the mournful little tent was discovered. It was partially snowed up and looked like a cairn, but in front of it were the ski-sticks and the bamboo mast of the sledge.

Inside were the bodies of Scott, Wilson and Bowers, the last two in their sleeping-bags in the attitude of sleep. Scott, who had died later, had turned back the flaps of his sleeping-bag and had opened his coat. The little wallet containing his note-books was under his shoulder, and one arm was flung across Wilson, his life-long friend.

Thirty-five pounds' weight of most important geological specimens collected on the Beardmore Glacier still remained on the sledge. They had retained them until the very end, though every additional ounce minimized their chances of survival.

When everything had been collected, the Burial Service was read and a cairn built over the tent, upon which was erected a rough cross made of Scott's own skis. In a metal cylinder was left the following record:

"Nov. 12th, 1912, Lat. 79° 50′ S. This cross and cairn are erected over the bodies of Captain

Scott, C.V.O., R.N., Dr. E. A. Wilson, M.B., B.C., Cantab., and Lieutenant H. R. Bowers, Royal Indian Marine—a slight token to perpetuate their successful and gallant attempt to reach the Pole. This they did on January 17th, 1912, after the Norwegian Expedition had already done so. Inclement weather with lack of fuel was the cause of their death. Also to commemorate their two gallant comrades, Captain L. E. G. Oates of the Inniskilling Dragoons, who walked to his death in a blizzard to save his comrades about eighteen miles south of this position. Also to Seaman Edgar Evans, who died at the foot of the Beardmore Glacier.

"'The Lord gave and the Lord taketh away, blessed be the name of the Lord.'"

Proceeding southward, they searched for Oates' body; but without success. Near the spot where he had died, however, they built another cairn and placed a cross upon it bearing the following record:

"Hereabouts died a very gallant gentleman, Captain L. E. G. Oates of the Inniskilling Dragoons. In March 1912, returning from the Pole, he walked willingly to his death in a blizzard to try and save his comrades beset by hardship. This note is left by the Relief Expedition, 1912."

Nowhere in Scott's last writings and messages is there the least trace of bitterness or jealousy, no cavilling at fate. In his letters to the wife of Dr. Wilson and to the mother of Lieutenant Bowers, he does the utmost to comfort and console them for their loss by telling them how magnificently their men behaved in the face of privation, danger and death. He had always been a poor man himself, and in his farewell letters to his wife, to Sir James Barric and other friends, he exhibits a deep and wholly natural anxiety for the welfare of his own and his companions' dependents.

The following few extracts from letters written with death close at hand do much to show his true nobleness of mind:

"I am not at all afraid of the end. . . . I may not have proved a very great explorer; but we have done the greatest march ever made, and came very near to great success."

"If this diary is found, it will show how we stuck to dying companions and fought things out to the end. . . . Wilson, the best fellow that ever stepped, has sacrificed himself again and again to the sick men of the party. . . . No one is to blame, and I hope no attempt will be made to suggest that we have lacked support."

"I want to tell you that I was not too old for this job. It was the younger men who went under first. . . . We could have got through had we neglected the sick."

"My thoughts are for my wife and boy . . . if I knew the wife and boy were in safe keeping I should have little regret in leaving the world, for I feel the country need not be ashamed of us."

"But take comfort in that I die at peace with the world and myself, not afraid . . . what lots and lots I could tell you of this journey. How much better it has been than lounging in too great comfort at home."

In Scott's message to the public he starts by summarizing the causes of the disaster; but the two final paragraphs may be counted among the finest pieces of writing in the English language.

"We are weak, writing is difficult, but for my own sake I do not regret this journey, which has shown that Englishmen can endure hardship, help one another, and meet death with as great a fortitude as ever in the past. We took risks, we knew we took them; things have come out against us, and therefore we have no cause for complaint, but bow to the Will of Providence, determined still to do our best to the last. But if we have been willing to give our lives to this enterprise, which is for the honour of our country, I appeal to our countrymen to see that those who depend on us are properly cared for.

"Had we lived, I should have had a tale to tell of the hardihood, endurance, and courage of my companions which would have stirred the heart of every Englishman. These rough notes and our dead bodies must tell the tale, but surely, surely a great rich country like ours will see that those who are dependent on us are properly provided for.

"R. SCOTT."

Scott's character was very complex. As a boy he was delicate and prone to outbursts of sudden passion, which flared up and then as quickly died away in a sunny smile and apologies to the subject of his wrath. He was always shy and curiously reticent, and as a man was subject to occasional fits of depression and moodiness, sometimes misconstrued by others as peevishness and irritability. During his second expedition he could never quite free his mind from the fact that some of his friends thought him too old for the task, a belief that was quite erroneous. Moreover, the anxious months of preparation and the thankless work of collecting funds by issuing appeals and begging at rich men's doors must assuredly have had their effect upon a man naturally sensitive and reserved. The second expedition, it must be remembered, was not financed by the Government or any rich society, and throughout it there must always have been a gnawing anxiety that funds might not last out. Even Scott's own pay and the sums payable for books, cinematograph films and the periodical news bulletins sent by the *Terra Nova* from New Zealand went into the common fund for the benefit of the expedition.

Added to this tremendous anxiety, the entire organization and the responsibility for the lives and well-being of his men rested solely upon his shoulders, while the *Terra Nova's* movements and every little item of the magnificent sledge journeys had to be studied and worked out in detail. In the little-known conditions there were so many things that might go wrong. The vagaries of the weather were bad enough; but nothing could be left to chance, and a single error, trivial enough in ordinary times, might bring about disaster and the loss of men's lives.

Scott always averred that he was naturally indolent, and in his youth hard work may have been an effort. But in his later life he showed an unremitting industry which amazed those who worked with him. His writings show his literary and artistic mind, a mind which was scientific as well and fully capable of grappling and dealing with any problem which came before him, no matter how abstruse and unfamiliar. He was not hot-headed or impetuous, but thrashed out every question which came to hand, considering it from every aspect before giving his opinion.

Essentially the driving force and master mind in both his expeditions, he was never severe without reason. He himself, through his naval training, was accustomed to rigid obedience, and expected the same unswerving obedience from others. To some, unused to discipline, it was unfamiliar and perhaps a little irksome. Chivalrous, essentially self-sacrificing, considerate and kind, he had a very attractive personality, and possessed a happy knack of makieg himself beloved by his followers by a few simple words of praise and encouragement. He had failings, like any other man; but by sheer determination, an innate sense of justice and wonderful force of character, he successfully conquered his weaker temperamental self.

One cannot but regard the *Discovery* expedition as the more wonderful of the two, for on this occasion, like many an Elizabethan mariner, Scott was venturing forth into the dim uncertainty of the unknown. He was the pioneer of all sledge travelling in the Antarctic, and where he had first blazed the trail others were sure to follow. It was sheer ill-luck that prevented him from being the first to attain the coveted goal of the South Pole, though its discovery was perhaps the least important part of his work as a great explorer.

He died, as he lived, an heroic character, and his last thoughts were not for himself, but for others. Loved and respected by those with whom he worked and came into contact, he gave his life in the cause of science, a faithful servant of his country and a noble representative of the great Service to which he belonged.

Quite apart from the dramatic circumstances of his death, his achievements have placed him on the highest pinnacle of fame as a Polar explorer. His body, with those of his companions, lies buried somewhere in the grim silence of that great white Barrier he knew so well. Some day, by the natural movement of the ice, those mortal remains will be committed to the boundless ocean, fit sepulchre for one whose fame is untarnishable and whose memory can never fade so long as the English language is spoken.